Life's a

LIFE'S A BANQUET

Robin Bennett

The Book Guild Ltd

First published in Great Britain in 2019 by
The Book Guild Ltd
9 Priory Business Park
Wistow Road, Kibworth
Leicestershire, LE8 0RX
Freephone: 0800 999 2982
www.bookguild.co.uk
Email: info@bookguild.co.uk
Twitter: @bookguild

Copyright © 2019 Robin Bennett

The right of Robin Bennett to be identified as the author of this
work has been asserted by him in accordance with the
Copyright, Design and Patents Act 1988.

Typeset in 11pt Sabon MT

Printed and bound in the UK by TJ International, Padstow, Cornwall

ISBN 978 1912881 680

British Library Cataloguing in Publication Data.
A catalogue record for this book is available from the British Library.

To everyone I've ever known: either in the best of circumstances or the less fortunate — it's all about how we are with others

A note on names

One of my concerns writing this book was I didn't want to embarrass anyone by their inclusion – unless that was my stated intention. Ostensibly, this centred around my closest friends, who already have enough to put up with re me. So, I took the decision to change many key names of people who aren't family, or simply not mention some by name – particularly those individuals I still see regularly and especially where literal accuracy matters not a jot.

A further note on names

Changing names also disguises my ineptitude at remembering them: once in a video shop in Wales I had to hide behind a giant cut-out of Kung Fu Panda to avoid a cousin whose name escaped me, and whose wedding I had been to the year before.

Our children

For similar reasons (relating to privacy), I decided not to indulge in any discussions about our kids – even description is a form of opinion, and their life is their own.

Contents

Prologue

This is a list of helpful Life Tips I sent to my goddaughter on her thirteenth birthday.

- A quite surprising number of electrical things can be fixed by turning them OFF and then ON again.
- Always do what needs to be done immediately. If you've got time to think about it, you've got time to do it.
- Never miss an opportunity to go to the loo (this one is basically the same as the last one).
- Polite and kind ALWAYS beats clever, and will win you more friends, jobs… pretty much everything. Trust me on this (I'm relatively stupid).
- Learn not to worry – everything sort of matters but no one thing matters *that* much. And the worst hardly ever happens anyway.
- There are twenty-four hours in a day: sleep for eight, work for eight and play for eight.
- Make friends with happy people.
- If you don't know what to do about a problem, it means it's not ready to be solved. Leave it until the answer comes. You'll feel it when it does.
- Your parents are always on your side – which I admit is hard to remember at times.
- Loving is a kind of giving.

PS Always be kind to animals, as I know you will. It is the truest measure of a person.

Chapter 1

The incident with the goose

How to live with an eccentric

When I was about seven years old, my father woke one morning and told me, in all seriousness, that not another day could go by without him tasting the sweet flesh of a goose.

He packed me, our cairn terrier Judy, and his shotgun into our rusting Morris Marina and strapped a canoe onto the roof rack. Then he set off for the river.

I had my doubts even at the early stages of this enterprise: it was November and freezing cold. On top of this, my father had never expressed a craving for goose before, so I felt pretty sure it would soon pass if the call was left unanswered. However, at seven, you just kind of go along with things – especially if your father is anything like mine.

We arrived at a bleak stretch of the Thames somewhere near Reading and prepared everything whilst watching the flock of Canada geese lounging about on an island in the middle of the river. Then we got in the canoe: me at the front with the dog; my father at the back, armed to the teeth.

The few walkers who were braving the weather that morning jumped in the air and looked about in alarm as the first shot rang out. Only the goose my father had picked for his dinner seemed unperturbed, as the pellets simply bounced off the thick mattress of breast feathers from twenty yards away.

Undeterred and completely unaware of the sharp looks he was getting from the bank, my father reloaded and paddled closer.

When the second shot rang out, taking the unfortunate goose's head off, people *really* stopped to stare.

Several things happened rather quickly after that:

My father (still armed) jumped out of the canoe, retrieved a limply flapping goose and threw it on my lap; he then jumped back in, sliding the shotgun down the side of the canoe; whereupon the shotgun's second cartridge went off, with a sort of muffled bang; *and we started to sink*. My father panicked: he threw me onto the bank of the island, along with the dog; paddled as fast as he could across the river in a leaking boat; jumped out of the canoe with the shotgun in one hand, the dead goose in the other; and scampered towards the car.

Then he drove off.

It had been an eventful few minutes, but the next part of the morning went very slowly indeed as I stood on that cold island with the dog and wondered what would happen next.

Eventually a put-upon-looking lock-keeper appeared on the opposite bank, got into a small motor launch and made his way across to where I stood. He picked me up, muttering something about a phone call, and took me back to shore to meet my father – who'd had time to go home, wash the blood off and hide the goose.

Two weeks later, we would be sitting in front of the TV with trays on our laps watching Tom Baker being Doctor Who and stuffing our faces with goose. The whole operation was pronounced a great success.

I sometimes think that eccentricity is being possessed of more sharply defined contradictions. Take the last point in the prologue (about kindness to animals): murdering geese in broad daylight could, very justifiably, be taken to being the opposite of that – yet it would be a task to find someone who likes animals more than my father, from our dogs to the tortoise. He even tried to bond with my sister's snakes, with their dead, prehistoric eyes and yearning for the small rodents we kept stashed in the fridge. But he also likes shooting and eating game, and brought me up to prize such free quarry over the miserable, mass-produced poultry in supermarkets.

True eccentricity is also a total unawareness of how you appear to others and the fact you are making a spectacle of yourself, and is the exact opposite of the Eccentric Presumptuous who gets up in the morning and puts on a loud bow tie precisely in order to get noticed.

If my father sported German lederhosen to mow the lawn in our quiet semi near Reading (which he did), took his dog into Mass (ditto), or obsessed about church architecture, whilst avoiding actual church like the plague, he did it for honest reasons of practicality or genuine desire – never, ever for effect. That is the point. I remember his clog phase unfortunately coinciding with his pith helmet period: this was the closest he got to looking like a proper lunatic – most of the time I thought he looked quite cool... but that might just be a family thing. He was fortunate to have been born with enough charisma to get him out of most of the awkward situations his behaviour got him into, and he taught me that charm goes a long way.

He had been the youngest major in the British army before he left the forces, then he went on to forge a successful career in business which ended up with him as a managing director at Remy Martin Cognac. Being a bit bonkers and having a successful career in a large, sensible company just goes to show what a liberal business business is.

Living with him was also an early lesson in the unpredictibility of life and the absolute necessity to be able to think on one's feet when everything seems to be going to hell in a handcart.

My brother Charles and I suspected he was different from other dads; he did things with us at the weekend that were alarming – more often than not – but interesting. Small boys will forgive a lot if they are excused homework and something irresponsible and mildly dangerous is on the cards.

And the truth was, we gave as good as we got. Cut to illegal potholing in Dorset, and a cave we stumbled across in a field. I dropped a hammer on my father's head and nearly killed him as he clattered down a shaft into the unknown. On another occasion, very close to the goose incident spot, Charles and I pulled a tree branch back as far as it would go and waited for him to come around the corner. When he appeared, we let go of the branch and it hit him square on the face, knocking him – dazed and probably very surprised – into the river.

The trick with my father's rages was to keep out of his way for thirty-eight seconds or more. The best way to achieve this was to run like the wind itself towards any kind of cover, but also to keep zigzagging, as he wasn't very fleet of foot. He'd catch us on a straight – but trees, old ladies with dogs on leads, and parked cars could be relied upon to slow him up long enough for him to calm down and hopefully see the funny side.

If he did catch you whilst he was still in a rage, it would be painful but short-lived.

This was the opposite of my mother, who would harangue you for what seemed like hours, until the infraction was long-forgotten but anything else on her mind had been given a good airing. She comes from Franco-Hispanic stock on one side of her family, so I have a lot of petite, rotund aunts who argue with each other all the time and who rush after small children in shops to cuddle them.

Opposites do attract in the case of my parents. She is middle class almost to the point of a cult, with all the self-awareness and social oversensitivity that can go with it.

But bourgeoise is more a state of mind than a birthright as most of her family history is inscrutable: obscured by anecdote, rumour and a middle-class angst that comes from knowing that one's forbears are not in the least respectable.

In my wine cellar in France there is a framed picture of a grand house in the style of an Atlanta planter's dream home. A cellar is a great place to keep guilty secrets, and the house, which belonged to my great-grandfather and generations before him, is most definitely one of those.

My maternal grandmother was born into a Trinidadian sugar plantation family at the start of the First World War. They had been there generations and my grandmother could trace her family back to the Tascher family – who were elevated to fame, if not fortune, by Rose Tascher, who became Josephine de Beauharnais and then shagged Napoleon.

By 1914 things weren't going so well for the family – presumably since the fall of the First French Republic and the abolition of slavery.

I was brought up to believe that my great-grandfather was a scoundrel who drank and womanised his way through what little remained of the rest of the family fortune. In the last few years there has been some revisionism, but not enough to obscure the fact that the fortune *did* disappear and my great-grandfather *was* forced to flee to Britain.

His choice of the UK was explained by the existence of a cousin who 'owned a chain of restaurants' in London. In reality, 'London' turned out to be Slough and the chain turned out to be one run-down pub in Shaggy Calf Lane that my great-grandfather was supposed to manage, whilst housing his entire family in a single room above the snug bar.

His solution to this reversal of fortune was to die right there on the spot; though whether through grief, rage or sheer bloody mindedness, I really don't know.

Dying might be an emphatic way to avoid one's creditors (and turn down a job offer), but it left my great-grandmother – a small, fierce Hispanic lady – with a large family to feed, nowhere to live and no money.

To where does a woman in this situation turn? Well, if you are Catholic and have been brought up with a strong sense of entitlement, you go straight to your local priest and move into his house.

Of her early years, my grandmother, who lived well into my late thirties, remembered very little from her Trinidadian roots, aside from songs her nanny sang her in creole, and some oddly francophone expressions for someone who grew up near Windsor. But there was a steel to her manner when riled that I like to think came from an upbringing that was precarious throughout her early years, followed by bringing up five children of her own during the Second World War – four of whom were daughters every bit as loud and strongly opinionated as her.

Coming from a family of slave traders and economic oppressors, I find it amazing that my mother grew up so unexcitedly middle class. Her family history shows that bucking social requirements works; but instead she spent the majority of her life rebelling by conforming to most middle-class social mores.

As for my father, who grew up in a comfortable family setting in Henley-on-Thames: one of two boys, with doting parents who liked gardening, keeping sheep and being members of the National Trust – I'm baffled why he isn't the normal one.

Chapter 2
Reading 1971

*In which I get around to explaining why I am writing
this thing. There is also a discussion of drains*

My name is Robin Bennett (for those of you who don't read covers).
I was born in Brunei and I've travelled about a bit. I am exactly fifty
years old. For a living, I write books and start companies. Whilst
people buy into my business ideas, they rarely buy my books.

But I don't let that bother me too much: I am one of the
more cheerful people you might hope to meet in life. I am also
lucky with and very grateful *for* my friends, who soften the
sting of my fractured family.

Accordingly, I'm a useful person to have around if you are
anxious or a bit depressed. Then again, this is not something
I have done on purpose: I did not wake one morning and say,
*Henceforth I will be trivial, yet upbeat; I will smile upon the
world and have really good manners. This will be for the
benefit of humankind... It is my gift.* Not on your life – I'm
jolly and generally nice to people because it makes *me* happy.
It's the opposite of a vicious circle.

So, why am I writing this book?

Well, to be read. However, the advice from my editor
was pretty stark, so I don't hold out much hope: 'For an
autobiography to make it, it has to be written by a celebrity...
but you are of course not famous.'

Oh…

He went on to say, in a more hopeful tone (although I don't know whether he was just trying to be nice at this point) that at least I am writing from 'a good place'. By that, I assume he means that my life, by most measures linked to health, wealth and happiness, is good, and therefore I should be dishing out advice. On the face of it, this makes sense: two of the things I am proven to be any good at – making money and being happy – are worth knowing.

'I think the answer to unlocking the potential of your autobiography is as a guidebook to how to negotiate your way through life – through education, through families, through business, through relationships and marriage, through failure and rejection.'

However, I've given it some thought and – nope – I won't be lecturing people: first of all, I don't have the energy and, secondly, I might be upbeat but I'm not conceited.

I think I can break down my writing this book into three distinct but mutually supportive goals:

1. How I got here
Life can be a little relentless: events (large and small) come thick and fast and there's never enough time to pick them apart, unless you *make* time.

The first time I managed to make myself well-off – in my late twenties – I did it wrong, and money was just a burden, a constant stream of demands on my time I did not really want. The next time I made a fast buck (starting with a spectacularly ill-thought-out but ultimately lucky investment in gold bullion), I managed things better, and I find it has bought me the best of all commodities – time itself… To take stock.

2. Self-knowledge

And hopefully a modicum of self-improvement. Understanding is not just a good reason to write an autobiography: it is, very possibly, the only reason – from the author's point of view. Wisdom has been described as a *torch* by thoughtful people. Holding anything up to the beam of scrutiny is to gain perception but, then, to turn it this way and that is to give it a radically different aspect with each twist of the light. For the reader, I think we like reading autobiographies, biographies, even obituaries though because people – *all* people – are faceted and therefore interesting.

It just depends how you hold them up to the light.

3. Travel guide

Especially if you harbour a deep, unassuaged yearning to know more about Reading, Berks.

With the leisure afforded by being financially fortunate, I'm going back to the places that marked the flashpoints in my life: the tarmac-scented streets of '70s suburbia, the high-hedge-rowed lanes of my schooldays and the flights to far-flung places that cast me out, then pulled me back to where and who I am today. It strikes me that these trips to places I once knew are as much about understanding contemporary me as my past persona.

I am looking for clues.

Present day

In the centre of Reading, by the old Kennet and Avon Canal, there is a shopping centre called The Oracle. It's full of teenage girls saying things like, 'I dunno, 'Chelle, what d'you fink?' On one level, I think it's a fantastic place: it's huge, warm, dry and packed with the sort of fast-food places that I'm only allowed to go to if my wife thinks I'm at the library writing books about elves.

I have an office in nearby Henley-on-Thames, so coming back to the first house I remember today is conveniently close. I've parked the car behind the row of houses where we lived on the west side of Reading, in a sort of cul-de-sac of garages where I remember we kept my father's Hillman Imp. Memories of that car are nearly all of being copiously sick all over the red plastic matting in the boot every time we ventured further than Basingstoke. Hot plastic and vomit has a smell that hangs about: after forty-five years, I can conjure it up in seconds.

Car parked, it takes me a moment to get my bearings, then I spot a familiar alleyway. Walking along it, to where I'm pretty sure our old house is, I stop by a drain poking out of the tarmac path and find myself looking at it very hard, feeling my first ripple of happy-sad nostalgia.

I'd forgotten all about it until just now, but this drain was once a big part of my life and it hasn't changed a bit (why would it? it's a fucking drain!). When I was about five, this marked the spot that was far enough away from our front door as to feel like we had made a break for freedom, but close enough that we were allowed to go here on our own. It's simple and somehow exquisitely familiar, this conduit of mulchy water and memory. We spent hours poking things into it, chiselling the earth up around its square corners, or boring into the chewy macadam and making up elaborate stories about what lurked at its bottom. This is a very satisfying discovery and bodes well as a start for this book, which I've just decided will be drenched in bitter-sweet remembrance, like *Cider with Rosie*... but much funnier.

As I walk around to the front of the row of red-brick two up two downs where we lived after we got back from Singapore, it is obvious that these houses – new when we all moved in – have not aged well: the brick looks cheap by today's standards, lacking in any patina of age and already crumbling in places. The wooden cladding on the upper floors is also pealed and

10

warped. But saplings have become trees, the gardens look cared-for and there is plenty of evidence of another generation of children (swings, bikes, trampolines) growing up happily here to give it all a cosy vibe. I could live here: it's close enough to town to walk to any number of shops, but only about ten minutes from the M4; it feels safe; and, because we're in England, there are at least three parks nearby and a pub.

But growing up in early 1970s Reading was every bit as grim as it sounds. Where The Oracle stands today used to be a semi-industrial no-man's-land of empty warehouses backing onto a canal with shopping trolleys and dead dogs floating about in it. It's another good reason to like the new shopping centre.

The early '70s still had a post-war feel in Berkshire, as if there was enough coal fire grime, peppery gents who'd fought, tin advert signage and Bakelite knocking about to transport you back to 1940 in an instant.

To go to school in the morning, I would walk quarter of a mile to the bus stop and take the Number 18 along the Oxford Road. Sitting on the top deck, watching the world go by through windows running with condensation, about one in four shops would be viewed by me with deep suspicion. Something wasn't right about them. The mannequins in the windows were oddly contorted – as if preparing to carry out a tricky Twister manoeuvre, or do yoga – and they would be wearing ill-fitting underwear and always, to my mind, sporting an accessory that seemed out of place, like a hat (with just pants on!), or they were gripping something that may have been a duster or a small cat-o'-nine-tails. Aged six or seven, I knew everything there was to know about pirates, and these weren't them.

The working girls on the corners in all weathers had no heroin chic, just very painful-looking cold sores and skinniness that inspired the mixture of fear and pity I usually reserved for the homeless in the centre of town who hung out by WHSmith.

Even by my parents' relaxed parenting standards, this was an alarming and possibly quite risky daily journey. I didn't know this was the Reading red-light district, I just knew I didn't like this part of the journey to school, past the sex shops and prostitutes to my stop by the newsagents (now a pharmacy) where I had to get off the bus and walk up the road in my bright red Catholic school uniform.

My father had left the armed forces in about 1971 and I imagine my parents had some adjusting to do. Life spent drifting between the officers' mess and country club in Singapore, where he served with the Gurkhas, had been swapped for a new-build semi in an insalubrious part of town and a daily commute to London on a perpetually tardy line run with decrepit rolling stock. His military career had been an entirely peaceful one and I do wonder if this was not a big part of why he left. The official line was his ambition of becoming a general looked unlikely when he had to go back to his main regiment, the then Green Jackets, and compete with a huge infantry corpus of other thrusting officers for the top job. I'm not sure I buy that: some soldiers are suited to the pink gin, golf and MG lifestyle; married quarters, army wife, the mess the centre of one's world; twenty moves in a career, but the same faces in each... and more gin.

Others want to fight, and I strongly suspect this was my father's ambition when he joined.

So, he left and took a job with Dewar's Whisky in London on the bottom rung of the sales and repping ladder. They can't have paid very well, because my parents, my brother and I ended up living where we did.

Genteel poverty makes me think of crumbling vicarages, Labradors for central heating and a sort of dignified respectability. You can hold your nerve as long as the Aga doesn't pack in. The reality – for us – was more boring: it meant eating a lot of cheese sandwiches devoid of butter, and not quite fitting in anywhere, really.

The estate we lived on had only just been thrown up and opposite was a brownfield site that had started to be developed virtually the day we moved in.

Even at that age it was obvious that we were outsiders. My big brother didn't have a gold stud earring, nor did we own a skinny Adidas T-shirt between us, or have a dad who drove a van with tools in it. Instead we had to walk into town via one or two council estates wearing identical blue corduroys and Arran sweaters with bobbles, the shame of which I still carry with me today. By the time I was six, friends on the estate and parents of friends were remarking that we were posh and, in a largely socialist Britain at the time, this was not a good thing.

Nowadays it's OK to be upper middle class and beyond: we have Hugh Fearnley-Whittingstall and the Queen. You can be posh unashamedly (Rees-Mogg) and even ironically (Boris Johnson). Back to 1973: being posh just meant you were an effete dickhead.

Not fitting in was coped with in different ways by Charles and me: I got stuck into being a bit naughty, Charles just got stuck in – that is to say, he took to carrying a large stick about the place and hitting people with it. Eventually, a posse of mums turned up at our door to complain that class war was fine as long as the toffs didn't fight back. My mother, true to form, talked *at* them for a very long time. Long enough for those mothers to realise that they were not going to get an apology, and they began to drift off in ones and twos, until the last couple of mums left on the doorstep were invited in for tea and turned.

Back here today, I'm attracting a few sideways looks from passers-by, which is understandable as I've been squinting up at my old bedroom window for a while. In future, I decide I will remember to bring Cooper, our springer spaniel, on these trips. There's something about having a dog with you, in England in particular, that immediately makes it OK to loiter about almost anywhere. If I go for a walk in the countryside, on my tod, lone female walkers will (understandably) cross muddy fields full of menacing cattle to avoid me; however, if I've got the dog they will come over and natter. This is fine by me – chatting is my third favourite pastime – but it's obviously nonsense: having a dog does not make me sane or safe, but it does break the ice.

Getting along with my peers when I was small, generally meant playing the fool as my stock-in-trade. It endeared me to other children, but not always adults. Famously, I was smacked by my granny on holiday in West Bay. It's a testament to my overall annoyingness that someone as kind and gentle as Granny Bennett, who had never raised a hand to a child in her whole life, was moved to wallop me – having spent three straight days in my company.

Whether or not being spanked shut me up, I don't really remember: probably for at least five minutes out of sheer surprise. I doubt it, though – very little did shut me up, with the possible exception of *Blake's 7* and *Top of the Pops*.

At my first proper school, English Martyrs, they sent a letter to say I was hyperactive and needed special treatment.

My mother was around there within the hour to explain that in no circumstances should I be given any more attention than the bare minimum to dispense an education, as anything else would just play into my hands.

Whether I was hyperactive or just a pain in the arse is hard to tell. Aged about six, I wound up in hospital with a case of constipation and vomiting that was so severe the doctors thought I had an appendicitis. The real reason for the state I was in is that I had decided pooing was a waste of precious time and so I gradually cut back until my large intestine resembled a boa that had just swallowed a goat. Several suppositories later, now feeling as light as air, I was driven home in total silence, put on a diet of bran and prunes and made to sit on the loo for half an hour after breakfast every day. Whether I needed to go or not.

So, I'm going for the pain in the arse theory, as this is what I usually got for being how I was, and life repays in kind as a rule.

This need to be on the move all the time (whilst providing a running commentary to anyone who will listen) has more or less carried on until this day. I am deeply perturbed by the passing of time and the possibility that I may be wasting it; I look about and see other people engaged in different activities and wonder if I might be missing out. I can usually be relied on to grab at the flicking tail of opportunity and tug without thinking about the consequences.

The upside is I can get away with five or six hours' sleep a night, much less if need be, and I get a lot done. The downside is that people around me for more than half an hour tend to switch off, even if I've got something really important to say. BUT I have learned to take a book into the loo – to take my time or suffer the consequences. So, that's something.

But Reading wasn't all bad and, anyway, kids – as the most disenfranchised, downtrodden and un-polled members of our society – tend to come with the built-in resilience to take things in their stride[1].

Frankly, it could have been much worse. It's only hindsight that makes me feel a bit sorry for the child I was: the fuel shortages, the strikes, Matterhorns of rubbish and Jimmy Savile virtually everywhere. At the time, it was just life, and there was enough that was new and interesting to ride over the bumps. We were still allowed to have a deep personal relationship with tarmac and cycle within a ten-mile radius of home. I'm pretty sure we *did* spend more time playing outside

---

1   … and the grace to forgive the things (and people) that get through this armour and genuinely hurt them.

with friends… and enemies, and learning to cope with these was the first great lesson, long before I learned to harness the hyperactivity into something useful.

One of the best things about our estate was its proximity to my maternal grandparents (of Slough and vicarage-pinching fame). I'm walking the short distance there now, down the A4 to a virtually identical estate of small red houses. Along the right-hand side of the road there are much larger, double-fronted Victorian terraces with leafy front gardens and nice hedges. I remember a lot of these being individual flats, but they're now offices and private outpatient clinics, which is a sort of gentrification, I guess.

Granny and Grandpa Budd (as opposed to the imaginatively named Granny and Grandpa *Bennett*) lived about five minutes' walk from ours in a slightly larger shoebox. My abiding memory of walking there is the smell of creosote from the rows of fences portioning off pocket handkerchief gardens with identical sheds, also liberally creosoted once a year.

You can do a lot in life if you know where you're from and whether you're loved, and both sets of grandparents provided this in heaps.

My grandfather was a retired officer in the Royal Engineers and, in those days, it was hard to meet anyone grumpier, or more tight-fisted. He had been known to wash up cling film and dry it painstakingly for re-use. At the time, I thought sitting in a corner of the living room watching the golf all day – breaking off to bark at my brother and me for making noise – was par for the course if you were old. However, about fifteen years later, he metamorphosed into another person altogether. He had a pacemaker fitted and his knees done, so he was able to walk about, and his temper improved overnight – as I imagine it would.

So now I know his bad grace was down to the fact he felt like shit. But Grandpa Budd lived until he was one hundred, and for the last twenty years of his life I was proud to call him one of my best friends in the world. I'm not sure why we got on so well in later years – in many respects we were very different people and, as a rule, old people don't like me: put me in front of anyone over the age of about eighty-seven and they'll be complaining it's time for their nap within five minutes.

The fact he lived such a long life is also a minor miracle and gives rise to a theory of mine about longevity: the harder one's life, the longer you live – provided you don't actually get shot at some point.

Francis J Budd was born at the start of WWI, the son of a meat wholesaler in Hastings, and remembers the troop ships going to northern France, hearing the guns and being very frightened about Spanish flu. He grew up just in time for WWII, where he dismantled unexploded bombs in London during the Blitz. As an officer, his life expectancy during the early part of the war was less than ten weeks; the main problem, he told me, was that nobody had any idea how to diffuse a German bomb. The only tactic they had at their disposal (in bomb disposal) was to dig it out, load it onto a truck and drive like hell until they got to Epping Forest. Once there, they would set it off, then go back to the East End and start again. The reason officers lasted so little time was that one had to be present during the disposal process – to supervise the squaddies who would probably get themselves blown up all wrong, left to their own devices.

As you can imagine, dislike of the people dropping the bombs ran very high during the Blitz. Grandpa told me of a German parachute coming down a few streets away from where they were working one day. By the time they had driven around the narrow Victorian streets to get to where the airman had landed, the local housewives had come out into the road, armed with knives, and chopped the man to pieces.

Bomb disposal did not stop after the Blitz. My grandfather was in the first wave of troops crossing to Sword Beach during

D-Day and was put to work making safe the booby traps the departing Nazis had left in people's homes for when they returned. This, I must confess, I do not understand: the war was lost and these were civilians. To lay bombs in ordinary people's porches and front rooms seems a petty act of murderous revenge on folk who'd already been through a lot and one that had no bearing on the outcome of a conflict that was drawing to a close. In Caen, the German engineers set up booby traps on top of booby traps, for good measure.

His duties took my grandfather all the way to Berlin. He spoke with great admiration of the remaining occupants of the city who were already clearing up the rubble and rebuilding whilst the Allies were still flushing out the last of the Reich. After being demobbed he started work with the firm of architects which designed the art deco clock you see when you come into London on the M4.

But civilian life did not suit him, so he joined up again and saw active service in Malaysia and Nigeria. About sometime in the 1960s I think he could have been forgiven for deciding the world was a madhouse and humankind was heading for oblivion. All he had known from an early childhood spent within earshot of the great howitzers on the Western Front, until now, was war. And Slough. However, I never heard him complain (about that, anyway – he moaned for weeks when I once reversed the charges to call him from a payphone at my boarding school).

I went to see him very shortly before he died in 2015 and we chatted easily over tea and cake until it was time to go. Even then, he was sharper than most people half his age and gave better, more objective advice than anyone I know. He was shortly to be awarded the Legion d'Honneur, France's highest order of merit, for his part in the Normandy landings. I asked him if he'd seen *Saving Private Ryan* and he waved away the whole idea of looking back on that period. In all the time I knew him, he never went to any of the D-Day reunions or military parades on Poppy Day. It was only rarely that he mentioned anything about the war, and it was usually anecdotal events that could have happened in peacetime. To be honest, I'm not sure it wasn't his way of gently taking the piss; so when I asked him about Northern France in 1944, he'd launch into a long pointless story about borrowing a bicycle.

When he died last year, it felt quite unlike how I'd felt losing my other grandparents; it wasn't until someone I had known very well for thirteen years committed suicide that I was able to put it into context.

When Francis Jesse Budd died on 12th June 2015, just shy of his 101st birthday, it felt like losing a friend.

If Granny and Grandpa Budd opted for middle-class comforts – central heating, wall-to-wall carpets (even in the bathroom) and a small patch of easy-to-mow garden – Granny and Grandpa Bennett were of a different breed altogether.

The fire was lit at 4pm for tea – not a moment before – almost everything was homegrown: from the lambs to the orchard full of veg and soft fruits that circled the sort of English garden you only see in costume dramas in which Helena Bonham Carter manages to look cross, whimsical and startled all at the same time.

They did have a Teasmade, to be fair: one concession to modern life that was otherwise steadfast country Edwardian.

They had moved from Henley-on-Thames to Bridport in Dorset when my grandfather took early retirement to become a gentleman farmer.

This was all made possible thanks to the one true entrepreneur our family did produce, my wealthy paternal great-grandfather who, by all accounts, was positively Dickensian and who had the sort of head for business only found in people who are single-minded as a religion and know they are right on account of everyone around them being idiots. Clearly.

His son, my grandfather, had a gentle nature that disliked authority or any form of bullying and hankered after the quiet life of a smallholder – albeit one with a large share and property portfolio that made all this possible. There's a saying I heard somewhere along the lines of 'I am a businessman, so my son can be a farmer, so his son can be a poet…' and there's some truth in that if my family is anything to go by.

It amused me, a couple of decades later, when the aforementioned Hugh Fearnley-Whittingstall put down roots at River Cottage to live the very same sort of life as Grandpa Bennett, especially as the backdrop to his pieces to camera in the garden of River Cottage was my grandparents' land.

For so many years of my life, my paternal grandparents' home, Woodhayes, was the rural idyll we all long for in some way. It was the place I looked forward to going to more than anywhere on the planet: for holidays that were a sort of freedom to Charles and me that you couldn't get in the Home Counties in a semi-urban environment; then as a refuge from boarding school on half terms; and, finally, as a focus for the nostalgia of childhood, on middle-age pilgrimages whenever I found myself in the area.

The living room, with its sponge cake for teatime, smelled of old sofa and old dog – which is great, if you like that sort of thing (my mother loathed it). The Aga gave us chilblains more often than not, but still felt like the womb of the house. I loved the thatch and the whitewashed walls, the smell of dust and oil in the barn, and the whole welly boot scraping, wind racking to the point of breath-taking, dried flower arranging, blazing fire, giant tractor tyre, dog-friendly thing. The garden was a miniature Eden (without the moral high ground, and my grandparents kept their clothes on to everyone's palpable relief). It had a year-round supply of things to eat: strawberries the size of a child's fist, gooseberries that made you wince, windfall Russets and Victoria plums we would split open with the heal of our hand to check for bugs then scoff on the sly.

At Woodhayes I experienced what it is like to have a spiritual home and how that anchor becomes a rock. Later in life it makes risk and disappointment easier – to have those memories and that grounding to fall back on.

On a practical level, I learned about how to keep lambs – the rudiments of ruminants – how to stalk a rabbit from a hundred yards and get a clean kill with an air rifle that shot like a banana, split logs, dam streams, spin for mackerel and shower in tepid water – even in mid-November, when it was cold enough for the soap to stick to you like paste.

I would go there for exeat weekends at boarding school and would never want to leave. I was never homesick, really, but leaving Woodhayes would be as close as I got.

We loved all of it; Woodhayes is my Rosebud...

In 1975, the petrol crisis hit Reading, and we had to queue outside our local Jet garage for a measly two gallons and a book of Green Shield stamps (we were saving for a bright orange yoghurt maker). My father's mortgage payments went through the roof with 30% interest rates, and everyone seemed to be on strike... but I had bigger problems.

My sister Amelia was born.

Any special protection I had of being the baby of the family was immediately out the window and I felt acutely what it was to be second or third best. My mother had yearned for a daughter, and I don't think she set out to be cruel to me in the process, but her delight in Amelia was obvious, as was her shift in focus. I remember being quite upset at the time and, at six, I hadn't learned to hold back: so I found myself blubbing a lot, then wondering how I had turned into such a big baby all

21

of a sudden. But over-sensitivity clearly got me nowhere, apart from being told off.

It was about that time I began to suspect that just getting on with it was the way to go. Keeping a lid on things is underrated, in my opinion.

About the time Amelia arrived, the nun who ran my primary school came to see my mother and spelled out just what she thought: Charles and I were 'gentlemen', English Martyrs in Reading was not the place for us and we were taking up free places children worthier could use. She advised my parents to send us to a good Catholic boarding school instead.

I'm back in the now (not then) and I'm walking back to the car, already fishing about for my keys. I'm thinking about how boarding school and Amelia's birth marked the end of that cosseted, almost dream-like period of childhood we most of us carry about – these parcels of memory in our personal sorting office of emotions and events both lost and found. I'm thinking how, aged eight, I had to get used to fending for myself at boarding school. This seems young, but the truth is it was not unusual for anyone my age, born when I was born: so not the revelation of this pilgrimage. What else have I discovered today, then?

Well, apparently, I still find drains quite interesting.

Digging a little deeper, as I slingshot around Reading's orbital, I realise that those early years were, on balance, most formative in the feeling of not quite fitting in, which has never really left me, if I am being honest: too posh for the estate, too poor for private school, as you will see in the next chapter.

If nothing else, it explains the fire in the belly, and one that I admit I tend to mask with jokes because then the drive does not seem too determined – or serious, heaven forbid. I can see that it was the start of wanting to get on with things, to prove myself in other ways than being funny – yet stay light, even frivolous. That drain or, more accurately, the life around it, where we fought and played and worked out where we would fit and how, was the well-spring of what I was to become — given the type of small boy I already was.

It was the nurture to my nature.

Chapter 3

Oratory Prep School

Falling out of trees and the benefits of being decent

Think Ron Weasley in patched bellbottoms and that was pretty much me at prep school.

But I didn't give a monkey's butt what I looked like: from the first minute I walked through the mock-Tudor doors of the Oratory Prep School in Goring Heath, I decided that this was the place for me. St Joseph's dormitory, of about fifteen other seven- to eight-year-olds in bunk beds with horsehair mattresses and sheets like sailcloth, still reminds me of that scene in *Oliver* (well, the musical movie version from the 1960s) when Oliver is brought back to Fagin's lair by the Artful Dodger. On one level, the school worked for us because the first rule of any good child's narrative is Get Rid of the Parents.

I went back a couple of years ago with my wife – not just to snoop about but because we were prospective fee-payers: legitimately nosey. The experience of returning and a) being taken seriously and b) getting to see what the staff common room looked like, was made even stranger by the discovery of two teachers still pottering about from when I had been there.

Not much appeared to have changed at all, in fact – and I was really chuffed about that because they were five happy years, by and large. These days, the grounds look more pristine and the pitches better-drained. I do remember an English jungle of giant rhubarb and parsley, next to some broken greenhouses that have both gone but the corridors have kept that warm wood and wax smell, and a quick visit to the bogs confirmed that Tusk is still a bender.

If I'm being honest, I thought the other parents we met had changed the most: in my day, it was doctors and local solicitors who sent their children here, or serving officers; and the car of choice was a wreck of a Volvo estate with a Labrador in residence and a little sister who never seemed to get any older. But, as said, parents were all but erased from our existence the minute the family banger turned around the corner of rhododendrons. These days, now the school is basically non-boarding, they are ever-present, well-heeled to the point of being almost vulgar and they seem to be consulted about and roped into everything.

Sending us to school took every penny my parents had. However you view private schooling, it was a huge sacrifice that ensured they never had money to spend on themselves and worried constantly that interest rates would go up, yet again, and it would become a choice of roof over their heads or school for the boys.

Back then, there were enough of us who attended the school who were from genteel poverty for it not to be a social stigma to never have had a holiday away from the grandparents' house, or not to own an Atari Space Invaders console. But ours was slightly the wrong sort of poverty: it was a bit too real and it lacked verve. Quite apart from the annual worry that I'd be taken from school because we could not afford the fees, especially when my second youngest sister, Rosamund, was born, we had no crumbling castle in Scotland, or title. We were just uninteresting suburban poor – but it would have been mortifying to say I lived in Reading, so our address in conversations was shifted down the road to Pangbourne. Then that was alright.

The school was run by a husband and wife team called Mr and Mrs Stow. In essence, I think they ran it out of a love for small, grubby boys. It can't have been for the money generated by a small boarding prep school not charging a fraction of the indexed fees they are making parents cough up now. This was real austerity and that included the food: we largely filled up on mountains of 'eggy' bread between meals where, if you did get meat, it was carved so thin as to be opaque. If your slice of grey-ish beef wasn't sunk in cheap gravy, it was possible to lift it up to the light like parchment and pick out the outline of the large draughty windows at the end of the refectory.

Aside from the Stows, there was the usual music-hall cast of trained, untrained, dedicated and – very often – wholly unsuitable teachers, gardeners, whiskery dinner ladies and matrons to look after our welfare or take advantage of a sort of care-in-the-(closed)-community environment the school afforded.

Quite a lot of the staff had fallen into a career in an unconventional school after their chosen path had not quite worked out. Or, in the case of one or two relics who took us for subjects like Classics, they were de-mobbed in 1946 and found themselves at the OPS much to everyone's surprise, including their own.

The 'beaks', then, were generally odd but harmless: like Prof. Philby, my first science teacher, who would make himself a cooked breakfast on the Bunsen burners if he'd been running late that morning, or Miss Mayne, our aging hippy art teacher, who never wore a bra despite having the largest areolae I had ever seen. In winter her nipples, which were located somewhere around her navel and pointed directly at the floor, would stand out like small flying saucers through her tie-dye T-shirts. Miss Mayne was clearly carrying on with the geography teacher, Mr Nevil. In their respective lessons, each would set us some long task – copying out descriptions of glaciers or drawing a pot –

and announce they had a meeting with the headmaster. Then they'd leave the class and sneak, quite obviously, in the opposite direction of Mr Stow's office. As soon as she was gone, we would crane our heads out the window and, sure enough, see the fuzzy silhouette of Mr Nevil leave *his* classroom through the frosted windows across the courtyard. They would meet somewhere in the middle of the rectangle of new classrooms that had been built away from the main school.

Presumably in the stationery cupboard.

Outside of class, Miss Mayne and the other teachers seemed remote – many were even older than our parents and therefore alien, to be avoided or ignored. But we were all in love with Tracey, the junior matron who cycled from the village each evening to help the head matron get us ready for bed. After lessons, our lives were ruled by this bad-tempered Spanish woman who looked part of a drag act, which required dressing a professional darts player up as Mrs Slocombe from *Are You Being Served?*. We didn't warm to her as she shouted a lot in Spanish and pulled our ears until the gristle in them creaked and popped. Instead we saved all our affection for Tracey who was strawberry-blonde and gentle and tucked us in.

I can't begin to imagine the difficulty of getting two score seven- to twelve-year-olds bathed, dressed for bed and asleep before 9pm each evening: I'd probably be tearing the ears off children with my teeth inside the first week. For the head matron we did what we were told, for fear of the feeling of your ear cartilage dislocating itself from the side of your head. For Tracey, with her freckles and ringlets, we did it for love.

However, most of the policing – the running of the actual school within a school – was carried out by older boys in a system that was more hierarchical than your average medieval Chinese court. For almost every activity – from sports to clubs – there was a captain and vice-captain telling you what to do and, depending on where you were meant to be at any given moment, there would be another boy about two years ahead of you in charge of your immediate surroundings – so each classroom had a monitor, ditto playground; and dorms always had their dormitory head whose main duties were to tell you to stop blubbing if you were homesick and organise dorm raids on other fiefdoms further down the corridor after Senora Slocombe had retired for the night to remove her makeup with a grinder.

Having an older brother at boarding school cannot be recommended highly enough. Through Charles, I was given an entrée into the ruling class of boys before I arrived.

I knew their ways and I knew their secret language.

KV for master/authority figure coming, from the Latin *cave* – to look out (and, yes, it really was that sort of school); *decent* meant you were OK; you'd just made a *bish* of something could variously mean you'd smudged a line of homework or taken your arm off at the elbow on a piece of twisted metal; and the cry *Quiz!* would get a chorus of *Egos!* – signalling someone had something to give away and the first to respond in the correct form would get it.

Come to think of it, knowing the right words to use in a highly targeted context has informed much of my childhood and adult life – from a basic requirement to fit in as a new tic, to earning a living in translation and being the amazingly versatile author – *hem, hem* – that I am.

And I do believe that however you might turn out to be: well-educated, good-looking, drab, strange, balanced, bonkers, fat, thin, objectionable, noisy, quiet, decent, dense; none of that matters if you can talk to people. Communicating with one's fellow human beings is a skill so vital that even if you have nothing else going for you, you will always get by provided you can master it.

For now, saying the right thing in the right way was to keep me from the bog washes, the lamp-posted beds, wedgies,

Chinese burns, dead legs and all the other indignities meted out to new tics before they learned the lexicon.

Language became my ally and has remained so ever since.

Knowing how far you can push your luck became another indispensable skill. Just before I left, the deputy house master at my public school confided in me that the only difference between privately educated boys and those who had gone through the state sector was the quality of the excuses, as far as he could tell. He said that a public school boy did all the same things as his state school counterpart, and was just as liable to be caught: however, he or she always had a rational explanation for whatever it was they were up to. Or at least a reason why they should not be punished. And that is probably why the white collar crime of, say, wiping out a company's assets – typically committed by posh people – cops a lower sentence than working-class misdemeanours that usually involve far smaller sums of money.

Therefore, most of us learned that if you were caught doing something, you started talking... until the donkey's back legs fell off: the more plausible, elaborate or downright outlandish, the better your chances of getting away with it. My favourite for absenteeism was: 'I was here the whole time, you just didn't notice me.' It was astonishing how rarely the teacher would pick you up on this but, then again, most of our teachers were just trying to get through the day and go home to watch *Z-Cars*, not score points off a nine-year-old.

The most talked-about infraction was good old-fashioned dorm raids. We spent days planning these but they were usually over in a maelstrom of split pillows and cries of '*KV!!!!*'[2]. They never quite lived up to their expectations, in my experience, and usually ended in three or four of the culprits being rounded up and beaten.

---

2   See page 28

Getting caned was a sort of badge of honour that made up amply for any pain and anguish caused by the anticipation of waiting for a very long time in a chilly corridor to be assaulted by an adult who wasn't a blood relation. Getting beaten, in our eyes, conferred status, but it was also deemed by us to be infinitely more preferable to the type of punishment that meant doing extra homework or lines – or anything that was boring and not in the least heroic.

This isn't an argument for bringing back corporal punishment in schools – I was beaten by too many teachers who took too much pleasure in the actual act for it to be healthy, and if anyone physically hurt one of our children without my express permission I'd *start* by kicking the shit out of them before deciding where to go from there.

However, I'm supremely cool with the tactics employed by the rugby trainers at my sons' club whereby bass tones (shouting), grabbing by scruff of neck, and moving from one place to another – generally instilling the idea you are much bigger and scarier than them and therefore to be respected – works on small and medium sized boys remarkably well and gets the job done without the resentment that is the result of lines, detention and nagging. Crime followed by fair retribution in short order.

Present day
It's several years since my last adult visit and I'm wandering through the grounds during the school holidays, trying to look nonchalant. This is easy because it feels like I've come home – and it was home for five years, and one I liked. I can't believe how well-kept it all is, though. This is a bit of a shame; I sort of preferred it scruffy.

'Hello!'

I turn around and my brain has to do a gear change. I had been half expecting an aged gardener to come hobbling across the lawn waving a rake at me. I hadn't been expecting a pretty girl: she could be seventeen or thirteen or anything in between. I'm getting to that age now where I can't tell anymore. And young girls all look exquisite to me... like miniature works of art... like my daughter.

'Oh, hello,' I say. 'Sorry, I thought it was half term.'

'It is,' she says. 'I'm a teacher,' and then she looks a bit pissed off. I wonder why, then realise there's a chance I might have raised my eyebrows ever so slightly when she said the last bit. About being a teacher.

'Oh, good!' (OK recovery, I think; almost sounds like she's just the person I was looking for). 'I used to go here!'

So what? her entire demeanour says.

'Just having a look around,' I plough on. 'It's looking good,' I white lie, and I can see her soften up a bit. I bet if I had the bloody dog with me we'd be chatting like old friends. I start to walk towards the car park, to leave without a fuss, and when she clocks this she relaxes a couple more notches.

'Really? Most old boys complain it's all gone a bit Health and Safety.'

'Well... see that balcony there?' I pointed at the window where the junior washrooms used to be.

'Hmm.'

'We used to climb out the window at night and drop into the bushes below, then run around the school and back up to the dormitory.'

'Ha! I don't think they get up to anything like that now – the whole place is locked down at night.'

'Oh well,' and I can see we tacitly agree this is a shame but it's not worth making a deal of.

As I get back in the car, I glance at the chapel in the courtyard and get my first and one and only rush of nostalgia. It was here I became a 'server' – a member of the Archconfraternity of St Stephen. I'm not sure why I went in for it – I wasn't an especially pious child. There was the benefit of doing a reading once a week, but I could never read out the names in the Bible like Nebuchadnezzar, Maher-shalal-hash-baz or Zerubbabel. Frankly, Joshua was a bit of a mouthful for me in those days – I was really very bad at reading. The new headmaster, a huge cliff of a man – Basque rugby player – would sit at the back of the chapel fuming as I jumbled up words and missed out whole sentences. Then he would bollock me after the service and make me promise to practise harder.

At the end of term we did get to eat all the leftover communion hosts, which is like bingeing on slivers of cardboard, but it wasn't school food so it was considered a treat.

Talking of food, as I coast down the driveway with its towering rhododendrons and laurels, I recall another one of my father's bloodthirsty activities that made me a life-long respecter of those who kill principally for the pot.

In the school holidays, when the school was shut and quiet, we would come up here in the family Granada Estate and shoot pigeons sitting in the ivy from its open-top roof. We were using a poacher's 4.10 shotgun, which is basically one up from a spud gun, but it still went bang and what we were doing was still illegal. The deal was we had to get six pigeons and my mother would cook us a pigeon pie.

After the first pie, this became a huge incentive for us all: up until then pastry for me had always been a tasteless slab – rock-hard on one side with the consistency of wallpaper paste on the other. But the late '70s was all about experimentation: cheese and wine parties (with pineapple chunks!), Wall's Viennetta and Spandex. So, my mother used puff pastry and we were hooked. The juices from the pigeon soaked into the pastry, which would already be melting in your mouth as you hit the rich, chewy breast[3]. Puff was the form a caring and generous Universe had always intended for pastry – the other sort had merely been an evolutionary process, consigned to a more basic and brutal past. Fluffy mash, fried carrot slices (never fucking *batons*), and cold milk to wash it down. We went through Oxfordshire's pigeon population like it was a zombie apocalypse and all the shops were shut.

Being my father's son, one of the first things I did, on arrival at the school, was set rabbit snares in the scrub between the 1st team rugby pitch and Out-of-Bounds.

Once I'd caught one, I then had the problem of what to do with it. I briefly considered presenting my kill to one of the school cooks in the hope she would skin, prepare and serve it on a platter, exclusively to me, instead of Sunday night fish fingers and generic-branded baked beans. But I suspected that, possibly, awkward questions would be asked, so I gave them to the school dog, which was pretty bloody generous given as the week before he'd stolen an almost full *sherbet dip dab* from my bare hands.

It got me thinking though, and when I came back from an exeat weekend at home I had pinched a lighter from my dad's cigar box and a very sharp knife.

I just needed a place to skin and barbeque the rabbits now.

This was not too hard: almost half the school grounds were wooded so I started scouting around. The main wood leading off down the hill that eventually turned into suburban Reading, looked like forestry commission pine: closely planted with sloping branches that almost touched the ground. I rejected this as being far too scary: even now, I get twitchy when it comes to being anywhere with less ambient light than

---

3   The distinct possibility of coming across spent ammunition just made it all the more exotic – like a sort of macabre figgy pudding.

your average supermarket or dental surgery. I opted, instead, for much friendlier beech woods near where I'd caught my first rabbit, and set about building a camp in a hollow.

I'd made friends with a boy in my year, Jack, and he agreed (reluctantly, and more from politeness) to help me build my camp. Jack was a gentle boy, with a nice temperament and a good sense of humour, but definitely not the outdoors type. I've made friends with him on social media in the last few years and I'd say he was more the *indoors with colour-matched scatter cushions and Italian boyfriend in micro shorts lounging on a white leather sofa* type these days.

I'm not sure he knew that the purpose of the camp was for roasting game, but he went along with the planning and building with enough enthusiasm that soon – by stripping some pine trees in the Brothers Grimm sector of the woods and making a basic a frame between two trees – we had made something primitive but pretty much waterproof.

In the end, though, my plans to create an outdoor kitchen were put on hold by another form of breaking the rules.

We'd been told that climbing trees was wrong – not dangerous, mind... the inevitability of gravity never came up. The Biology master at the time had read the Roald Dahl story where a man invents a machine for listening to the suffering of plants – either that or he was off his rocker. The main thrust of his objections was the damage it would do to the yews growing opposite the headmaster's wing of the school. By damage, there was a strong hint that the Bio master meant mental anguish. But the fact is, yews are almost perfect for climbing: they have lots of branches and nothing to scratch, sting or snap. So, any objections to us climbing the trees were overruled in our heads because amusement trumps common sense every time.

Indeed, one of the great things about yews is their inherent *bendiness*, which is why they made such good bows for shooting at French people during the Hundred Years' War. Bendy – as opposed to solid or, worse, brittle – is a great quality in a tree for a small boy. One of the biggest thrills was to climb right to the very top and start rocking backwards and forwards until it felt like you were on the top mast of a tall ship during a violent storm. I couldn't, quite frankly, think of anything worse these days but it's amazing what you'll dream up to pass the time before you're allowed to drink beer and have sex.

One of the hardest climbing tricks to master was the 'Ladder'. This involved edging along one the highest lateral branches and then launching oneself forwards towards another branch below, which would bend under your weight, allowing you to grab hold of the next, lower branch, and so on… so we could go from the top to the bottom in a series of downward flexes.

One day, I demonstrated that enthusiasm in no way makes up for skill, by completely overshooting the first branch and falling forty-odd feet onto hard ground. I was extremely fortunate to get away with just a broken arm and two cracked ribs. The yew's thick foliage broke most of my fall and, on landing, my kidneys narrowly missed being speared by a series of old stumps sticking out from the packed earth like those prongs you see on a stegosaurus' back. As I lay there in terrible pain and anguish, looking at what could have skewered me fatally, my first thought was if I went to hospital my reputation would be ruined.

The fact is, I was harbouring a shameful secret – and, with me gone, it was bound to be discovered. I cursed my luck but, lying there, I mainly cursed myself for not having the strength of character to stop sucking my thumb. The problem with this (which was bad enough in itself) was that I needed to accessorise.

I had a comfort blanket.

It even had a name: I called it my *boff*. The thought of the humiliation to come was the reason for the hot tears running down my cheeks; it even managed to outstrip my incredibly painful breathing through broken ribs.

As I lay on a trolley bed at Royal Berks hospital waiting for the results of my X-rays, the first thing I implored my mother to do was drive to Goring Heath, break into St Joseph's dorm and steal my comfort blanket before my bed was stripped by the matron and my secret was out. Standing about four feet behind her, looking somehow out of place in his hacking jacket and britches, my father rolled his eyes heavenwards.

But somehow my appalling secret was not discovered[4].

When I did get back to school, with my arm in plaster, I enjoyed one of those brief periods of great popularity that come and go (interspersed with periods of the exact opposite). Like in life, everyone has their opportunities to be popular at school, and you can also bet that sooner or later, whoever you are, the bullies will come for you. Granted, there's less respite in a boarding school, but the rules are pretty much the same in any institution. We all get picked on, but that's not the real problem: it's choosing how you deal with it that dictates how long it goes on for and how severe it is. As I would later find out.

Anyhow, it turns out that being bad at climbing trees makes you into a minor celebrity, especially if you've got a plaster cast to sign. I've still got that cast somewhere and, when I occasionally come across it whilst looking for spare socks, what strikes me is this: with arms that small, falling out of trees was inevitable; and, on reading all the misspelled messages, what a fundamentally nice bunch I was lucky to find myself amongst.

But let's face it, attending a prep school that was run on a shoestring in the '70s wasn't ideal – it was freezing bloody cold most of the time and the food was atrocious. The teachers

---

4   I'm sure the matron was kind enough to be discreet. As it happened, I carried on sucking my thumb until I was eleven and – yes – no doubt it *was* all down to something darkly psychological.

and matrons may have been very dedicated; but if you suspect that that is no substitute for living with the two people who love you more than anyone in the world, you'd probably be right. Yet the way we coped with being away from home at such a young age I'm slightly humbled by, when I look back – we didn't complain nor did we brutalise ourselves. In fact, during my recent visit, thinking back on how we behaved towards one another, the ethos in the dorms and the lexicon, reminded me that this was far from being the heartless and inhuman place of many boarding school memoires – *decent* was the description we aspired to: it meant you were honest and honourable and respected the rules (not the school rules, rather the code of behaviour). Bullying was frowned upon unless used as a policing method to bring someone back in line, for cheating or lying beyond the pale. I can't help feeling regret that I was certainly much nicer in those days.

Looking back on who I was and how I feel about it now, the Oratory Prep was an idyllic time. And the discovery, at just eight years of age, that I could stand on my own two feet for much of the year stood me in good stead for Life in General. Apart from my thumb-sucking shame, I needed to suppress very little of who I really was and work only on doing my best, which is pretty much what I achieved in my final year, aged twelve. I hope.

If we could have stopped the clock there, that would have been just right – for I was my best self then, I strongly suspect: kind, but old enough to be faceted and therefore interesting.

We were all nicer – most eight- to twelve-year-olds just are – but fervently I hope that some of that affability and goodness has remained to this day. And I do look more favourably on people I know who have been through the prep boarding mill: those of us who found it made sense and signed up to the system seem more resilient and more comfortable in their own skin because they were given that confidence early on that being courteous and fair was OK. And that they could cope.

As I was driven off in the ambulance, Jack immediately set about preparing for my return by marshalling – and I'm short of the collective noun, so here goes – a *grubbiness* of small boys to complete our camp in the woods.

When I got back from hospital, I found that the four by eight structure we had created was now merely the entrance hall to something the size of a largish bungalow in Virginia Water. A lean-to had morphed into a headquarters.

I'd pinched a couple of my dad's cigars when I was at home and, at the first opportunity, about fifteen of us sat around a fire toasting slightly stale bread filched from the kitchens, spluttering away on expensive King Edwards. It's one of my fondest memories.

However, change was on the horizon. My father's civilian career was taking off and he'd got a new job with Remy Martin Cognac.

I would no longer be able to look out of my dormitory window from my bunk and take comfort in seeing the water tower at the end of my parents' road, or go home on a Sunday for six straight hours of stuffing my face.

My parents and younger sisters were off to France.

Chapter 4

France

Égalité, Fraternité… Canapé? Life's a banquet

Present day

Whilst I was at university, I made an important life decision never to get up before 8am, unless I had a plane to catch or the house was ablaze. My reasoning is thus: it's no longer pitch black by that time, unless you live in Norway, and it is not so late as to induce guilt. I need little sleep, but that doesn't mean I don't like lounging about in bed. We've got three children and other pets, so I need to cheat these days: the alarm goes off around 6.45am and I'll spring out of bed, go into the children, make sure the right number is there, that they are awake, have pants, etc., then I'll half fall, half run downstairs to put the coffee on. Whilst fighting off the dog, I'll throw some boxes of cereal on the kitchen table, feed the cat, Dennis, then dash upstairs with two cups of coffee – a normal one for me and basically a bucket full of milky water for my wife.

If it all goes smoothly, I can be back in bed by seven sharp, which gives me almost a whole hour to lie in. It helps if you can shout encouragement loud enough to be heard around the house – those high French ceilings help.

If I don't have to take the kids to school at 8am, I'll get up, throw on my clothes from the day before and walk the dog for half an hour. At our house near the Pyrenées, I've got shooting rights across the woodland and fields around the village, which suits the dog – an English springer spaniel, Cooper – just fine. He relishes wings, feet and heads. I think that pigeon breast on toast is a fantastic Sunday evening meal, often whilst watching *Antiques Roadshow*, a programme I can take or leave but Hélène loves. Pigeon goes remarkably well with baked beans and a roughish Madiran, the local red. It's tender, healthy and *free*.

By 10am I'm usually sitting in the study at home reading emails and checking the sport pages on the BBC. Since living in France, I talk to the main office in Henley-on-Thames as soon as they get in at 9am their time. I've set up around fifteen functioning businesses over the last twenty years, but I've cut that down to four now, to keep life simple. I've got very good staff and I give them space to be grown-ups and make their own decisions – that is the key. My role these days is to oversee what is going on but keep my nose out of any day-to-day stuff. Again, speed and focus are of the essence; it's amazing what you can get done in two hours if you concentrate. Generally, I don't get involved unless something goes spectacularly wrong or spectacularly right.

On Wednesdays, the kids come back for lunch. The boys are massively into cricket right now – they've even got the French kids playing it at school – so we'll usually play that in the stable yard until it's time to lay the table and sit down. Hélène is French and so the midday meal is the big one – three courses, including cheese, plus whatever fruit is in season.

The best bit of the day is walking the dog again, this time for longer in the mountains, if I have time to get in the car.

Moving to the Pyrenées was an interesting choice – it's not a part of France either of us knew much about. We live near Lourdes, which is ghastly, but the surrounding countryside is breath-taking and it does feel quite spiritual. The peaks are somewhat lower and gentler than the Alps and there are scores of hidden valleys, natural oubliettes and precarious meadows perched on mountainsides.

After lunch, Hélène and I will swap. She gets the office (she is co-director of the translation businesses) and I'll go upstairs to write in my favourite chaise longue next to a large window that looks out on countryside.

By about 5pm the children are back again and Hélène and I will take it in turns to ferry them about the place, to sports, or music or whatever activity is on the cards that night. We all eat a light meal together around 7pm (usually soup and charcuterie). I'll try and sneak a cold beer in before supper and we'll have wine with the meal. If drinking every day is too much, then I am a bit buggered.

Much as I love them, though, it is a sense of great relief to get the children into bed and join Hélène in the living room. I'd like to say I read a mind-improving book, but I *love* TV. If I was allowed to, I'd watch practically anything. I have a lot of time for, and I live in hope for, another golden age of comedy soaps. I think American box set series like *Homeland* and *Game of Thrones* are the best thing, not just on TV but on any screen these days. My wife will watch anything where someone is making improvements to where they live: I can take about eighteen minutes of someone discussing curtains before I get up and fiddle with the fire or pick a fight with the dog. However, we generally agree on detective series. If nothing is on in that vein, then it's a gritted teeth compromise.

Bed is around 11pm; the dog often insists on sleeping outside, so I'll turf Cooper out and then I will read for about half an hour before turning out the light and remembering, moments before I drop off, that all the lights are on in the barn.

If this sounds like a comfortable and fairly pleasant existence, then you'd be right, but...

… 1979

'If you don't apologise, the whole street is going to hear about it!'

Tonight's argument was louder than usual, but the format was par for the course: my mother is shouting and my father is sitting there mute and thunderous.

Moving to France had given our parents' fights a whole new edge: they were conducted at home over dinner, in front of the TV, in the car on long journeys, at friends', in restaurants, on walks, in shops and, worst of all, late at night, when we would lie in bed and listen to our parents finding new ways of expressing how much they fucking loathed each other, wait for it to die down, then try and think about something else to get back off to sleep, because pretending something isn't horrible is the way children tend to cope.

At times, there really was no place quite like home.

We suffered in silence because there is a stoicism to children – on the outside they will accept almost anything and not complain, so then everything is fine: obviously. But children are also amazingly fragile within themselves and their inner lives. They take things much more to heart than they ever show and that is why they deserve the best of us.

Rows suggest a tit-for-tat exchange of views, but my father rarely, if ever, said anything beyond, 'Oh, why don't you just shut up, you bloody cow!': most of the time he just looked annoyed and pretended to read, or concentrated on the road, or he simply walked faster, away from the blotchy-faced shouting.

Being ignored would, understandably, make my mother more annoyed and she would up the ante and the volume until something gave – usually my father would storm out, but just sometimes he would erupt back and we would know we were on for a big one. Then us children would avoid looking at one another, especially if we were in public, wrapped up in our own minor level of misery because however much time you have to get used to the fact that your parents' relationship is basically no fun at all, it still feels really shit.

Jealousy was at the heart of it. My mother seemed almost to enjoy the imagined scenarios of debauchery my father would get up to whilst away on business; at a glance she could read the minds of wicked women who had only one object in mind: she was utterly convinced each and every one of them had a plan to steal him away. The more she thought about what the possibilities of infidelity were, the more outlandish the real motives behind their smiles became, and the surer she was that only she could see – only she was not fooled.

Jealousy doth indeed mock the meat it feeds upon, and my take-home point – even at that age – was master your thoughts, for fear of the ones that will surely master you.

I think my mother also missed England with a vengeance. On arrival in Cognac, her French was as good as anyone's of her era (abysmal), and she doesn't have that love of all things foreign of a type of Englishman or woman: TE Lawrence, Isabella Bird, Lord Byron, for example.

And, in some respects, I agree with the notion of: why would you want to leave the Home Counties?

There is a period in England, roughly between April and May, when the countryside is at its loveliest. Provided the sun is shining and it hasn't decided to snow, there is no better place to be anywhere on the planet. It's a frantic awakening, like a time-delay shot: nature as a jack-in-the-box.

France does not have this season so much. Where we live it pretty much rains all the time in spring; then, one day, you wake up and it's summer. Wallop – or, Voila!

My memory of arriving in France, aged eleven, was of sun you don't get in the Home Counties. The track outside our house was crushed chalk, which coated my Start-rite sandals in fine white powder as I scuffed along, squinting through the glare. By the time I'd gone one hundred yards I was half blind and dopey with the heat.

The grass in the back garden felt like hessian on my bare toes and was booby-trapped with termite nests and a kind of two-toned ant that would dash across several feet of open patio for no other reason than to bite you very hard.

By August, a cricket ball, correctly pitched in our back garden, would rear up and hit your brother in the face just like you were Bob Willis.

We were renting a '60s house that sat on its own mound of earth like the houses in Asterix. I thought it was great but it only had three bedrooms, so it meant we were all sharing again. Charles and I had bunks, like at school, and just enough room for a bookshelf and somewhere to do homework.

We were inseparable, but we still had to be separated sometimes for our own safety. Our fights really got into their stride around this time. Charles was still taller and stronger than me, so he would win eventually; but my strategy was to inflict as much damage early on as possible, then hold out for as long as I could. I sometimes overdid things: after one particularly attritional game of Monopoly, which Charles won, I grabbed his hand and bit it so hard I hit bone. For years afterwards, quite possibly until this day, when Charles tanned, you could still see three thin white lines running from the first to the second knuckle joint where my teeth had scored deep grooves.

I tried playing with my sister Amelia, but gave it up as a puzzling waste of time. When I bit Charles, there was no lingering anger or recriminations – we were both far too interested in what his finger bones *actually looked like* as he ran the tap over them, and we rarely involved our parents. With my sister, the rules of the game were entirely different and quite the opposite of what I had with my brother: our play looked like war, but was bonding. Play with my sister looked innocent enough and involved things like shops or role play, but it always felt like a power struggle about much more than just selling plastic apples or pretending to be a waiter. Baffling rules triggered tears, my mother was regularly roped in and I got told off a lot, regardless.

Playing with my sister was a minefield, and I came to learn, in time, that she was my mother's property, not mine.

Unsurprisingly, the food was a revelation.

In England, unless it was Sunday or somebody's birthday, we ate for fuel and moved on. These were the days of *Smash* for mash, gravy that was essentially brown salty water, and yoghurt that smacked of rotten milk, and then there was Blue Nun.

Living in France we suddenly had courses. I was never going to eat salad, in fact I have managed to get through fifty years of my life largely without vegetables of any sort – however, I did discover that soup didn't have to be oxtail and out of a tin. I'd probably heard of such a thing but never imagined that fish soup could be delicious and not actually taste fishy but not exactly meaty either; and I never stopped to think why adding grated cheese to it worked, it just did – as did the croutons: very stale roundels of bread that were deliciously salty and crunchy on the top, but soaked in juices underneath.

The key in France is not to stuff your face – I admit that it can be extremely satisfying to load one's plate in the manner of the type of person who gets banned from all-you-can-eat diners in the US. The Anglo-Saxons are great *pilers* and mixers of their food: we are free marketeers in everything, especially when it comes to building up our plates at a buffet. Where the French will take no more than three items, then come back for more – if they are starving – the British at a buffet seem to be quite happy creating a sort of Plate Edifice. It starts with a coleslaw and potato salad foundation; lower level sliced ham floor and turkey mezzanine; chicken drumstick and carrot baton uprights; throw in some smoked salmon and tiramisu to fill the cavities because it's impossible to see these as anything but luxury items – although both cost less than bubble wrap these days – then cover it all with trifle.

We eat, especially in open buffets, not so much like it is our last meal but on the well-founded fear that it will be cleared away by grumpy members of staff after five minutes.

I learned in France to savour individual items: my French mother-in-law still dishes up the potatoes and meat as separate courses. It makes for very long meals, which I complain about bitterly at Christmas where you start eating at 11am and finish long after it has got dark and too late for a decent walk. It makes for patient children, though, and you do get to mull over the flavours, to savour and study how well the endives have turned out this year, if the meat really is good or just heavily seasoned. I've heard French people very seriously discussing a meal in depth that took place years ago. They remember meals like we remember cricket or football matches. And alcohol was everywhere; people in France don't seem to guzzle like we do, or binge, but booze formed the backbone of life in Cognac and we seemed to know a lot of people who were functioning and just-functioning dipsomaniacs.

Aside from the shambling alcoholics, the lifestyle in Cognac itself was remarkably glamorous compared to the UK. In the '80s there were more millionaires living in this relatively small enclave of the Charente than in any other part of France. My parents happily reverted to the expat lifestyle they had known in the army, and we went to lots of English garden parties in upgraded stone farmhouses with pools, lavish dinners, carol services in the winter, and had to put up with the endless gossip between the big Cognac houses of Hennessey, Remy, Martel, etc. My father's career was on an upward trajectory, and we found we had money and, remarkably, status.

46

It was a far cry from Reading: at twelve or thirteen it was not unusual to find myself driven somewhere to play tennis with the heir to one of the big French drinks dynasties. And they were all frantically expanding out of hard liquor and into wine, champagne and anything else they could lay their vast wealth on. It was sort of like *Game of Thrones*, but with less sex and more alcohol.

Whilst my early memory of France is of the glamour – the tasty food, skinny wives in sparkly clothes and our first colour TV – even in Thatcherite UK there was a feeling of coming out of the '70s grime and into the light of the poptastic '80s. At that age, I had better things to think about than social shifts, but even I could see change was afoot just by taking, as an example, one area that interested me more than most. Music. Suddenly we didn't need the escapism of glam rock anymore, or the protest of punk. Songs, and the people singing them, were generally fluffier. Singers stopped wearing space costumes or blood-soaked T-shirts and started singing catchy three-minuters about falling in love and dancing with your girlfriend. And they all had very clean hair. Cliff Richard was back in vogue, and all you needed to get into the charts was a synth and a pastel jumper draped casually over your shoulders.

Up until then, apart from music, my idea of culture had been limited to what was on TV for kids for two hours a day. I loved television in a way that you love a morphine drip after an amputation. Charles loved it too, but for the other twenty-two hours a day, when he wasn't beating me to death with his plastic light sabre, my brother liked nothing better than sitting down with a good Hornblower book or almost anything by Alistair MacLean. I couldn't see the point. All efforts to get me to read up until then had utterly failed, with no exceptions.

Reading meant concentrating on something *inert*, it meant sitting still and, above all, it meant not talking.

In short, there was nothing – to my way of thinking – that recommended books.

Whenever I did try and read, within less than two minutes my mind would have wandered. I would struggle on gamely for another page or so but the words just became a meaningless jumble of symbols – like in *The Matrix* – interspersed with dots, dashes and squiggles I knew came with rules, but ones that I didn't fully understand. I was probably the only eleven-year-old in 1979 never to have read Roald Dahl of my own free will.

However, it took a move to France, terrible TV I couldn't begin to follow and abject boredom to lead me to the one activity I can enjoy to this day that is entirely simple, blameless... and quiet.

I've learned with our children that telling them they *have* to read something is the absolute slayer of any actual desire *to* read. The only way is to leave enough books lying about the place and hope. And read to them before bed.

My own reading career started with leafing through my mum's old copies of *Country Life* and the romance stories in the back of *The Lady*. Armed with a thorough knowledge of the housing market and flawed, yet terribly attractive men, I moved on to fiction.

Now I don't, as a rule, like animal books – especially those written from the point of view of an animal (usually a dog, or a cynical cat), but *White Fang* literally grabbed me by the scruff of the neck. I picked the book out of the bottom shelf of the bookcase in the hall because it was a large hardback with a yellow spine and hard to miss. I then read it through in less than two days. I've never read another Jack London since... but, reader, he was my first.

After that, I moved on to Len Deighton, Jack Higgins, and I borrowed my brother's Alistair MacLeans when I could. I quite enjoyed all of them, but it wasn't until I discovered

Dick Francis that I found an author I could stick with. If I'd been a more careful reader, I would have realised that he had mastered the most important trick of all in writing: character. Create someone the reader cares about and you could have them stacking shelves in Tesco's for the next two hundred and forty-two pages and it would still work.

My parents, who had always read a lot, noticed that with a book in my hand I became less annoying and so started plying me again with stories they thought I should read, which was more a reflection of their tastes than anything else: this meant I went through a lot of Daphne du Maurier and Jerome K Jerome before I rebelled and regressed.

This took the form of reading all the books I was meant to have read at seven. Around the age of twelve I was comfort reading *James and the Giant Peach, Fantastic Mr Fox, Danny the Champion of the World* (with whom I felt a strong affinity on several levels) and anything else I could lay my hands on by Roald Dahl.

I hadn't learned a word of French (outside of school) but, ironically, France taught me to love the English language.

As awakenings went, it didn't end there. At twelve, I was caught between being a child and noticing things. Mind you, I didn't exactly have to look far: we went to the beach a lot, and any number of my mum's friends who we'd meet up with would dump bags of towels, picnic baskets and umbrellas next to where I was sitting and take off their clothes. Every last stitch, in some cases.

Up until then, my appreciation of the female form had been limited to family members racing from bathroom to bedroom, dawdling through the lingerie section of the Mothercare catalogue when I thought no-one was looking and, one dull Sunday, the discovery of the English master's porn scrapbook hidden in a classroom. This had been typically '70s kitsch:

lots of Kate Bush lookalikes standing in fields next to horses, or drippy girls, in soft focus, gaping into mirrors. Their nipples were normally obscured by leaves or the long tresses they were pretending to comb, and each appeared to have a small marsupial between her legs: pants made of hair that left everything to your imagination. The Mothercare catalogue – particularly the maternity bra section – looked positively hardcore by comparison.

But it was now the '80s and depilation had come to France somewhat earlier than the UK. The upshot was you could see *everything*: smooth mons – like statues I'd seen in museums – pouting labia, and breasts that made the slightest movement excruciatingly exciting.

This was also the first time I had been exposed to the less than perfect form of the female body and, in real life, they seemed to be even more in the nude: childbirth bellies, hefty crotches and dark nipples. It was shocking at first, then thrilling.

I looked on from under my blonde fringe at these magnificent women in their thirties and forties: drinking ice-cold rosé, gossiping and scolding children, whilst they slapped cream onto areas that swayed and puckered erotically in the fresh air. What was most appealing was their French insouciance – they were utterly confident in their bodies and all their imperfections: they knew they were sexy, but that wasn't just it – they were also there to talk, to drink, to eat, and bring up their children. They had other stuff going on.

My mother and the other English mums looked on like they'd just stumbled onto the set of a saucy B-movie, where nudes frolicked and quaffed and children did what they liked. These Home Counties women remained steadfastly on the sidelines, clutching the cheese sandwiches they'd made earlier, squeezed into dark M&S one-pieces, their bodies like *boudin blancs*.

Sometimes they remembered to chew.

Who knows where it would have ended? Probably in some sort of stumbling declaration two years later to a flustered woman in her late thirties.

Then I fell in love. Proper in love – as only you can do at that age.

Amy was the blister-pack American teen, except she was Canadian. She was Britney Spears whilst Britney Spears was sane: clean-limbed with cobalt eyes, she seemed more like a cartoon than a real girl. I'd probably never met a girl who was prettier; I'd definitely not encountered anyone as spotless and healthy. She and her sister spent their time outdoors doing Activities, which meant that by April they had flawless honey-coloured skin that smelled of sun cream... and *girl*.

Amy's mother was a Martha Stewart divorcee who rented a cottage each summer in the village next to ours. When she found out about two nice English boys who were roughly her daughters' ages, she immediately invited us to play tennis with them and afterwards come home for pizza and fruit juice.

Amy was thirteen, which might as well have made her thirty-six in terms of personal development compared to me.

Charles and I were still at that matching sandals and socks stage (coordinating with *each other*, as well as *each foot*) and it must have seemed like her mother had invited two nine-year-olds over when we turned up in our mother's car with two baby sisters.

Unsurprisingly, that first afternoon was a disaster. Amy and her sister, whose name I forget, did little more than make fun of our accents, hit the ball to each other and talk about things we couldn't quite follow. That feeling of being emotionally out of your depth with girls and not knowing what to do with your hands lingers with us men – I think we are haunted by it until we hit our late forties – it probably explains a lot of affairs.

As we were driven home, whilst avoiding my mother's more searching questions, I was certain that this would be the last time we ever saw them.

However, when a second invitation came just a few days later, Charles and I knew we had been given a second chance to raise our game. And we had a secret weapon: Charles had had a birthday and, enshrined under French law (presumably Napoleon himself had drawn it up), early adolescents who were only a few years beyond riding a bicycle without stabilisers could, immediately they turned fourteen, race about on mopeds to their hearts' content, some of which went above a gentle jogging pace.

Turning up to the tennis on anything that might have leaked oil on their pristine micro-shorts was clearly the stuff of heady rebellion.

Secondly, we had refined our act: if we were going to be English, we might as well make it into an asset. In short, we hammed it up.

Thirdly, all four of us actually enjoyed the tennis. A few years of boarding schooling and the public school obsession with sport paid off: when the girls deigned to hit the ball to us they found we could hit it back.

So, tennis became a regular fixture, as did the healthy drinks and pizza.

I can remember their house even now – certainly better than a lot of the flats I've rented over the years. Everything seemed slightly marvellous, from these two miniature Charlie's Angels, to their apple-pie mum and the giant fridge that dispensed ice. It was open-plan in a way that encouraged families to talk and discouraged anything else we might have had in mind. We'd walked into the set of *The Brady Bunch* and had slipped into British cameos.

Amy's mother had decided we were a *good thing* for her daughters and she fought our cause with compliments, home cooking and lots of shared social engagements to pool parties, more tennis – in fact anything that kept us outdoors, lustily engaged with one another – but not too lustily and with hands visible at all times.

By the second summer in Cognac, Amy and I were essentially friends.

Unfortunately, at that age you're also just hormones: a set of synaptic responses, with hair and clothing, all firing in one direction. Except at thirteen you've no idea what to do about it.

I liked Amy, she was pretty good fun to be with: unlike some girls, she never screeched or complained if you pushed her into the pool, and she'd virtually stopped saying she thought my accent was cute.

But I also really, really *liked* her.

Crushingly, I didn't have the vocabulary to put that into words – that ability to know how to get a point across with careful hints that tells the other person how you feel (but not in so many words) and invites them to drop hints back: the sort of non-verbal green light which says *it would be OK to kiss me… if you can reel me in.* I had an inkling that it was a process: a series of stop and proceed signs that I would have to read right; but boys aren't given a map of the heart when it comes to girls and I guess that's part of the adventure. At the time, when you are young and clueless, it's more puzzling than thrilling.

Nevertheless, I was almost certain Amy felt the same way too and assumed, as she was a bit older, she might take the lead. In the end, she sort of did, but not before our relationship entered a brief, intensely puzzling phase that might have been extreme sexual tension were it not for the fact that we had no idea what *that* was and, anyway, it was never exactly *that*: my memory of that semi-erotic awakening is less a physical thing, and more an internal dialogue between different parts of my brain. It felt romantic.

Before I grew up into a cynical capitalist, bent on conquering the world one small business at a time, I used to fall in love very easily, and a big part of my growing up experience later in life was learning how to deal with that fact.

Back then, I had no idea how to, so (instead) I started pushing Amy into the pool a lot more than usual.

Then something happened one evening at her mother's house.

I remember there were a lot of people around the table outside for dinner and it had reached a point where most of the adults' wine and food intake was perfectly balanced: they were relaxed to the point of lethargy, pleasantly intoxicated but not boorish and, more to the point, totally unaware of the time.

This is the stage in the evening when small children curl up to sleep on laps and older children slope away to watch illicit things online. However, pre-internet, or access to anything with more computing capacity than a Casio calculator, the teens just sat around and rolled their eyes at each other.

I must have been feeling quite drowsy myself because I only became aware that someone was standing behind me when Amy rested her hands – ever so lightly – on my shoulders. It felt funny because the gesture was an almost adult one: it was the same as I'd seen some parents use when they wanted to express affection and possessiveness without making it obvious. I could sense her fierce concentration mirrored by my own because it created a sort of bubble around us, like a sound filter. The grown-ups talking and the music playing all became background to what she was doing that was somehow more important because it had come out of nowhere.

Then, ever so slightly, Amy pushed her hips forward as I tilted back in the chair as carefully as I dared and, by the minutest of degrees, I gradually rested my head on the fleshy mound between her legs that I had no name for. I stayed there, with just enough presence of mind to feign nonchalance, concentrating so hard that my breathing was matching hers as my head softly moved in time with the rise and fall of her pelvis.

By and by, her small fingers squeezed my shoulder blades, just the once, her palm brushed my cheek and she moved away, into the house. And I didn't move a muscle. I wasn't really sure if I should follow or whether the squeeze meant that that was it, the moment was over.

What the hell had just happened? I didn't exactly know, except for at some point I had become aware of her pushing against me. Her mons had felt soft, but underneath was the hardness of her pelvic bone. This juxtaposition, and the revelation of a part of a girl's anatomy I had only ever seen, was completely and utterly thrilling. Had she done that on purpose, or had it been an accident? I had no idea, so I just stayed put: drowsily aroused and dazed.

Then I literally thought of nothing else for seven straight days.

During the moments when I believed Amy had allowed me to nestle like that on her loins (urgh! but for want of a better word), I had kind of assumed that this would be the start, that a line had been crossed between us and that the confusing bit would be over – it would be easier now.

But, about a week later, they came round for lunch and Amy ignored me from start to finish.

After lunch I followed the girls on their walk, my chubby, still-childish legs reddening in the heat, carrying our blow-up dinghy all the way to the small river near our house, hoping we could float on the slow current and… I didn't know, talk? Or something. No sooner had I got the boat in the water than Amy pushed past me, jumped in with her sister and disappeared downstream, with my brother and I looking on like a couple of oxen.

As they got in the car at the end of the day, nothing was said; in fact I don't think we ever uttered another word to one another or touched again from the moment her hands had squeezed my shoulders.

For some reason Amy's mother never came back to Cognac after that summer... and I would have to wait another three years before I even kissed a girl. It had been one of the most intensely sensual experiences of my short life so far and also one of the most baffling.

I'm aware I haven't made a present-day pilgrimage back to Cognac, but I don't feel the need. I spend half of every year in the same *département*, and that corner of the country still feels distinctive and mine.

From the off, France has done more to form my tastes than any other place. In my experience, the happiest people are the ones who have an emotional and material largesse, those who laugh and those who share. And whilst the Gallic psyche can tend towards the depressing and the petty, the way they would like to live in France curiously makes it possible for others (like me) to immerse themselves in the life of a *bon viveur*. This way of life seems to be on the slide, but they understood, in those days, that what really counts in life is how we get on with others: if we are inclusive, if we are generous with what we have, if our thoughts and feelings are open and kind, we will be content... it's that simple. Epicurus said it all: Life *is* a banquet.

It was in France that I learned that yelling at one another solves nothing. Communication, I was yet to learn, is alchemy and was to be the source of my success on every level. For now, I was just beginning to suspect (after the incident with Amy) that it was far subtler than I'd given it credit for and often used no words at all... but it was a while before I got to grips with that language. If ever.

I also learned that the best things in life come, as often as not, from the senses: from our appreciation of what is good to eat, to read and to look at. I learned to lose myself utterly in someone else's words: to be still, to be quiet and to appreciate what another human being has to say, for a change. I was drunk from those first summers by all there was here to imbibe, lulled by the heat, befuddled and seduced by women the likes of whom I had never encountered nor fully understood. And my heart had been broken, which is about as big a deal as it gets.

On the upside, how I dealt with the event horizons – the no-going-backs from these milestones – was more in my control than ever.

What I can see now is that it's hopeless to cling to the past – to mourn the child I obviously no longer was quite fully – but at the same time it's impossible to leave him or her behind.

How to manage this dichotomy: the liberty and the ligature would be the next challenge.

Chapter 5

Downside Abbey

In which I come to grips with the fact that not everyone has to like Robin all of the time

---

If you stand about in a wet field for long enough, you start to be able to distinguish between the different smells of wet mud, wet grass, wet hawthorn and wet spaniel. In this respect, driven shooting is educational.

Then again, standing still, in silence – anywhere – is enlightening.

For the last five minutes before the actual shooting bit of any drive, there's a sense of something between trepidation and high hopes: the beaters close in, like an advancing line of Buffs, sticks beat the grass and dogs punch through the brambles as some of the more nervous birds make a break for it. Then guns snap shut and the blood rushes a little faster through head and heart. For a good twenty minutes before all of this, though, I often wish I still smoked. Or I'd brought a book.

Today, I've got something else to take my mind off the dead time between the guns getting in place and the beaters slowly covering the broken ground, across cover crop, corn stubble and coppice.

I'm back in drizzly Somerset, and Downside Abbey, whose shadow loomed over me most days for five years, sits on the grim brow of the horizon: stodgy and square, like an ecclesiastical urinal.

That's a bit unfair: somewhere else it could be beautiful, somewhere the sun shone more often – as part of a former city state in France or Northern Italy, its blockishness diluted by quainter buildings. Here it's too heavy to be elegant – in the way that Salisbury Cathedral achieves – and not well enough sited amongst parkland to be truly grandiose – like Blenheim.

But for five highly formative years I called it home, and the friends I made there are more like family today. We squabbled through boyhood and adolescence – from dormitory to study, sports pitch to pub; regrouped after university in shared hovels; drank through the London Years (as paupers, at first, then with cash to burn); settled down to marry each other's exes; and became godparents to children who miraculously get on as their parents did.

As I said, with my friends I know I am very lucky. And very grateful.

Coming back to this rainy corner of Somerset twice a year to blow unfortunate poultry out of the sky feels a bit like coming home.

From the age of about nine, I had been aware that the goal after prep school was Downside. My father, a life-long atheist who had gone to St Edward's in Oxford, seemed relaxed about sending me to what was then considered the top Catholic boarding school in the country. He'd been in the army with someone from the school (an *Old Gregorian*) and had approved of him: quite what the criteria were, I have no idea, but the school in the early '80s had a reputation for a sort of loucheness and extreme empowerment that allowed boys after sixteen to slope about like they were already at Oxford – thus there was a pub on campus (this is a *school*, remember), boys who kept beagle hounds and digs in nearby Bath... and a plentiful supply of soft drugs. It made for a lot of eighteen-year-olds walking around in tatty morning dress, period drama waistcoats and hair by Jim Morrison. I was going to Fancy Dress School.

I'd been briefed by a few people before I went and quite liked the sound of the bits I could grasp, but I had to get to this nirvana of upper-class entitlement first and that meant getting a slightly-higher-than-average result in my Common Entrance.

I have little or no recollection of what the Common Entrance entailed in those days, save for two terms prior the headmaster had hoicked me out of the lunch queue and told me I didn't stand a chance of getting into the school of my parents' choice – perhaps I'd consider somewhere for dummies.

And it was true, my mock exams had been pitiful. Somehow this had escaped my parents' notice in France but not that of my great-aunt Millie.

Now, Great Aunt Millie... was actually called Hilda. Hilda Harding. She was a blue stocking with a penchant for clumpy shoes, woollen shirts as thick as a well-made Axminster and Extreme Hair – by which I mean she must have superglued each strand in place somewhere around 1953 and there it remained, in all weathers, until she died in 1994. Yes, she may have been a lesbian, but it was never mentioned – not out of any early political correctness, simply because it wasn't relevant as pertaining to *all things Millie*, in our eyes. She was defined by practicality, marathon baking and horticulture and nothing else came into the picture – and that's the way it should be.

Great Auntie Millie shared the guardian duties of Bennett Minor (me) with my grandparents. Childless and unmarried, she took the whole thing extremely seriously. Millie – as she was generally known – had been the world's first female bank manager and, in retirement, she ran a market garden in Shiplake near Henley-on-Thames. The property had belonged to my great-grandfather and she shared it with her brother, my uncle Ted.

Frankly, I'm not sure I ever heard the poor man speak in company. When I was quite small, I would go down the lane to see him in one of the long greenhouses: Victorian and over-engineered, they were dank as Borneo, even in November when the mud froze in tyre ridges and the ice on puddles felt like you were walking on panes of glass. Ted would be at the end of the hothouse, fiddling with a stub of a pencil. He was always good for a tomato and would watch me in companionable silence as I sucked out the seeds encased in that tangy jelly. He never asked if I was working hard at school, or what my favourite subject was, or patted me on the head and, for that, I had all the time in the world for him.

Whatever Ted didn't say, Auntie Millie made up for in heaps.

The publication of my woeful mock exam results must have coincided with it being her turn to look after me over an exeat weekend.

I didn't exactly get a bollocking, but it was made abundantly clear that *Failing Common Entrance Was Not An Option*. My uncle Andrew was over for a visit and, between them, a martial plan for my impending academic triumph was drawn up.

Children thrive on the right sort of attention and this was pitched perfectly: no-one was saying I was an idiot (who ever *really* knows?) or lazy (I was, too). Instead I was reassured that the results, whilst a fair reflection of my progress *on the day*, in no way reflected my *potential*, which was surely spectacular for a Bennett.

In short, I bought into it: they sold me on the idea of my promise, what I could achieve… and that, Ladies and Gents, is the trick with all education. Any education.

The next item on the agenda for my very own Aunt Agatha was a man on the inside. This proved to be Mr Woodruff, the science teacher at the Oratory Prep, who reminded me of Gerald Durrell, and who had a soft spot for me. My aunt made sure his head was in the right place with a few well-timed visits to the school after church, a cured ham and a succession of Silver Jubilee '77 cake tins with Victoria sponge or lemon drizzle inside when you prised the lid off.

In the knowledge I was being monitored, I applied myself. For the first time in a very long time I started to enjoy school work and take pride in it.

As said, I have little or no memory of the Common Entrance. During my last term at the Oratory Prep School, Auntie Millie carried on making her pilgrimages to Great Oaks to check on my progress, but announced before the end of May that I would sail through.

So, I turned my attention to being captain of the cricket team and generally lording it over the new tics.

My last day at the school was a bit of a zenith: I won a book on the Kings and Queens of England for being the most improved student; a cup for taking the most wickets; and heaps of praise from a proud aunt and a science teacher who might have been fooled into thinking this pupil had been worth it. I had passed the Common Entrance – just – and was off to Downside, the unsuspecting school of my choice.

As for Millie, she went back to her quiet life in Henley, sorting out the accounts for Uncle Ted and looking after the garden.

I never thanked her once.

I was far too busy basking in a glory that was to be short-lived[5].

---

5   It's one of life's heartaches that we rarely get the chance to redeem ourselves in the eyes of elderly relatives for things we have done (or haven't), until it is too late and they have gone. That, in a way, is fitting penance, I guess.

I'm thinking about all this whilst waiting for the pheasants to come over – how a possible through line of this book is that being a bit likeable does not mean you are always going to get an easy ride.

As I was about to find out.

The monks for all their goodness[6] had finally learned that you shouldn't be too easy on boys who are learning to be men. In fact, some argued that you could learn as much, if not more, from the negatives in life: the twin crucibles of failure and conflict are two of the most potent catalysts for success. Some disagreed and wanted to carry on spoiling us. So, I arrived at a great school struggling to redefine itself, get rid of the drugs and the general *languidity* and insert some rigour and conformity into the agenda.

More worryingly, arriving at the school I discovered that the older boys were basically men, that my peers were nearly all smarter, better at sport and more mature than me – and I had no allies, as almost no-one from the Oratory Prep went to Downside in those days.

Downside had taken some hard knocks in the press in the early '80s (ditto of late), but had a new headmaster, Dom Philip Jebb, who remains one of the strongest personalities I have ever encountered (and I once spent ten minutes being grilled by Margaret Thatcher).

One of the decidedly less pleasant side effects of this new, stricter regime was that bullying was somehow allowed to creep in and, for that, I was woefully unprepared.

As I say, my experience of the harsher side of boarding school life, up until then, was as a policing mechanism: very often kids got bullied when they somehow deserved it – so antisocial behaviour (selfishness, stealing, not playing by the rules, 'sneaking'…) was the most commonly punished offence.

---

6   I'm sorry to disappoint some readers but they were that in the main.

More often than not, the offender mended his ways and the pack moved on.

Doubtless I had been lucky up until Downside – my small prep school had been a cosier place, nestling in the gentle folds of Oxfordshire countryside I was familiar with – here it was the wilds of the Mendips: brooding cows and driving rain.

I felt isolated like I never had before.

Without knowing how I managed to achieve this feat, within a week I had several enemies at Downside. I hadn't gone out of my way to upset anyone – but it was alarmingly obvious that I was attracting the wrong sort of attention.

Looking back, I think it was down to maturity. Being twelve or thirteen can fall one of two ways for boys: in the way you behave, the things you say, you're either a teenager or you're still basically a child. I was the latter and this annoyed the hell out of the more mature kids, and the pack's attention caught me off guard.

I started to panic.

Every time I opened my mouth in this new school or made any sort of move, I was doing something wrong, but I could never work out what until it was too late. Perhaps if I got angry with this growing tribe who seemed to get riled up for the mere fact I had just walked into the common room… that might work?

So, I tried fighting one boy, picked the wrong one and got the shit kicked out of me in front of everyone in a corridor.

So, I tried being upset instead. This took the form of blubbing.

Frankly, at this point, it was just going from bad to worse.

Thereon in, I was so taken aback at my failure to get people to like me, I acted like someone I had never been. I became invisible. Everything I did from the middle of that first term was designed to keep me unseen, in the shadows… and meek.

I would have turned to my brother, but he was having an even worse time than me. In fact, compared to him, I had nothing whatsoever to complain about.

A year before I arrived at school, Charles had been taken out by a visiting brother of a friend in his year. He was thirteen, and the 'adult' in question was barely twenty – so, naturally, they went to the pub. On his return, a drunk Charles decided to slide down the banisters from his dorm but, instead, tipped backwards and cracked his head open on a radiator beneath the banisters.

For some reason my father was first to be informed, whilst he was on business in Brazil. I don't even like thinking about how it must feel to receive a call when you are thousands of miles away and be told by a secretary at the office that one of your sons, although she did not know which, was likely to die from a head injury long before you were able to get on a plane and fly back to the UK.

By the time my mother did manage to get over from France (now knowing it was Charles), he had been moved off the 'certain to die' list and was now in the 'certain to be a vegetable if he ever woke up' category.

My mother moved into the nursing home near Frenchay Hospital in Bristol and sat by his bed for three months. There was really very little else she could do but wait, day in, day out, hoping things might improve.

And, little by little, they did. Charles woke up after an operation to remove the blood clot in the front of his brain, then he started showing signs of recognition and awareness of his surroundings: this was a miracle in itself. Then he showed a desire to speak and even walk and the doctors were amazed (in a good way).

A few months later he was discharged from hospital, still very ill but alive, and – against all predictions – with all his marbles.

I can count myself extremely fortunate that there have been a few lottery-winning moments in my life, when something incredible has happened against the odds. This was one of them.

I saw Charles when he eventually came home, and I was old enough to politely ignore the huge scar running from the nape of his neck to the top of his cranium – a hairless strip of pink and white flesh, like an access road cut through a wood. We also pretended not to notice the slowness of his speech and his new, lopsided way of walking.

If minor spills and breaks make you into a hero in a boys' school, major injuries seem to have the opposite effect. Charles was sent back to Downside a couple of terms later, to find himself in remedial classes, banned from rugby and all but friendless, thanks to his status of school invalid.

In a nutshell, he had more important things to worry about than the fact that I was on the receiving end of name-calling and the occasional wedgie.

Hence the coping strategy: not to say a word to anyone in my family and avoid my peers as much as was feasible when living in boarding confinement.

Downside had a higher academic standard than I was prepared for and most of the kids were at least a year ahead of me academically. This may as well have made them university professors. Perhaps my former headmaster had been right and it wasn't the right school for me: I found myself in bottom sets for almost every subject (even after Millie's attentions). In Maths, in particular, I discovered that bullying wasn't confined to boys. Mr Northon had started life as a full back for Arsenal, become the school gardener, then fell into teaching when he was asked to stand in for a teacher who was sick.

His methods were effective, I grant you that. I have never before made such strides in any subject, but for a long time my inner life was divided into when I was actually sitting in a lesson with Mr Northon (fear) and the time in between that (dread).

The three pillars of his teaching method were: rote, ridicule and corporal punishment. Obviously, the one that sticks most in my mind is the last. His preferred method for minor infractions was to hit us over the knuckles with the sharp edge of a ruler, so that the backs of your fingers would have puffy bruised ridges running across them after each lesson. For anything major he would make you stand in a bin, with your feet wedged together at the bottom. He would then kick you smartly in the backside, so you toppled over. It would have been very funny – like on TV – had it not been a child he was kicking.

Oddly, I don't think he was an especially cruel man: he kept up a banter in his lessons throughout, a sort of bonhomie that suggested he thought he was being firm but fair – like a sort of jocular but violent game show host.

It wasn't like I was a stranger to corporal punishment, either. Both my parents hit us and, over the years, many of my teachers had beaten me, but there was a sort of relentlessness to Northon's lessons that was deeply unsettling – a quick-fire series of questions and knee-jerk punishment – and it came just at the wrong time, when everything else was falling apart.

I am really bad at maths, so by the end of the lesson I would have been up the front several times and I would already be feeling slightly sick at the thought of the next lesson.

The sense of being stranded in this cold, unfriendly place became who I was.

I lived with it when I woke up and immediately judged the day on whether I had Maths. If it was a Maths day, I would think about what happened in the last lesson and what might happen in the next, as I showered amongst boys with pubic hair, found my towel in a puddle, got dressed in silence and went to a refectory where I didn't know who to sit next to.

As anyone who has ever been unpopular will tell you, mealtimes are tricky: this is one of the exposure points of the day, when your total lack of friends is out in the open; there is a choice, taken three times a day – every day – when you turn from the queue and have around sixteen seconds to admit defeat as you go and sit in a corner or decide that this time you will fulfil the desperate urge you have to fit in and try to sit next to someone. If you're unlucky you'll be told to piss off and you have the shame of having to turn away in front of everyone and go and sit by yourself after all, or you might get away with it and simply be ignored until you get up to go and someone will casually remark you are a spastic as you walk away, breakfast ruined, something else to think about. To be honest, being ignored was the best I could hope for in those days.

My timing was off: my remarks would make people roll their eyes, my jokes would come out wrong and reveal themselves for what they really always had been – pleas for popularity.

So, I would shut up, locked in loneliness and, to take my mind off it, mainly think about maths. Then I would collect books for lessons I couldn't do but found bearable as long as they weren't with Mr Northon. Each day I would go to the classrooms early, to be on my own. In break times I would find empty corridors and haunt corners. My new-found total lack of confidence affected my ability to play sport, so I became one of the ones who didn't, if I could get away with it. I discovered a far-flung classroom no-one went to, near the science wing, that had an ancient TV, and in the afternoons I would skip games and sit on my own and watch old episodes of *Murder, She Wrote* or *Bergerac*, and drink in the bright escapism of the washing powder ads that showed a world of sunshine, families together and normality. After lessons were over, I'd wander outside around grey buildings, beneath a grey sky, because being cold was better than being pinned to a bed until you blubbed. In that first year I *was* my unhappiness. And I was alone.

One day, on a monastery tour, we climbed the abbey tower. Standing at the top, I got an urge to jump. I wandered about for the rest of the day knowing things couldn't go on like this; I'd never been this miserable in my life. So, the next morning I drank several cups of tea very quickly and took myself off to the 'San', saying I had a temperature – which the tea would do. 'You're in a bit of a state,' the nurse remarked. 'I think you could do with a few days in bed.' I suspect she knew I was faking, but I like to think she could see I needed a break.

I had been there about a day, when a senior boy slouched into my room and sat on the end of my bed and didn't say a word. Even so, rumour travels fast and I knew who he was, but I hadn't got a clue what to say to him, so we sat there in silence until he got up and left. Like Charles, his problems dwarfed mine: the Sunday evening before, he had been walking down the main road outside the school we called the Fosse Way, with a girl he knew from a nearby school. Quite correctly (according to form), he had been walking on the road side of the pavement, but the girl complained she was getting slapped in the face from branches that hung over the wall that bordered the school grounds, so he offered to switch. A few moments later, a car mounted the kerb and killed the girl outright…

I'd like to say I learned a valuable life lesson in the sick bay and by looking on at my brother's plight: that it taught me to think a bit less about my woes and more about what others might be going through and, importantly, how I could help. Unfortunately, I had to wait a few more years for that.

Two good things did come of it, though: firstly, I got some breathing space, which gave me the clarity to see I needed to toughen up… and fast; secondly, I decided to concentrate on my school work and, in doing so, pull myself up from being in lower sets in everything to higher sets that would mean feeling less of a loser all round.

Interestingly, I remember my main concern with being unhappy was that my parents and grandparents must not find out how miserable I was. Worse than being a bit unpopular was it being discovered, then aired. I didn't want to have to explain it to anyone at home. With my grandparents close by in Dorset, half terms and weekend exeats were when I could leave it all behind. My grandfather would pick us up in his electric blue Capri on Saturday morning (a somewhat incongruous car for a gentleman farmer) and drive my brother (monosyllabic) and me (queasy) back to Woodhayes. I would have the next day and a half to rough shoot, chop wood, stuff my face with homemade cake and generally pretend everything was rosy.

A few years ago, I came across a box of my school reports. My junior housemaster's report for the end of the Michaelmas term said: 'Robin is a popular boy who mixes well with his peers without being unduly influenced by them.'

Even the monks thought I was popular, which made it bearable.

In that sense, I had got away with it.

Coming back the next term, things began to improve. There was no moment when I finally stood up to the bullies, I just got better at not annoying people, took things less to heart and improved at maths so my knuckles didn't look like a war zone.

I still avoided the times when I could be an exposed target: this meant not playing sport to a level where I got on any teams or had to get on a coach. I learned to use my new-found love of reading to good effect by sneaking off to the library when not in class and, most importantly, I kept my trap shut.

As with prep school, the day-to-day geopolitics of the place outside of the classroom was run by the boys – school prefects even had the right to beat the junior house pupils when I arrived. Luckily for us, this 'privilege' was rescinded shortly after.

Unluckily for us, a lot of the sixth-formers, who'd been tied to radiators and beaten with fencing swords when they were in the first flush of youth, found it unfair and frustrating that they weren't allowed to dish out corporal punishment when their turn finally came. Thus, the 'no beating junior boys' rule was often seen as no more than a guideline.

In my second year, I was once hung, head first, over a deep stairwell for not making my *fagmaster* coffee to his taste. I was also made to run about in the snow with just my slippers on (forget why) to get shot at with an air rifle for being cheeky (he was a rubbish shot and missed). At this point, it would not be unusual to say that all this had the opposite effect of being character-building. However, the truth is it just rounded off the toughening process that my father had started years before.

Mention fagging to my non-public school friends and you normally get sniggers or the sort of knowing-cum-pitying look Robin Williams spends most of the film directing at Matt Damon in *Good Will Hunting*.

Aside from having to make an older boy coffee two or three times a day and yank his duvet more or less straight, it was generally a cinch; you also got paid and had the use of a study when your fagmaster was not using it.

I even did some illegal fagging in my first year – another ruse to get me away from my peers in Junior House – on a corridor of studies called the Dragon Floor, so called because of a large dragon mural they'd allowed to be painted on the wall. It was surprisingly good artwork. Over the years a few more murals had been added about the house: I remember a reproduction of the album cover of King Crimson's *In the Court of the Crimson King* and Caravan's *In the Land of Grey and Pink*.

The Dragon Floor was a virtual no-go area for masters and monks alike – a throwback of '70s hip when Downside was much more liberal and cool. I loved this cross between a Moroccan tent and a gentlemen's club – it felt like freedom up there and nobody called me names; I was liked there, at least – by the older boys. It was where I was introduced to groups like The Doors, Jethro Tull and Free. I also puffed on fags and chomped magic mushrooms, whilst listening to *The Wall*. Becoming a sort of mascot for the more senior boys made me feel a lot better about life.

If drugs were still around in certain parts of the school[7], alcohol seemed to be slopping about everywhere. The easiest way to get pissed was to get on the rota for serving at the sherry party after Mass on a Sunday. This was when the great and the good of Somerset would descend on the headmaster's rooms for an hour or two, before redistributing themselves to various Georgian mansions in the county for Sunday lunch. Junior House boys were tasked with bringing trays of sherry from the kitchens upstairs to the drawing room on the ground floor. On the way down, we would sneak one or two glasses for ourselves and, in this way, you could count on being shitfaced for Sunday lunch in the refectory. This was easily the best strategy to getting half a kilo of badly roasted potatoes down you – if only to soak up the pint of Budgens Spanish sherry you'd just necked.

---

7   Re street drugs, I never saw anything harder than dope during my time at Downside, although that didn't stop us experimenting with anything we could lay our hands on: magic mushrooms were the natural pharmaceutical of choice, but there were enough stories about bad trips to make it a rite of passage drug rather than an actual habit. Being resourceful we tried a lot of other things – Tipp-Ex thinner and spraying deodorant through a towel were probably the most common and it's a minor miracle no-one set themselves alight because, on top of this, we all smoked.

So, like the prep school, teachers taught, boys policed... but it was quite hard, at first, to work out what the monks did. Granted, some of them taught lessons and a few more of them ran the houses, but that left quite a number you'd see striding about in flapping black habits, like rushing rooks, going through doors you never got to see behind. The monastery was a mystery.

In my five years, I never quite got used to the habitual shock of coming around a corner and being borne down upon by one of the monks with their cowl up. I have a feeling it was one of the perks of the job, especially at night.

When not scaring the pants off us, I reached the conclusion that the monks were there to set the tone of the place as much as anything. Most were old boys who had come back to the abbey after brief stints at university or the forces, and they were steeped in Downside lore; it was rather like they were prefects who'd conveniently forgotten to go and find jobs after they graduated. I can see the attraction; the role of a Benedictine monk seemed to be quite a jolly one – they had most creature comforts, could pursue any number of hobbies the vast resources of the place enabled and, for around a third of the year, hadn't any of us lot to contend with. There always seemed plenty to do, without anyone dying of stress; this included a few parishes to run, a farm or two around the school, and the monks' library, which is one of the most important in the country.

Not bad, but there's no getting away from the fact that not being able to have a house to call one's own, small children who marvel at everything you do, and sex – especially with someone you love – is still a huge sacrifice in return for three square meals per day, a job for life and lots of terrible sherry.

We all agreed that the monks seemed to split evenly into two categories: those with a genuine vocation who had given up good careers, prospects of potential wealth and a lofty station, to live in a rainy monastery in Somerset and not shag; and those who became monks because, quite frankly, no-one else would have them.

Sadly, for everyone, Father Winnoc epitomised the latter. He was my senior housemaster and we made the poor man's life a misery; more than anything he just wanted to be liked and respected but, deep down, he was *not* a particularly pleasant or godly person. I'd had him for Religious Studies before I joined my Senior House and found him to be spiteful. Mr Northon bullied everyone, which I almost respected him more for, whereas Fr Winnoc tended to pick on the pupils less able to stand up for themselves.

I didn't much like him and the feeling turned out to be mutual.

Then there were the powerhouses, the monks who had forged careers or had the potential to excel in the outside world but had turned their backs on this to try and make gentlemen of us. Head of it all (in the school, that is – the Abbot ran the monastery) was Dom Jebb[8]. He moved about the many polished corridors at a perpetual jog, like one of those sharks who might drown in his own inertia if he stopped. Jebb had the uncanny ability to sprint around a corner just as you were lighting a cigarette or preparing to sneak out of the back door to the abbey to get out of Benediction.

I once tried knotting sheets together and climbing out of a second floor window, really just to see if it worked. It did, but I got to the ground, grinning, only to jump out of my skin when I turned to find Jebb standing very quietly right behind me.

He cultivated the notion he was telepathic, and it was incidents like this that gave weight to the rumours. By way of example, a few years earlier some boys had scared themselves

---

8   *Dom* (being the honorific of any ordained Benedictine monk as in 'Dominus' or 'master', which is cool because it makes it sound like we were being educated by Jedi).

witless playing with a Ouija board. Instead of telling them to stop being so daft, he took the whole incident in extreme earnest. The boys were convinced they had called someone or *something* up who meant them a very great harm. By the time anyone reported it to a monk, virtually the entire Caverell House was in a state of manic hysteria.

So, Jebb stepped in to perform the necessary exorcism and, whether the effect was real or simply a spiritual placebo, it all died down, whereupon Jebb became a hero for generations of boys to come. God had triumphed! Showman's trick or not, by confirming their superstitions about the existence of pure evil, he made believers out of a generation in one evening. Not bad.

Jebb was certainly impressive in more worldly areas – he was considered one of the best heads in the country and, as a young man, he had mentored Siegfried Sassoon through his conversion to Catholicism.

He wasn't the only monk with famous connections. Father Anthony, who would later become the first person to seriously encourage me to write, was on close terms with many of the royals, including Princess Diana who publicly cited him as her favourite priest. He would go on to become the headmaster and frequently appeared in the press and on Radio 4's *Thought for the Day*. His fall from grace would come later, but he was, without doubt, the finest teacher I have ever had.

Another monk who deserves attention is Father Daniel, dead now, God rest his soul – and I mean that. Dom Daniel was unusual for being an outsider in the school. An Irishman of humble origins, he looked like how we all imagine a monk should: tonsured, rotund and beaming – basically Friar Tuck. He had no important friends, nor old Downside family connections, he was just a very good man who happened to be a monk. He once tried to explain the idea of vocation to me. I don't think he had wanted to be a monk at all – I think that coming from a large family must make it very hard indeed not to have one of your own. He explained that his vocation was more than just an idea that wouldn't go away. It literally entered into his head like a voice and simply talked *at* him until he answered the call.

Obviously, Father Daniel hearing voices telling him to be something either makes him sound a bit of a nutter or a bit of a fibber. However, I don't think I ever encountered a more balanced, saner, basically human and humane being in my life – nor more honest, for that matter. If it hadn't been for kindly Fr Daniel, countless small, somewhat frightened boys, myself included, would have had a much harder time away from home in those first terms.

As junior house master, he was, at times, the closest thing we had to a parent, and he lived up to our trust by being the same soul in all seasons.

Priests – and monks probably especially – are all suspected of being closet paedophiles. But it's obvious the vile come from all walks of life, all professions, social classes, all ages and upbringing. There were over forty thousand registered paedophiles in the UK in 2014 – and the police think the number should be nearer a quarter of a million if we caught them all. It's lazy but more satisfying to concentrate on making this appalling aspect of all our humanity into a philosophical kickabout: so, it's easier to condemn politicians, priests and teachers as paedophiles, when you could just as easily mention the same criminal statistics for bakers, lawyers and gas fitters and make something of that. We are never likely to hear anyone saying, 'Fred West, that bloody agnostic!' or 'Peter Sutcliff – typical stock clerk!'.

There was a case whilst I was there and, to their lasting shame, the monastery took professional advice, were told (unbelievably) they had no legal obligation to report it, so dealt with the matter without going to the police or any higher authority than the Abbot. Even worse, their way of 'dealing with it' was to make the monk in question promise not to do it again.

When he inevitably carried on abusing children supposedly in his care, they *still* neglected to tell the authorities and simply moved that monk away from anywhere he would have anything to do with us. He was only gaoled some twenty years later. His name, Dom Nick, turned out to be prophetic.[9]

This was a criminal act of putting an institution before the needs of the children it was meant to be caring for. When it all came to light in 2010, the Abbot resigned (although he had nothing to do with the original decision) and a lot of monks who I knew, including Dom Anthony, were quietly sequestrated by the order. Not so much too little, too late as entirely the wrong people, too late.

I think that first year was characterised by the bullying. However, I learned how to blend in when called for. This is the exact opposite to my natural state, so all the more surprising – and useful. Mooning about the empty parts of school to avoid people, and spending a lot of time reading, made me comfortable in my own thoughts, which has turned out to be a good thing. Later, after I had re-grouped and matured, I learned to stand up for myself.

Looking back, I feel sorry for that small-for-his-age, unhappy boy... *but not too sorry – and I certainly don't mourn him.*

He couldn't have survived much longer, in any case, this immature, over-sensitive child... Or, if he had somehow

---

9   The parents of the first victim had also agreed to sweep it under the carpet; the second only complained when it came to light that Downside had already known what the monk was. Fact is, if Dom Nick had been locked up in the first place, the second boy would not have had to suffer as he did. Terrible, unforgiveable and a lasting stain on an institution that has otherwise done so much good.

endured, he would only have done me harm. I feel sympathy for him because he was generally likeable, but I don't much like him because who he was made me so miserable. The world is a properly harsh place for many, but I hadn't been born in a Mumbai slum or police state – and if being hit on the knuckles twice a week and called a few names hurt him so much, then he had to go.

Chapter 6
Downside Abbey, Part 2

In which I learn that generally, at some point in life,
you just have to grow a pair

Once in the house system, in its cosier environment, I began to find my feet and make real friends. I'd finally begun to get the measure of the place, its disparate and sometimes confusing cast of characters... and, more importantly, of myself.

And I still have those friends I made in those last three years at school. An inner circle we can, each of us, always go back to... or possibly a vortex, although we do have other friends – as good, just not as old. We tend to meet once a month on average and, even for those of us who do not make regular appearances – owing to the fact they live five thousand miles away, or have proper jobs – it's satisfying how we can pick up where we may have left off three years before.

Being cool at school relied to a fair extent on how well you played sport. I'd pretty much stopped growing by the age of about fourteen, and rugby, when I did venture out onto the pitch, just became a painful exercise in humiliation. After I broke two teeth in a ruck, I gave up and tried my hand at fencing.

This was definitely *not* a cool thing to do. Fencing was usually the sport forced on the kids who had nowhere else to go: the myopics, the pale ones who wheezed into inhalers, the very fat, the very thin, the small and the weedy (a category in which I was uncomfortably close to being). But my father had fenced in the army and all I'd ever played at school was team sports, so I was keen to try it out.

Foil was my chosen discipline, and the first thing I noted was that being stabbed with the pointy end of a blunt sword felt very little different to actually being stabbed: my ribs were dotted with blood bruises as if I'd been repeatedly pinched by horrid, sharp-fingered children. If I didn't want to get hurt quite so much, I'd need to improve. And I found I did get OK at it reasonably quickly – I had decent hand speed, although, to be fair, the in-school competition was nearly always interested in just getting it over with and going back to something that wasn't sport.

By the end of my first term I'd improved enough to get on the school team, then I got a county seed and, much to everyone's surprise, including my own, I found myself in a hotel in Brighton preparing to fence against other Under 16s from France and Italy.

I lost every bout of my first international, but it gave me a national ranking and I was really pleased about this at the time.

Emboldened by my success at stabbing people whilst wearing tight-fitting breeches, and experiencing an improving social life, I began to enjoy school again.

The following term, I decided to give the Combined Cadet Force another go. I'd always been drawn to the idea of following in a good proportion of my family's footsteps and joining the army: at five I knew most of the names of British weapons of choice and theatres of war. And (thanks to my father's Sunday morning easy-listening tastes) my in-depth knowledge of German military marching bands was spectacular, although I had the good sense to keep that under wraps.

At thirteen, I had been looking forward to becoming an officer cadet, but my first year of the CCF at Downside had been a disappointing exercise in standing about waiting for the minibus. None of our uniforms ever fitted, and the only interesting thing about parades was who might faint first. In the first year, it was also compulsory, so everyone had to join either the army, the navy or the air force; it was therefore generally considered a huge chore to be carried out each Wednesday afternoon with the least commitment possible.

After several years at boarding school, most of us were virtuoso shirkers. *Dad's Army* had nothing on us. Whilst giving every semblance of keen application, we fumbled rifles dangerously, tore maps, contrived to misunderstand the simplest instructions and generally fucked about until the officers in charge gave up and put us in a classroom to show us safety videos. Sometimes they exacted their revenge by giving us long lectures on radio waves or gun cleaning, but we didn't mind – at least it was warm and dry inside. However, once a year we also went on exercise.

This was our opportunity to really shine.

The usual drill went like this: bussed, en masse, up onto the windswept Mendips, we were handed ancient Lee-Enfields that hadn't changed in basic design since the First World War. We were given some army rations, three blank rounds and told to go and pretend to kill one another.

As soon as we were given our orders, it was absolutely essential to get as far away from the 'commanding officers' as quickly as possible and hide. You only came back when you saw the coaches draw up in the car park as it began to get dark. Hanging about was madness – although probably a lot less mad and disorganised than actual war, where running away and hiding is also an option[10], albeit one that will get you shot as opposed to a Wednesday detention.

---

10 A study conducted after WWII concluded that a sizeable percentage of combatants engaged in 'posturing' – i.e. pretending to fight and rarely, if ever, actually shooting at their targets or using their training for anything other than coming home in one piece.

We all knew that the annual exercise was simply an excuse for the older boys to muster the third-formers into private armies in order to fight each other – it was basically Afghanistan under a system of warlords... but in Somerset. To avoid becoming cannon fodder in a prefects' turf war, we legged it.

The second thing to know is that whilst a blank round does not actually have a bullet, it can do a surprising amount of damage at close range. The wadding comes out as a plug of paper, and there would be boys emerging from bushes with it in their hair, like smouldering confetti, complaining, adenoidally, that they had gone deaf. A Spanish kid went one better and shot at a cow. First, he put a lead pencil down the barrel. To everyone's surprise and consternation, including and especially the cow's, the pencil killed it.

I can't remember what actually happened to the boy, except we were all quite surprised when he wasn't expelled. Quips along the lines of *goes to show, sir, the pen is mightier than the sword, sir!* were met with stern looks, but if there's one thing I learned about public school, you never took anything seriously – even dead cows shot with HBs.

However, I remember very little about my first exercise. I was sheltering behind a stone wall over which someone jumped and dropped their rifle on my head. The rest of the day passed in a sort of concussed dream state, as I tottered from one set piece action to another, whilst thunder flashes went off and smoke grenades made a muffled bang through the ringing of my ears and my one and only migraine ever. I would have felt like Charlie Sheen in *Platoon*, except the movie hadn't come out yet, so I had no choice but to suffer without a Hollywood reference point.

Coming back to the army version of the CCF, a couple of years later it seemed to have transformed into groups of *regulars*: boys who wanted to be there. Smaller numbers freed up the budget to do more interesting things that involved helicopter rides, firing anti-tank Milans, ditto heavy machine guns, sleeping in trenches, potholing in Cheddar Gorge and all sorts of things a fifteen-year-old boy will engage in wholeheartedly if he has no internet access. We even knuckled down to the discipline, seeing it as a trade-off that led to better things.

Then I heard about the Army Scholarship Scheme. In essence, if you received an award, it meant free schooling, a second lieutenant's salary through university and a guaranteed place at Sandhurst afterwards: all in, it constituted an unbelievably generous investment in one boy. The tricky bit was finding a sponsor, as most regiments would not take you unless they thought you were in with a chance of passing and therefore a good PR opportunity. I had wanted to apply for my father's old regiment, the Green Jackets, which was an infantry regiment. However, I was persuaded that my twin talents of loafing about and making myself agreeable would be better suited to the cavalry, so I went for an interview with the 13th/18th Royal Hussars. At some point between the wars they'd very sensibly stopped charging at people on horses and climbed into nice sturdy tanks. So, that was good, too.

Before my interview I read everything I could lay my paws on about tanks and regimental history. Then an extremely genial colonel (semi-retired) picked me up at Winchester station in a crumbling Volvo and took me to the pub. Over cold beef sandwiches and bitter, he quizzed me about hunting, ostensibly to find out how well I rode (not at all), my family regimental background (none at all) and my knowledge of current affairs (scant). When I asked him a pre-prepared question about kinetic and chemical artillery rounds viz. the new Chobham armour, there was a shocked silence – as if he was a solicitor and I'd just asked him to grout my bathroom.

We looked at each other in dead silence, until he rallied and asked if I wanted another pint.

Later, we had tea in his office, after which he ran some errands with me in the car and we talked cricket: I began to feel less like a potential officer, more like his grandson.

On the train back to school, I was pretty sure I'd blown it, so it came as a surprise when the regiment wrote to the commander of the CCF at school to say they would be happy to sponsor me, provided I learned to ride.

The next thing on the list was a mini-RCB in Westbury. The RCB (Royal Commissions Board) was (and probably still is, for all I know) the principal means of filtering people for entry into officers' training at Sandhurst. I genuinely think it's one of the saner tests of an individual out there, and companies, universities and other bodies, just generally, ought to adopt something similar. In essence, it tests you on ingenuity, communication and leadership – all of which is on the day and under pressure and there's absolutely no way you can revise for it. It's tough, but life tends to be tough, too.

Everything went reasonably well for me: the written paper was easy enough, then I gave a short talk on why brains not brawn counted as a soldier which, whilst it didn't say anything outstandingly clever, raised a few wry smiles on the panel, and I even managed to succeed in my command task (by using my leaderships skills to get a group of other people [other than me] to do something tough whilst I made purposeful comments). Unfortunately, on the last part of the day – the assault course – I managed to get myself and a box of ammunition wedged firmly in a wire tunnel because I went the wrong way around the assault course.

Thankfully, the Armed Forces are one place where being a bit of a clown can be seen as an advantage. I can only assume that it's useful for morale to have people around to make you laugh when lots of other people are doing their best to make you dead. Having someone small, who can be relied upon to find a way to wedge themselves in a tunnel designed for burly men to crawl through, also means there's a natural selection in play: your best guys live to fight another day, whilst people like me slow up the enemy advance.

So, being spotted as potential comic relief and/or cannon fodder meant I was in the final stages, and the school began to take a real interest in my progress, as did my parents who were now very excited at the prospect of not having to find the price of a new kitchen every year to fund my mediocre progress through the private education system.

I was prepared for my interview by Jebb himself and, let me tell you, it was a far more gruelling experience than anything the British Army had to throw at me. At this point, I began to think that I was in with a chance.

The last stage of the process was a series of reports sent for consideration to the board: one from my CCF commanding officer, one from the MOD panel which interviewed me, and finally one from my housemaster. In a sense, this stage was the formality, to make sure all the paperwork was in order and pushing in the right direction: my Cadet Force officer would always issue a glowing report; likewise one's housemaster for all the honour it would bestow on the house; the MOD, based on its interview, was probably the only wild card in the pack, but I'd saved my best until last and felt I had done well in front of the panel of retired officers who were more avuncular than fierce.

But Father Winnoc was about to get his revenge.

I first thought all was not right when I passed Dom Winnoc on the stairs one evening and he refused to meet my eye.

To this day, I have no idea why he gave me a report that ranked me so low in terms of my fitness as a potential officer that the board had to sit up and take notice. Fr Winnoc had his tormentors but I wasn't really one of them.

The Hussars were mortified, the dear old colonel who'd given me lunch was on the phone to the school, and my parents were insisting I would still make a cavalry officer in the Hussars even if I did not get on the scholarship scheme.

Up until then I had thought Fr Winnoc merely a weak man and petty but not bad. Scotching my chances with the MOD was spiteful, and in fact I think it hurt his reputation, too, as the board thought something was up and they instigated an enquiry into Fr Winnoc's report. However, by then the MOD had decided to move on to less troublesome candidates.

I'd like to say our relationship has improved over time, but whenever I have come across Dom Winnoc over the years – at reunions and the like – his face darkens and it feels like it's about to snow indoors. He used to head the Downside Alumni, and whenever I have done something of note, like get married, have a child, or write a book, you can be sure it is left off the list of achievements for old boys at the end of the year.

I don't really know why he doesn't seem to like me in the least. I am of course aware that sooner or later we all rub someone up the wrong way, and it's usually a measure of our self-centredness that we often have no idea why. Rather than it being an *actual* great big mystery. When we are hurt we remember; when we hurt we tend to forget. And I wish I could say I don't especially care if someone I don't like doesn't much like me. But I have to be honest and admit it bothers me – I'm not cut out for having enemies.

On the upside, caring about others' opinions is a start, even if also knowing why they are thinking one thing or another would be better. Like I say, back then I needed to toughen up, but I'm glad I hadn't become a rock.

Going back to this army scholarship thing, in fairness I think my parents and potential commanding officer were more upset than me. Having a high opinion of oneself has certain advantages when it comes to making rejection someone else's problem. I could see other plus points as well: the mini-RCB under my belt meant I was a virtual dead cert to get into Sandhurst and, much as I liked the idea of being in the cavalry, one of the benefits of not being tied to the Hussars meant I could at least take a look at other branches of the army, such as the Guards (infantry, not tanks) and the Gurkhas – the regiment my dad had been seconded to when I was born in Brunei.

But at the same time, just as I was mentally preparing myself for a role where there was a 37% chance I'd end up getting shot at for a living, quite another side of the human condition, away from all the mayhem and madness, was stealing up on me and it was all down to a combination of PG Wodehouse and Edward Thomas.

A few years ago, my wife, Hélène, and I decided to track the source of the Thames. I do realise this is not the sort of undertaking on a par with wading up the Nile on the back of a camel or fighting indignant pygmies for a glimpse of the prime Amazonian tributary, but it was tough – in an Ordnance Survey kind of way. We got lost: maps were unfolded, found to be depicting a square mile just north of Birmingham, and folded back (poorly). Regrettable things were said. It was not our finest hour as a married couple.

Then (in the best tradition of what came next) I saw a name: *Adlestrop*. And a tin sign with the opening lines of a poem. This was one of those unexpected moments it turned out I'd been waiting half my natural life for. The words on the sign were a soft punch to the belly, like the physical translation of the moment you realise you really (*really*) like someone. For those of you who don't know the poem, it goes like this:

Yes. I remember Adlestrop—
The name, because one afternoon
Of heat the express-train drew up there
Unwontedly. It was late June.

The steam hissed. Someone cleared his throat.
No one left and no one came
On the bare platform. What I saw
Was Adlestrop—only the name...

The language and the rhythm are so simple and tidy – words bedded in place like well-tended plants in neat borders outside a village train station. Nothing much is being said, but this, for me, is the most satisfying love poem to England I know.

Only later did I learn that this was Thomas's first proper foray into poetry. Up until then, he'd been a minor everything: critic, prose writer and husband. A chance encounter with Adlestrop unlocked the lyrics in him that can only have come from a deep personal connection to this country and, in doing so, opened up a world of poetry to many readers since, including me. Germany does philosophy, France melancholy, Italy love... whilst we seem to have a talent for the commonplace: green plastic watering cans, shopping streets, rural branch lines and thrushes – the objects of our endearments are often no more than the mundane things around us. There's very little fundamental difference between *Adlestrop* by Thomas, *Sumer Is Icumen In* (Anonym) and *Penny Lane* by The Beatles – in style or substance – just eight hundred years, roughly.

And willows, willow-herb, and grass,
And meadowsweet, and haycocks dry,
No whit less still and lonely fair
Than the high cloudlets in the sky.

And for that minute a blackbird sang
Close by, and round him, mistier,
Farther and farther, all the birds
Of Oxfordshire and Gloucestershire.

I'd always wanted to visit Adlestrop, since I read and re-read that poem all those years ago, and now I'd stumbled across it quite by chance, looking for something else. Perfect.

I got very excited and started talking about fate: Hélène's mouth went sort of straight and she didn't look convinced, but we got out of the car and took a look around and she eventually had to admit it was quite pretty.

Then we got back into the car and found the source of the Thames, which was also quite pretty – a lush crucible of reeds in a field full of spotted cows, under a large oak – but the highlight of the day had been Adlestrop, and remembering my fourteen-year-old self being delighted that modern words I could understand without a stretch could convey so much that was beautiful and important.

In response I wrote a longish poem called, simply, *Snow*. In execution it was probably more Pam Ayres than Edward Thomas, but my English teacher, Father Anthony, read it and his encouragement for me to write gave me something outside of sport to be proud of. And I'm very grateful to him: I wouldn't say that his encouragement made me into a writer (I wouldn't say I was necessarily a writer anyway), but the first filigree roots of self-belief were needed, and he provided just that.

Then the discovery of PG Wodehouse, at about the same time, when I was made to sit out a rained-off tennis match in a locker room and I picked up a book left lying on a shelf, was equally influential – but in a different way. I saw the proof-in-print that being amusing was often more about the way you wrote things than what was going on. I was also pleased to discover that it was quite acceptable to write about nothing more important than a cow creamer, buying socks and lying in. If I was going to write, I would keep a light touch, I decided.

But writing felt like a guilty secret. The day Roald Dahl came to the school was the day I was meant to go beagling with some people from my prospective regiment. To the dismay of my adult self, I opted to miss the talk, which was brilliant, apparently. And I don't even see the point of beagling – it's basically cross-country running in wellies, following a pack of beagles who are pretending to run after a hare that I've never seen them catch.

'Roald Dahl,' remarked one of the officers, when I told him what I was missing; 'he's a complete weirdo, isn't he?'

It's not a stretch to see how a military career and writing could be compatible, it was just that at sixteen I couldn't.

So, O-levels came and went[11]. I looked set to go through school without great distinction, but it wouldn't be a disaster.

However, I didn't twig at the time, but things were starting to unravel in the classroom: it seemed popularity and good grades were not compatible. Also, my choice of Modern Languages at A-level was a bit of a problem: I wasn't much good at grammar, especially when it was German.

Having spent nearly twenty-five years in the field of translation, I have concluded that there are two types of linguist. There is the technician, who sees languages in terms of an internal combustion engine, each constituent part acting on its neighbour, so (by way of a very general example, with European languages): the personal pronouns affect the verbs; the nouns can dictate the type of article used – whether it is masculine, feminine or sometimes plain neutral; prepositions the case. Like an engine, it is a human construct – so it is imperfect, idiosyncratic, idiomatic and, at times, infuriating.

---

11   Mediocre nine, for me – virtually all Bs, no As. Bloody typical.

However, if you are a class of *mechanical linguist*, like my father, who must be on his eighth or ninth language by now, once you get a global overview of how the language fits together and works (and this gets easier with familiarity of groups of languages over time), you just need a good memory for vocab.

Then there are the chatterboxes.

My A-levels of French, German and English were 50% grammar and 50% literature-based, the latter of which was their primary attraction, but I also loved talking. Obviously. I find, even to this day, that I can pick up a spoken language quite quickly if I spend time in a country: it's word and sound osmosis, and after a couple of weeks of fumbling through Italian, Portuguese, or even Mandarin, it suddenly gets easier, sentences seem to click into place and words you never knew you knew pop into your head. I think the human brain is an incredible thing and language is one of its crowning achievements. We are all linguists; you just need to be a Homo sapiens, and a couple of million years of evolution does the rest.

But I was never the world's greatest linguist – with the exception of English, my choice of A-levels didn't even include my best subjects: that dubious accolade (based on me not ever having excelled at anything) would have gone to Biology, Chemistry and probably History – going by my O-level results. However, my choice of A-levels was the equivalent of me running a flag up a mast for literature and language: they were based more on who I wished I was, than who I actually was. It would have also helped if I'd worked.

The upshot of this would have some fairly calamitous consequences in the short life of RS Bennett Esquire. However, in the long term I'm glad about my choices. They were made for romantic reasons, and they're as good as any[12].

---

12 This is ignoring the fact that it seems inherently foolish to have an education system that pretty much sets the tone for the rest of your life by your A-level choices at sixteen or seventeen.

Talking of romance...

Having no girls at school, and being surrounded by monks and open countryside as far as the eye could see[13], meant we had almost no access to members of the opposite sex of any sort, unless you counted dinner ladies, who are an entirely different species. By way of proof through research of this last point, I have just googled 'naked dinner ladies' and come up with not a single relevant hit, unless you count a picture of Victoria Wood, who was very much clothed. So, even in the arena of the internet, which caters for tastes even the most depraved or jaded imaginations can concoct, it seems there is no-one yearning for the whiskery person who dumped mashed potato and cheesy ravioli onto their plate for the best part of ten years.

By the sixth form, if we behaved, we were allowed to go to dances at girls' schools. As can be imagined, these could only take place in the parallel universe that is a Catholic girls' school and would be heavily policed by female monk equivalents... *fonks*... haha!, only joking... nuns!

As with all early school discos, these were pretty excruciating for the first hour. Frustratingly, once the ice was broken (usually about three songs from the end of the evening) and we finally started to dance with girls instead of moving awkwardly from one foot to another ever nearer the bowl of Frazzles, the nuns would swarm in and man/nun all exits – in case we tried to escape with their charges over our shoulders, like Viking raiders.

However, the girls were usually one step ahead of us. Our nearest school was St Mary's in Shaftesbury and one of the girls came from a farming family close by.

When the invite came for a party in an old Second World War temporary Post Office on their land, I couldn't believe

---

13   *fields and trees* as far as the eye can see, not clerics.

my luck. To this day, I have no idea how twelve of us firstly managed to get out of school, and secondly how we found the field a good thirty miles away where the old prefab building was located. All I remember is it involved a lot of local buses. Sara, whose parents owned the land, had told her mum and dad about the party, but we never saw any sign of them until the next morning. We just turned up and it was laid out for us, as if by elves: there was alcohol, food, bedding. And lots of girls our age, practically looking like they were pleased to see us.

Going to church three times a week for ten years had finally paid off. That night it was good to be Catholic. God was benevolent and we were being rewarded with all the ingredients of a perfect night and more trust to behave ourselves than we really deserved. We just had to try not to screw up.

Amy had long-since gone back to Canada, never to return, but I felt older and wiser to the ways of the fairer sex now.

Actually, this was the first time I realised what a benevolent effect a litre of warm scrumpy and Katrina and the Waves has on social interaction: Laurie Lee had a point (about cider, not 1980s' pop bands). And I have fanned the flames of this precious knowledge ever since.

About midnight, the girls – by prior arrangement, I'm guessing – stopped their Brownian motion of dance-flirt-flit-dance again and settled on one of us they liked. This took us by surprise as we were just getting into pogoing to The Vapors' *Turning Japanese*, and it took the girls a little longer to drag us away from bashing each other up than they planned. As a dance form, pogoing is in truth just a good way to jump up and down and thump your friends at the same time. However, they were persistent and, eventually, I found myself standing outside at the edge of a field with a girl called Connie who had a shock of frizzy hair, like Orphan Annie. She was pretty and she held onto my arm, which was pretty cool.

Others joined us and, as someone struck a match to light a cigarette, a girl I hadn't noticed before was briefly illuminated in the flare. She had dark hair in a rather severe 1920s' bob and a slightly disapproving look on her face. The match died and Connie was asking if she could put my jacket on because she was cold.

She made a lot of finding my glasses in the side pocket and of trying them on. Over her shoulder I watched the dark-haired girl walk back towards the house alone. Then, like in all the best movies, she turned and glanced at me just before she slipped inside.

It was a measure of how innocent it all really was (and how well Sara's parents had probably read the situation) that when we all started to feel tired, we simply went to bed in rows on the floor. It didn't turn into an orgy, and most of us went to asleep.

However, I lay there feeling a little hard done by because Connie had suddenly announced she was leaving to stay somewhere else, so I was on my own.

After a few minutes of sulking on the hard floor, I saw a slim silhouette above me and the girl with dark hair slipped half under my blanket without a word.

I froze. I simply lay there as the gears in my brain crunched, then seized… and the world stopped spinning on its axis.

And so there we were, wordless for what seemed like half the night. I don't even remember breathing to start with.

A real girl was in my bed.

Sort of.

Then, by the minutest of increments, I rested my hand on her side, feeling her ribs through her cardigan as her chest rose and fell. It took an eternity to happen but we kissed just the once, not even a real kiss, our lips just touched and her small, soft mouth parted a fraction.

Then she turned over and I lay there listening to her breathing even out before falling asleep myself.

At around 5.30am, I remember waking as Francie[14] got up. I listened to the diesel chug of Sara's father's Land Rover outside, as he drove off with her and another girl, then wriggled over to her bit of the carpet, which was still warm and smelled nice.

Could you fall in love like that? As I dozed there that early morning, I knew you could. Up until now, most of my love had been unconditional – limited to family and pet hamsters: you loved them because that was the rule. However, I'd assumed that, later, when it came to girls, I'd have choice – as long as I wasn't too picky. Except I hadn't had any say, *per se*: the girl had chosen and, with no words spoken, and just one hovering kiss – more shared breathing than anything – I now felt sort of, I don't know, a bit funny, and I had a longing to have said something to her or held her or be back there now luxuriating in the warmth of her nice soft cardigan.

I have had no more than half a dozen parties that will stay with me like that night, and the early morning, when I slipped away from my friends and walked down the damp road smoking a dawn cigarette, my hangover (thanks to a pristine liver) evaporating with the dawn mist. By chance, an early bus to Frome came along and I got on it.

As it slalomed down the lanes, I fell into a daydream: a Rolodex of images and cutaways from the night before; my eyes unfocused as the hedgerows and cowslip peeled past, replaying, instead, scenes and conversations from the evening as I remembered the heady buzz of alcohol, the beat of music, her rising and falling ribs, the beat of her heart and a kiss.

For the first time there were no vigilant members of the clergy hovering in alcoves, no waiting bus to curtail things – all in, it felt like we had crossed some kind of threshold. But it was the girls who had made it work; they had planned it and they had set the tempo, the tone and the terms of engagement.

---

14   As I later found out.

I'm still in touch with many of them from that set – most mothers now, with their pictures on Facebook, wearing woolly hats on slopes, lining up with children next to grandparents at family dos, or red-faced, on holiday, eating in tavernas with friends: a bit frumpy, but settled and, by and large, they look happy, which makes me happy, too. Behind the middle-aged blandness, you can decipher the young girls they once were and, like so much youthful recollection, the noticing is bitter-sweet: memories of another me and them, the phantom of feelings past whose summoning makes them seem fresh once more and then a little sad because falling in love will never again be so new, or exciting... or unexpected.

Present day

The shoot is over and we've gone back to the lodge for some cake and tea. Getting out of the battered Defender, I look across the blurring Somerset fields at the monastery in twilight.

After five years, the drizzly countryside and the looming abbey had become as much a home as anywhere in my world.

But it was an odd sort of home, all things considered: the whole structure was cold as a witch's chuff for nine months of the year, and no-one gave you a hug – unless they oughtn't. The corridors and the classrooms had all the ambience of an 1830s' workhouse, with their decades of polish smell, and the semi-industrial radiators arranged against the scuffed wooden panelling that ran the length of the corridor. Then there was the graffiti. You could stop at any of the window ledges and pick out scratched statements in the stone: who had spent time there or who deserved invective; information that could have come from last Thursday or an entirely different generation that went to war and never came back.

In that last summer term, the abbey finally began to look beautiful in my eyes. In sunlight, not streaked with rain, the stonework looked closer to Cotswold honeyed than hewn granite, and the countryside softened as the fields and hedgerows filled out with fresh growth and wild flowers. Between November and March, Somerset mud seems to get into everywhere and onto everything. Come May, footpaths, which had seemed like routes through Ypres, were now pleasant places to walk with a book and some study notes to find a hollow of flattened grass in which to lie down awhile and fail miserably to revise.

My days here had not started well – at all – but I really had needed to mature. And I reached the helpful conclusion that if a situation is unbearable and there is no obvious way to change it, then modifying yourself is always an option[15].

As a result, Downside was going to end on a high, just as my prep school days had. I had fallen in love, the exams were over and my career was mapped out: university, army and comfortable retirement to write deceptively comic poems in front of a fire.

But there is something else.

When I look back today, mulling over the abbey in the gathering gloom as I drink my tea, it occurs to me that this was when the rot had set in. The first layers of innocence had been stripped away and I had become harder, more knowing and less knowable. The reed-not-oak coping strategies I learned at Downside – of retreat, toning down, then modifying – were a clear compromise and one I have used successfully in life: in business it has made me willing to try new things and make opportunities, but I do wonder if in my personal life it doesn't make me a bit too much of a chameleon. I've always admired those people, like my brother, who go through life just as they are. It is truer.

---

15   I say helpful because, later in life, we are all pretty much forced to abandon the simple solutions and entertain the possibility that a) there are no answers to some problems or b) *we* might be the problem (more likely).

Signing up to that public school thing of not taking anything too seriously helped me endure, though I'm very far from convinced it improved me as a human being. But I didn't really stop to consider this at the time; all I cared about was that I had won, of sorts: first I had worked out a way to live with the bullies, then I had made good friends. The ever-present monastery; the black monks striding across the quadrangles like cormorants of stern purpose; the refectory with its smells of stewing and broiling; the dank locker rooms; the stony, frigid showers that would transform thrice a day – before morning prayers, after games and in the evening – into a hammam of noise and pink bodies looming in the steam; and the sense that nothing really existed outside the walls except the village, a few fields, then... space. It defined me in those days.

But I was leaving.

Chapter 7

London

At seventeen, the world expects very little of you. If you're going to screw up, this is about the best time

The trick to getting your first grown-up job is to *nod loads* – basically be prepared to do anything.

When I started out in the job market, this was not a long-term sentence, because the sort of jobs you got when you walked into the Fulham Job Centre in 1986 and told them you were desperate were either cripplingly boring, psychologically harmful, fraught with danger, or all of the above. You never stayed long.

So, within the space of a few short weeks of my first summer holiday after my A-levels, I was: a dishwasher in a commercial kitchen serving unhappy Fujitsu staff; a dishwasher in a small, very exclusive nightclub-cum-restaurant in Chelsea serving a leathery Joan Collins; an office cleaner (between the hours of 4am and 7am); a map folder for a deeply unpleasant printing firm in Fulham; a temporary gardener for an elderly gay couple in Earls Court; a silver-service bartender at private parties, where I met Annie Lennox, saw my first cocaine and was given a tip by Bob Geldof of some dope; and... best of all, a general labourer on a building site.

This newly discovered work ethic was the result of wanting to go Interrailing and meet girls on beaches.

I got to this last job as a labourer after three weeks and promptly decided I would stay put: the pay was marginally better than the others (dot on £100 per week) and they had as much work as I wanted. Better still, I got to wear a hard hat and smash things with a sledgehammer.

We were a team of around four students working under an old and very grumpy Caribbean foreman, and our job was to gut large London houses before the real tradesmen moved in and turned them into expensive flats. In the weeks I worked there, I must have created, then shovelled, several tons of rubble into skips. And I also developed a good head for heights: a lot of the work was up the sort of scaffold that would now feature in a Health and Safety clip online, called something like, *Look What These Idiots Are Up2* or #darwinawards. The boss restricted the flooring on each level to just a couple of planks, which were hardly ever secured to anything so, more than once, I was five floors up when a plank slipped from under my foot and I had to catch hold of something solid and then try not to burst into tears in front of everyone else.

Each morning, I could remind myself what I had been doing the day before simply by blowing my nose: if my snot was red, I'd being taking out brick walls; black, fireplaces or ceilings; off-white, plasterboard.

Thanks to the generosity of wealthier friends at that time, I was also going out every night and drinking several pints of beer. I told myself it was to flush out all the Victorian dust I had taken on board during the day, but I was fast replacing it with nicotine from all the fags I was smoking.

A seventeen-year-old chap is more or less indestructible – or imagines he is, which is pretty much the same thing; I never stopped to consider the ill effects of getting pissed every night (I don't exactly dwell on them today, although I have given up smoking and spending my day up precarious scaffolds for a living). We all laughed off the total lack of safety precautions on site, until one of my workmates went through a floorboard and tore open his scrotum, leaving one gory testicle hanging from a hole in his jeans. I'm still squirming.

After that, things improved on site. A bit. But I was nearly at the end of my stint anyway: I'd banked enough to live on bread and tuna for a month whilst travelling, plus the cost of the Interrail ticket. This 'deal' was great and I hope it still exists: it allowed unfettered travel through the European railway network to tens of thousands of teenagers every summer – it was basically as if the SNCF had agreed to babysit Europe's population of middle-class semi-children, before they went off to universities in towns mum and dad would struggle to locate on a map.

After Interrailing, the next stage of the summer was pencilled in to visit Francie[16] in Germany, where I'd almost certainly get to see her naked, before jetting off for the start of my gap year in Uruguay where my father had found me a job. Life was looking very rosy at this juncture.

Our first stop was to descend on my long-suffering parents, who were renting a place south of Avignon.

As the train went south, the weather improved, and it began to dawn on us that we had the whole of Europe to choose from and just enough money to make it feel like our first real taste of freedom – the better for having earned it. We could lounge on beaches, camp in woods, drink and watch the sun go down or come up – just as we chose; in fact, the sun was shining on a bright future as we walked the last mile up a chalk track towards my parents' villa.

And I was about to get a massive wake-up call.

---

16   After *that* party, I had made contact and we'd been out in a rather chaste way in Bath a couple of times, which didn't stop everyone assuming we were an item. I thought about her a lot but I don't think that counts.

I had sort of known all along that my A-levels were unlikely to make my family swell with pride. Apart from some early promise in German, where I mastered the trick of *sounding* like I was German and had a knack for learning lots of new words, my grasp of grammar was on a par with the extent I understood Applied Maths or made light work of Computer Programming. I had only taken up the subject to get out of Latin, because I couldn't tell my genitive from my genitalia; but by the time I had realised that German was basically a stroppy version of the language I was avoiding, it was far too late. Bit by bit, I'd resigned myself to a low D or high E. Either way, I was counting on French and English to keep the ship afloat: I needed two Bs minimum, but I was great at those subjects – I'd probably get straight As.

Standing in a payphone somewhere near Avignon to hear, from my brother, that I got an E in German, a D in French and a C in English was not that pleasant. It would almost have been better had I completely ballsed up (then I could have claimed an exam meltdown, hay fever, broken heart, morbid fear of invigilators... anything). Instead, this just made me look a bit crap and lazy. Never fail moderately.

I didn't have time before we arrived at my parents' villa to think up any good excuses.

Initially, my parents were very nearly sympathetic... until they found out that virtually all of my friends had failed their A-levels too. Then – and quite unfairly, in my view at the time – they blamed the monks for letting us do nothing very much for our last two years. Looking back, I am surprised (and obviously very grateful) that my mother and father didn't beat me to death using the first thing that came to hand the moment I told them (rented villa BBQ tongs, probably). I knew the amount they paid in fees and the sacrifices they had made in the early years of prep school to keep me there but, now that they were very well off, I just assumed they didn't have anything else better to spend it on. I also assumed that they would now sort out a 'crammer' for my retakes. That way I could go back to enjoying my month loafing around Southern Europe.

Quite rightly, both my parents and my brother flat refused to lift a finger: the first part of my punishment was to go home immediately and start interviewing for retake colleges in London.

And so that was my short-lived Interrailing experience.

I said goodbye to my school friends sunning themselves on a beach near Cannes and, to make matters several times worse, got back home to London to find a postcard from Francie telling me I was dumped: she had found a proper boyfriend in Germany and, whilst I was still welcome to come over, she wanted me to know it would be entirely platonic[17].

In those days, making international calls cost the price of a small farm in Wales, but I got permission to ring and had a stilted five-minute conversation with Francie. Francie was sorry to hear about my A-level results, but I could tell the serious and applied German in her was disapproving, and perhaps a tad reassured, that she had made the right choice dropping me for someone who had probably passed all their exams and always made the most of his opportunities in life.

Fucking twat.

That's the fictitiously stodgy German boyfriend – not Francie, for whom I still have a soft spot. Although I am not sure why I do – as first loves go, it was a bit of a stretch: we barely got to know one another, we never officially went out and, as a rule, I'm a sucker for blonde, articulate, arty girls – not quiet, slightly geeky brunettes. Ho hum.

Closer to home – i.e. *at* home – I was not very popular.

---

17   Teutonic platonic

Present day

I'm in Fulham. The timeline is converging: the me then and the me now are getting ever closer.

As always when I come back here, I can't quite shake the memory of that grim start to the academic year in 1986. I was almost an adult, and the way I felt about things then comes unbidden and fresh, so it affects my mood as I walk from where I parked the car on Parsons Green to Elthiron Road with its large Victorian terraces, 4x4s and pricy shrubs in minute front gardens. It has the same feel: the houses aren't that nice when you really consider them – you could be anywhere in a UK town – it's just expensive because in 1984 Chelsea became unaffordable for the upper middle classes, and all that sets it apart from Luton or Liverpool are the delis, the lack of all-day breakfasts, Sky Sports in pubs and some really nice furniture I can't help noticing because no-one seems to have net curtains anymore.

I'm not sure what to make of London these days. It's a young person's game, I have a sneaking suspicion. Now, when I go into pubs and bars, I feel old and it's too noisy. When I walk along the street, people seem to be in my way, and I look up more. Like a tourist. I still know the place like the back of my hand, thanks to eighteen years cycling, then motorbiking, from Wapping to Watford, Tooting to Turnpike Lane – but that just feels like useless information, a party trick. It's because I tend to pop in and out these days, I never loiter and so nothing feels lived in – the knowledge of the backstreets and cut-throughs, so laboriously acquired, is useless.

However, I still happen to think it is the greatest city on Planet Earth. If nothing else, nowhere has its range: its sporting mecca of Wimbledon, Lords, Twickenham and Wembley, spiritual homes of four of the biggest sports in the world, not to mention the iconic football clubs; music venues that saw the advent of most of what mattered in popular music culture from about 1965 to the present day; the busiest financial exchange centre in the world; and more restaurants, more pubs, more youth, more languages, more parks and more icons in the form of Big Ben, busbies, peppery gents, red buses, Tower Bridge, taxis, barrow boys, bric-a-brac and bobbies. There are twenty-six other female monarchs in the world, but it's ours who is being referred to when you mention The Queen.

I'm coming to the Thames now, where I lived on a houseboat for three years. Walking the mile or so to get here, it's packed with memory – ghosts loiter on virtually every street. A lot happened to me in the two decades I spent here, I realise. I can't go anywhere without passing places I did odd jobs, houses where friends lived, pubs I frittered time and money in. And I've just changed my mind; I still love this place and I'm proud that London is in my country and was once my city.

But back in 1986, I was barely eighteen and London didn't feel like a young person's place at all. It felt like it was full of people who knew just how they fitted in. And me. For the first time since I was eight, I was living at home, which didn't help.

My allowance had been cut to £20 a month and my money from the site work was all used up, so I had to think up cunning ruses. First up, I hawked my record collection to the second-hand shops in Notting Hill and then I callously went through toys and books. It was obviously pre-eBay, so this all had to be done with small ads in local papers, so it wasn't unusual to answer the door to a six-year-old (with his mum) who'd come about the Tonka Dump Truck for £2.50.

My parents were understandably annoyed with me nearly all the time, and my failure to pass a relatively easy set of exams (given the education I had received) was constantly there – either because I reminded me, or they did.

This wasn't the first time I noticed that, whenever anything bad happened to me throughout my childhood – like I lost a toy or broke something – then I had it coming to me *because I never took anything seriously*. And now this was all beginning to look perfectly true.

I found this hurt because they never understood something fundamental about me: making jokes and conversation was considered a sign of not really caring but, worse, of shallowness.

I didn't have the verbal artillery at that age to refute this, so I let the fact I was considered pleasant but a bit lightweight carry the day. On the basis that we are defined by how others see us, the definition stuck.

It took me a while and a lot more maturity to learn to stand up for myself on this issue but, even at the time, I *knew* that making a joke of things was a sign of the opposite of not caring – that it was actually a mechanism for protecting yourself from caring too much. Because I did mind a lot about a lot of things: for instance, I cared deeply about my exams and I hated the failure. I also cared about my friends, my books and, I guess it is shallow, I cared about being liked. The crux was that, as well as owning up to failure that year, I was also coming to terms with the fact that my parents didn't think much of me.

So, I made a joke about that too, and the bonkers things my parents said or did became the stuff of amusing stories for my friends in the pub – and that way I found the unevenness and the unfairness didn't sting quite so.

But perhaps I was over-thinking things. It is obvious to me now that I needed the sort of simplicity and perspective evidenced in the prologue but, at the time, everything was a muddle. When you are eighteen everything is a contradiction because that is what you are: still a child, but in an adult body, with your thoughts ping-ponging between the two. It's not life that is complicated, it's you.

For the record, education wasn't helping; it all seemed a little obscure as to how all these lessons helped turn me into a better person, a better adult. To make matters much worse, it was also impressed on me that everything I did was vitally important.

Not knowing quite why you are doing something that you are also not terribly good at, whilst being told your whole life depends on it, is quite stressful.

Then – not now – I needed some of my own advice.

I mean, I liked learning things – or, at least, I liked the idea of getting more intelligent – and I am quite nosey, which means I can be engaged by a subject fairly easily. All in all, I'm not hard to teach, but I didn't like the way I was being taught, because a great many of my teachers were really crap. I'm sorry, but it's true.

I think that any subject is fine and I don't have a problem with the current curriculum – run your finger down the descriptions of the Key Stages and they all seem perfectly reasonable to me. However, a really good teacher will take the framework of any subject and add themselves to it: that is, their experience, their dedication and their feel for the class as individuals. A well-delivered lesson about almost anything is really about life and, at its most fundamental level, teaching should focus on showing us how to learn. Now that *is* a skill worth having.

Amongst my peers, what is striking is the inverse relation academic success has had to material and spiritual success as a proper grown-up. For the most part, people I know who did well at school and university didn't do much for the next twenty years except commute each day and receive a 5-10% pay rise every couple of years.

What is so noticeable to me is that nearly all the academic failures in my peer group have done so much better than their 'brainy' counterparts. There's only two possible reasons for this: early failure is good insofar as it provokes a desire to prove one's detractors wrong; or academic results are not reflecting ability – thus education failed at least 80% of people I know.

Bit of both, I daresay; but education rewards conformity and, worse still, doesn't reflect real life, which is more about having the confidence to go your own way (believe me, it really is). Not just reflecting; it's not best preparing us for the real world.

One of the best things about British private schooling is constantly being told how marvellous you are. In between beatings and the mental anguish of being very far from home with strangers who are on low pay to look after you, teachers and one's peers constantly remind you that you are in an elite cadre.

But that year – at least to begin with – no-one was rubbing my ego up the right way.

However, in a sense, it all came at just about the right time of my life. It wasn't just that I richly merited pretty much all the bollockings I got (it was me who failed my exams, no-one else) but this was my first big failure, and luckily I had a whole year to sort it out whilst being cushioned by the fact I wasn't living on the street and I didn't have any greater responsibility than to remember to get up in the morning and knuckle down.

Much worse things than my first set of A-levels have happened to me in my life, both before and after that year. But it was key, I think, to me, because this was the year I learned to cope with the stark reality of having no-one else to blame but yourself.

Coming right after the entitlement training at Downside it was probably the best life lesson I could have had right there and then, and it's a good thing it happened when I was young enough to use what I learned at the start of my adult life, before things got too serious. Failure followed by uneven, shouty parenting came along when I needed it most: it gave me just the right concoction of a wake-up call and teenage sense of injustice. Get over your requirement for life to be unbiased, then get angry, then make sure you stack the odds in your favour in future.

And so I hope my children make mistakes early and I get pissy about it.

By December I decided I now knew what failure felt like; it hadn't killed me, and if I was going to fail in life it would never again be for want of trying. If I was going to screw up, in future, it would be energetically, spectacularly... and with flair.

Marsden tutorial college was housed in a fading Georgian townhouse, overlooking the Queen's Club on one side and a row of rusty railings on the other. That whole district – wedged in a triangle between Barons Court, the eternally squalid North End Road and the A4 – hadn't quite made up its mind about whether it was upwardly or downwardly mobile: posh slumming it or slums with airs 'n' graces.

The same goes for where I was retaking. Marsden itself was supposedly run by an eponymous ex-Eton housemaster with impeccable manners, and he was the first adult I had met who seemed completely relaxed about my results and certain that I would turn things around. However, apart from the first interview, where we'd chatted about Sartre and cricket, I hardly ever clapped eyes on him again. It was only much later that I learned he had been a champion rower well into his forties (astonishing the rowing world in the 1950s by beating the Russian Olympic silver medallists in the Double Sculls at the Henley Royal Regatta), a stockbroker, farmer and decorated wartime spy.

Instead, he seemed to leave the daily running of the place to the tutors, who were hardly older than us, mainly Oxbridge educated and, for want of a better word, a bit Byronic.

Josh Phelps, in particular, was the teacher you always wanted – unless you were teetotal and a firm believer in classroom education only. Josh was a socialist of conscience who happily took our parents' money then spent it on us in the pub.

After a few weeks of sitting in a classroom we all of us realised there was nothing to stop us moving to a more comfortable environment that sold beer and little bags of pork scratchings. So, we had our tutorials in the local. My fellow students were a mismatch of A-level failures, or Trustafarians who lived in mansions in Chelsea with the sort of enlightened parents who wouldn't dream of sending their children to boarding school but found the local comp was just a step too far. Finally, there was a minority of the mildly brilliant, who were being fast-tracked through A-levels.

Had my father – or anyone else's father for that matter – twigged what was going on, our tutor would have had a lot of explaining to do, but perhaps not. I like to think Josh would have appealed to my father's tendency not to do things by the book.

And the key thing here was we were learning two important lessons: firstly how to manage one's alcohol consumption so that you could spend three hours in the Front Page Tavern, then still go home and write a coherent essay on Baudelaire; and secondly that you can learn a lot of French actually speaking the language, smoking Gauloises in a snug bar whilst tucking into London Pride.

The rule was simple – we could indulge in a two-hour drinking tutorial, as long as no English was spoken and no-one subsequently handed in an essay that was late or sloppy.

Thanks to Josh jumping down my throat whenever I said something flabby, within two months I'd learned how to set out a rigorous argument on paper and, more importantly, not to open my mouth unless I had something meaningful to say.

Josh had that whole intellectual hard man thing going on, so when he wasn't getting pissed, smoking roll-ups and reading *Les Fleurs du Mal*, he was off lifting girders. He could be as physically intimidating as mentally, and he made sure we respected him enough to want to do well, whilst making it clear he was on our side through thick and thin. It was a balancing act, but he had it off pat.

In short, he was exactly what I needed after years of being taught by nervous monks, retired majors and masters who had been so long away from an exam that any empathy had been bored out of them by what must have seemed like a relentless tide of arrogant yet generally mediocre boys.

Marsden was also co-ed.

It was the first time I had learned alongside anyone remotely attractive since I was about seven, and it made for infinitely more interesting lessons. Within a few weeks, I proved how shallow I was when, quite miraculously, I found myself thinking of Francie hardly at all. Being in the dazzling orbit of the dozen or so girls of sparkling prettiness and urbanity was just the tonic I needed for a bruised ego – as opposed to a broken heart. These debs sloped in and out of lessons or the common room with knowing looks on their faces, talking about the shopping in Harvey Nichols, weekend parties in Kensington, and the terrible hardship of finding a taxi in Chelsea after midnight.

Typical of most of my sex, I was still basically a nine-year-old in terms of what I enjoyed doing, and here I suddenly was, standing about with actual young women who dressed liked adults and had a bored, cosmopolitan attitude that was very different from the nice farmers' daughters I had known in Somerset. They were alluring.

I soon began to lead a sort of double life that you sometimes do when growing up and are still unsure about exactly who you are.

During the day, at home, I was caught somewhere between childhood and adolescence[18].

With the thin, dark house in Fulham to be avoided at all costs, in the evenings I threw myself into pub culture up and down the Kings Road in Chelsea: attempting to pick up the way these young tutors, all fresh from Oxbridge, had of not appearing to say much but still managing to come across as clever and very funny. In truth, I was more ribald than witty, more Falstaff than Faber – although I was sure I had pulled off the look of intellectual bohemia with my father's old dress shirts, a military greatcoat and cavalry mess boots. I probably hadn't. I probably looked like a dickhead.

Truth be told, I don't think I'll ever be wry. Heaven knows I tried. And I think these tutors put up with me with a sort of sardonic lenience because, whatever else, being a bit of a clown buys indulgence.

On the other hand, I still had my Downside friends and spent weekends either in Oxford, pretending to be an undergraduate, or in the country in big chilly houses belonging to schoolfriends' parents, doing country things like repairing quad bikes, lamping, and walking the dog as an excuse to smoke cigarettes.

I was starting to like London but was rarely there for longer than two straight weeks. I had no computer skills, so 'VDU' work was out of the question, as was working in a pub since I couldn't add up a drinks bill unless I had a maths teacher standing at the end of the bar to hit me with a ruler. So, during the winter I earned a bit of extra cash chain-sawing firewood, and in the summer holidays I helped with haymaking on a friend's family farm. Coupled with a summer on building sites, I went from being very skinny to only slightly very skinny.

---

18   … it's a hump some of us never quite get over. Depressingly, perhaps it is true and we do not grow up properly until our parents die.

On the home front, through hard work and being quite a lot brighter than most people he comes across, my father now found he was unexpectedly wealthy. This was pleasing, but essentially odd, as we'd got used to being a bit poorer than our peers – it was how we self-identified as a family. But the move to France had paid off and he had reached the lofty heights of managing director at Remy Martin Cognac, with all the trappings of wealth expected from a company exec in the 1980s.

He still never quite managed to pull it off convincingly. I think his underlying eccentricities, which hadn't diminished over the years, would always make him an unusual sort of businessman. In fact, climbing the corporate ladder so successfully surprised everyone – not least him, most probably. But he has just the sort of strategic mind that company marketeers love, especially when he would couch corporate argument in military language from his days in the Gurkhas. In my experience marketeers love nothing more than pretending that marketing is like a Napoleonic battle, because it makes selling wet wipes sound dangerous and manly. He's also got this thing he does, which is to adopt a manner which is a cross between Lawrence of Arabia and Bertie Wooster – it makes people somehow overlook the fact they are discussing a deal worth several tens of millions with an Englishman wearing a fez he bought at the airport because he genuinely thinks it looks nice.

He never spoiled us in the way that other captains of industry might their privately educated children. After years of hand-me-downs, we didn't really do indulgence. Any expensive holidays we went on were a disaster for the simple fact my father clearly loathed any hotel that was comfortable, served nice food and didn't involve some kind of terrible ordeal to get there.

Don't imagine he is puritanical; in many ways, we did lap up the new luxury – literally: for four years we drank champagne by the gallon. I don't think he ever fitted into the corporate body politic, though. The oceans of bubbly came about not so much via his new-found wealth or prestige but by a schoolboy prank much more in keeping with his usual bad behaviour. We basically pinched it from the company cellars during a move.

I think my father tried quite hard to play the rich industrialist but his one foray into hedonism, the purchase of a boat in Henley – a real gin palace – was a bit of a disaster. It was this great plastic bauble that was freezing in winter when it sweated condensation and so hot in summer it made us all angry and argumentative.

Truth is, I think he missed his canoes.

Ironically, that last year I lived with my parents – the first and only year I did so since they packed me off to board – was the year we grew most apart. Frankly, it must have been a nightmare for them, too. I can only imagine the self-restraint required to put up with their exam-failing son who spent a great deal of his time in The White Horse in Parsons Green dressed like Adam Ant's mum.

My toothbrush was at home, I usually ate breakfast there, and supper sometimes, but the rest of the time I was out.

One of the places I spent a lot of time in was Wimbledon.

Tim was one of the more down-to-earth students at Marsden in that he didn't own an acre of Chelsea or have a nascent drug habit. His parents still had a very fine *vicwardian* house on four floors overlooking the tennis club and a full-size snooker table upstairs. This is an important detail. Tim liked music even more than I did, and we would spend all evening in the pub then go back to his parents' house to play snooker and listen to Radio Caroline, which still played Led Zeppelin, early Genesis, Bad Company and bands from the '60s with names that sounded like they could be characters from a Teletubbies spin-off.

Once in a while, Tim would invite us all round for dinner, cooked by him. I liked going because it felt a bit grown-up and, for an eighteen-year-old, Tim certainly knew his wine.

The only rule in his parents' house was that once on the top floor, you stayed on the top floor until the morning. I don't think I ever saw any of the bedrooms – most nights we drank ourselves silly and crashed under the snooker table.

Sometimes, but not nearly often enough, girls would stay, and Tim had a sister who was pretty if you could get around the fact that she looked like Tim but with a pair of breasts. So, that was never going to happen. More than once, anyway... or twice, tops.

Towards the end of the summer, one girl started hanging out with us more than others, which was surprising, as the evenings had got steadily more blokey – more *real ale* and *rugby* – as the year went on. But this new girl seemed happy to go to the pub with us most nights, smoked roll-ups and she bought her fair share of rounds.

Her capacity for fags and alcohol was all the more amazing given she only weighed about six stone.

Pardice's parents were very much part of the London Catholic Mafia. They all went to Farm Street Catholic Church in Chelsea, or the Brompton Oratory where you could still get a good old Tridentine Mass: sung in Latin, three priests, with their backs to you, like rooks – Catholic Hardcore. Pardice had been to St Mary's Ascot and had an accent you could etch granite with. She was pretty but, most of all, poised.

Her usual haunts (when not pretending to be virtuous at Farm Street) were Harvey Nics, Sloane Avenue and Notting Hill, which made it all the more surprising she wound up in Wimbledon, playing snooker with two blokes who talked pretentiously about existentialism and the blues (I'd recently been to see BB King in concert – in Croydon, of all places – so that was pretty much all I could talk about).

The evening in question, Tim's parents were away, and when Pardice announced she was going to bed it turned out he had a special papal dispensation in mind when it came to sleeping arrangements. 'You can sleep in my room,' he suggested, a tad more magnanimously than he should. 'I'll just crash upstairs,' Tim added. None of it was very convincing.

Pardice narrowed her eyes at Tim and announced she would take the spare room. 'You must have several.'

I think Tim was so ashamed of his transparent ploy he agreed to show her to a room without any excuses and came back a few minutes later, still looking sheepish.

'One more game?' he said, putting a brave face on what I think he had hoped was an evening that was going to end well.

'No, thanks…' I don't actually recall, but I almost certainly gave a theatrical yawn at this point, 'I'm bushed.'

'Oh, OK,' said Tim. 'Goodnight, then.'

Darn right, I thought. Before she had walked out the door, Pardice had turned and given me a *Look*.

The minute Tim pissed off, I snuck downstairs and looked for a light under a door.

When I slipped into bed beside Pardice, I found her slim body, thrillingly, completely naked.

The truth was, for all our artifice, our privately educated self-assurance, we were probably both a bit nervous: fifteen minutes earlier we had been friends and now we were doing something neither of us was quite sure of – although Pardice was probably on the surer side, to be fair, as she had already taken off her clothes. After a few minutes, she took the book from my hands and kissed me. I felt her small nipples against my chest as she leaned over and… some things are the better for being private.

Prosaically, the experience lived up to the expectation. Physically, at eighteen, there's no such thing as bad sex because any sex is brilliant and, five minutes later, you're raring to go again… and do it much better.

This event marked a change in fortunes across the board.

Shortly after, my retake results came. I took myself off to the park and opened up the envelope. Well, the B in French was a disappointment and so was the D in German. So, my tally was BCD; I knew that no self-respecting university would accept me on results alone, so I had to pin my hopes on the clearing system. Essentially this was (may still be) like waiting outside a posh restaurant and nipping in every five minutes to ask the busy maître d' if there had been a no-show.

It turned out that Royal Holloway, which was part of London University, potentially had a place for me to study French and Italian. I'd been there about six months before and quite liked the place because it looked like a real campus: the Founder's Building was modelled on the Chateau de Chambord in France, except in red brick because it was built by the Victorians at the bequest of Thomas Holloway and they wouldn't have dreamt of using actual stone. The overall effect was of a large, pink birthday cake sitting on a hill near Windsor. The countryside around was manicured Surrey and I saw a deer in the grounds.

However, as I did not have a Maths O-level[19], they would need to make me sit a Latin exam before letting me in.

It seems ludicrous, now, that my place at university was going to be determined by a persistent failure in one subject (Maths) that had nothing whatsoever to do with my chosen degree course, and a resulting exam in another subject (a dead language) that I wasn't likely to look at again in my life unless I was in a garden centre or I wanted to become a wizard.

But the only other option was Leicester, so I got on a train to Egham and walked up the hill feeling nervous. I really wanted to go here.

---

19 Whilst at Downside I had managed to set what must have been close to a national record of six straight fails.

After the exam, I was given a grilling by a busy but sharp female professor in the French department and asked what I would like to do with a degree in Modern Languages. Finally, this was a question I had prepared for and, fifteen minutes later, whilst I was still talking, the professor held up a bony hand to stop me mid-flow – but she was smiling. Yes, she said, they would love to see me at the start of October; a reading list would be on its way. She looked forward to my inevitable verbal contributions to her 17th and 18th Century Literature seminars.

Being a chatterbox had won the day. Importantly, I hadn't tricked the lecturer into believing I was keen – I had just vocalised my very real love of something (books) and thereby made a connection with someone who already agreed with me. Rubbing people up the right way is pretty much the most effective and pleasant way to get on in life. And, thanks to that, I was going to a respectable university that had the huge bonus of having a 60/40 split of girls. I could also indulge any Sebastian Flyte fantasies on nice lawns, or in turrets that overlooked ironwork and statues.

But first we had the summer. And what a summer it was.

I found work with Fulham Council as a gardener, which meant I was outdoors all day, honing my skills mowing up empty packets of Benson & Hedges and dog poos around the various council estates that had been thrown up after the war in bomb-damaged south London.

Council gardeners were run along military lines in those days, in that we convened for tea, smokes and swearing at 7.30am each morning in the 'mess' in Normand Park, just off the North End Road. Then we went out in 'sections', assigned to various grids in the borough that needed tidying up. That's where the military bit stops, unless you happen to be in the Italian Army.

In 1986, council gardeners who were all part of a strong union were generally about as feckless as you could be: white, male, cockney and Conservative (Thatcher had let them buy their council homes for a song and most now had a large nest egg to retire on). They spent half of each day in the pub sinking pints of lager, or playing golf in Ealing, then a couple of hours driving around the borough very slowly, pretending to be on route from one job to another. The final portion of their busy working day was watching the temporary gardeners, like me, do their work from the safety of their van whilst they read *The Sun*. When they got back to the mess, they filled up jerrycans with fuel for their cars and nicked whatever bulbs, seedlings, etc. were hanging about the depot for their own gardens. Had we even worked half the hours we were paid for, Fulham could have been Eden itself.

'I don't know what they must make of you,' one of my friends remarked in the pub.

'They call me Brainy Cunt,' I replied, still, after eight weeks, not sure how to take that.

In fact, they were tight-lipped for the first week or so, then invited me to the pub one day out of the blue and, after about a month, dinner with their wives and children.

Dishonest, but loyal to the hilt if they liked you, foul-mouthed, surprisingly sentimental, sharp – especially when it came to money – yet as superstitious as the gypsies they despised... Whilst being appalled by these post-modern cockneys, I found I also liked them a lot.

That last, long summer before university, which marked my leaving home, was long and hot and life really did seem there for the taking.

That year's Henley Regatta had a sort of *Brideshead*, coming-of-age feel I would have recognised had I been bothered to read the book. My Downside school friends and I had been up and down to Oxford all year visiting girls from the secretarial college and, as their term ended, so the regatta started.

This is one of the few times when the plastic gin palace my father had bought by mistake came into its own, and we clambered aboard: a dozen boys and girls looking like extras from the posh contingent in *Half a Sixpence*.

I have known Henley all my life[20] and I'm obviously aware of how it is seen by the rest of the world. But if you can get over shitfaced toffs at the regatta, it's one of the nicest spots on the planet and there's enough of the serious business of rowing very fast in a straight line to satisfy the true sports fans – namely the Old School Henley, who row the course with a picnic hamper, tether to a post and spend the day reading the papers and eating sausage rolls and Bakewell tarts.

I remember that day through a haze of alcohol and bright sunlight. We drank ice-cold beer and champagne, squinting because the reflection off the water was so blinding it was easier to half close one's eyes and let the world pass by, filtered by your lashes. I remember when the heat got too much we stripped off and swam in the chilly water, then scrambled aboard in our boxers – almost, but not quite, sober again.

One of the girls, Lucy, had become my first real girlfriend and I was looking forward to spending the rest of the summer with her. Strawberry blonde, loud, warm and very funny, she had the youthful looks of a milkmaid. She also pulled off that trick some girls have of being both lithe and shapely and completely unaware of how sexual she was.

We went back to Oxford that evening, probably leaving the boat looking like the Raft of the Medusa, and slept late, rising only to go to The Trout and say goodbye to that chapter of Oxford.

---

20 Let this record that I wish to have my ashes scattered in the Thames when I die.

Life seemed to be forming a pattern that has been with me since: another chapter starting badly but turning out alright. There had been nothing to worry about, after all – and perhaps there's something to learn from that.

Was I grateful to the tutors who turned my results around or the parents who, even though I clearly really pissed them off, still forked out for my failures? I can't remember, so I probably wasn't. But even I had a vague sense that I had got away with it. Again.

And so, I was off to an arched and turreted university to complete an education that had started, far less salubriously, in a run-down corner of Reading.

Chapter 8
Royal Holloway

In which I learn how to drink irresponsibly but with intellectual rigour... and that there are literally thousands of ways to make money if you put your mind to it

---

University instilled many habits in me – good and bad – that I maintain to this day. One of those was the habit of writing (good).

I've been scribbling things down almost every day since 1986 and you'd have thought by now I'd have made some progress. My first (titchy, scrap of) success at it was not until 2002 when I sat down during a rainy holiday in Sydney to write up how I'd got into starting businesses at a relatively youthful twenty-three – ostensibly, before I forgot the details and basically started making it up. The book's first print was called *Start-up Smart* (my publisher's title, nothing to do with me) and it had an orange cover that was so bright you could still see the blockish title for several seconds after closing your eyes.

It took a while to find favour, though. At the time, everyone was starting technology companies with private venture capital, with the aim to grow fast and sell quickly. I was never really into that, partly because if I was going to put my heart and soul into something for five years I wasn't inclined to flip it on to the highest bidder, and partly because no sane venture capitalist would invest in me, and the insane ones (of which there are multitudes, believe me) are to be avoided at all costs.

With no money and no safety net (more about that later), I had no choice but to learn how to set up low risk, low cost businesses that started earning cold, hard cash pretty damn quick, or go and get a job in Tesco. They were all about organic growth and instant profits. Anyway, that's what my first book was about and I had to wait until the recession in 2008 before anyone would listen.

On the other hand, I also like to write about elves.

And however odd that sounds, as a Brit, I'm not alone in this. Normally, the British are never happier than when they are making money, getting drunk or picking fights with other people. Yet these decidedly unliterary preoccupations have produced a nation of eccentrics who excel at stories about things that patently don't exist. Of the thirty-five best-selling authors worldwide in any genre, sixteen write fantasy – of these sixteen, an astonishing thirteen are British. Curiously, it is a legacy that not only explains a lot about us, but unites Britain as a nation – at a time when it seems to be fragmenting. I even made a documentary about this, called *Fantastic Britain*. In that, I got up one day and started filming bits to camera and, around six months later, I had it finished. No-one at the BBC picked it up, but it won an award – in Hollywood, where I got to go on a red carpet, then speak to a very big room full of people – and although learning my lines was very nearly the death of me, it goes to show that, living in the free world, most of us can do stuff like this – if we fancy it.

Anyway, back to writing.

The general aim at the outset was to write one book on entrepreneurism, followed by one fantasy or children's book.

Fact is, writing and starting businesses are very similar creative pastimes that are not at all hard to combine.

I'll explain. With the help of bullet points.

- Both need a very clear central purpose or goal to stand any chance of success from the starting blocks: 'this business sells fish'; 'my book is about how to deal with unrequited love... in space/medieval Britain/Watford'. In both cases you have to create a personality: for a business it is the image or brand, in a book it's a central character or characters, then work to establish these creations as something people will be interested in. Again, if you can't do this, forget it.
- Once you have done that successfully, you are well advised to have a good backstory: 'I went into ice cream because my grandpa made the best ice cream in our village and I prised the secret recipe from his cold, dead hands before my cousins burst in' or 'this story preserves the traditions of the Beaconsfield Folk. My people'.

Nonetheless, to be a truly successful writer today takes more than just the above – a sort of alchemy that turns stories into legend as they catch fire and sweep through countries, across continents and language. Doing what I do and knowing who I know, I read a lot of books in development, and there are masses of books that cover all the essentials described above: good books – some even great – but very few get published, and the ones that do make it through rarely take off and sell more than a few thousand (if they are lucky) copies. So, it is clear to me that I am very unlikely to earn as much from writing as I do from my investments and the companies I've started. In fact, it would be a close race as to whether I died of boredom or hunger first if I had to earn a living solely from writing.

Financially, I'm not alone in this: recently, whilst on a short sabbatical from looking at pictures of naked women on the internet, I came across an article in *The Guardian* online that said that 54% of traditionally-published authors and almost 80% of go-it-alone writers are making less than $1,000 (£600) a year. Intrigued and depressed in equal measure, I did some more digging and found out that much less than half of the two hundred authors (worldwide!) who are extremely fortunate to sell over a hundred thousand copies are very rarely new authors, rather the usual suspects like James Patterson, Harper Lee and Alex Comfort (*The Joy of Sex* – Full Beard Edition). But even that is not much to write home about (assuming you can still afford the stamp, and the shoes to walk to the postbox): the sales figures from even the very small percentage of top-flight authors will basically earn you no more than what a reasonably busy local accountant or solicitor will earn in a year. The rest of us starve in garrets.

So, why do I write – if it's very unlikely I'll get much material gain and not many people are actually reading my books (except this one, of course, which is amazing and is sure to sell by the truckload)?

Fuck knows.

I still love reading, as much as I did when I started uni – and happily my French degree at Royal Holloway provided plenty of that. Unhappily, I then had to write essays about all these books.

'You are the ideal intellectual.' Professor Malcolm Smith had called me into his study for a tutorial. He'd been reading my first essay of my university career, on Michel de Montaigne, and was beaming at me. I beamed back. I'd drunk and shagged my way through Freshers' Week and now this. 'This,' he enthused, 'is the best first year essay I've ever read.' *I love university*, I thought. *Finally, they recognise my genius.*

Nevertheless, two weeks later I was back in his study, the beaming smile replaced by an anguished look on his face as if he'd simultaneously sat on a drawing pin and dropped his keys down the sink: Malcolm was Cross & Sad. I looked down at my second essay being handed back to me.

'*Patently un-markable!*' was scrawled across the top of the essay in angry red pen. Other comments, further down, were no less complimentary and he'd obviously given up after a few hundred words.

'Um,' I said.

'*Um*, indeed,' he said, not quite meeting my eye. 'I'll give you another week to rewrite this, and we'll not record the result right now.'

For a whole week I lived the blameless existence of a nervous spinster. The essay was on Rabelais, and part of the problem was that *Le Quart Livre* just isn't funny (it is meant to be hilarious). Fart jokes are great, but sixteenth-century fart jokes, made by a monk, will be stale.

But that wasn't the crux of the problem – as far as I could gather, my method was. I compared my structure between the first essay and the second and couldn't see much difference. In both I tried to get away from the classic, define the question in the first paragraph and how I intend to answer it, then one paragraph per point (with illustrations from the text), and a conclusion that gathers it all up in a nice pithy final paragraph. A-level stuff. Yawn.

Obviously, I had tried to be too clever, I decided – I had got away with it once but hadn't pulled it off the second time, so I went back to basics.

I even did some research and quoted MA Screech, the pre-eminent critic of Rabelais at the time, liberally.

'Hmm…' said Prof. Smith, second time around his face clearly showing we were no longer friends. He'd handed the re-marked essay back after a long interval, during which I'd got back into the swing of things, imagining the terrible essay had just been a blip, whilst mentally preparing myself to raise my game in future. '… it's a bit better, I suppose… I've given you an E.'

And so went the whole of my first year at university: I lurched from being considered exceptional to being the fresher year dunce and back, without ever understanding what I was doing wrong (or right).

It bothered me only as far as I knew I had to perform reasonably well in the first-year exams or I'd be kicked out. If I got through, then I wouldn't have to sit another exam until I got to finals, in my fourth year. But I liked what I was doing so, optimistically – or stupidly – I assumed that my enthusiasm for French Literature (from the tenth century to the 1960s) would shine through eventually and my marks would get more consistent.

I might have got depressed about it: a surprising number of people do in their first year at university. I say surprising because, on the face of it, the first year of university should be one of the best years of your life: you've worked hard to get there for at least two years – and you've done it! You are usually studying the subject you love, you finally get a chance to lose the embarrassing nickname you carried about since Year 3, to re-invent yourself as someone cooler with a wide circle of friends and romantic conquests back home, and no-one can stop you having Ready Salted crisps for breakfast.

Thanks to the previous year – I was forearmed for failure. I had reached the conclusion, after my crap A-levels, that nothing is ever *one* thing: nothing is all good or all bad, or at least not consciously so. The point being is that Life does not have it in for you. Life does not set out to victimise us, because it is not a conscious thing. We *are* sentient, and the conclusion I took from that – whether it is sound or not – suits me.

And it is this.

You've always got a choice and, when viewing the slings and arrows, that basically means *interpretation*. You can choose to add events up and decide to make of the world what you will – there's no right or wrong answer, just a conscious shift in your perspective. I usually choose to be optimistic about things, assuming they will get better because it's the one thing that affords me the most pleasure, and I've pretty much always found this to be the case, anyway. Shallow perhaps, but I don't care.

Also, choosing to see mishaps as rungs on a ladder: you go up, down, down a bit more, but eventually get to where you are going *feels* about right. A step is not a precipice. At nineteen, this world view made sense to me because, whilst you're still drawing breath, things can *always* change for the better.

Obviously, this was neither particularly ground-breaking, nor was it the result of some great philosophical moment: it was just me thinking up ways to keep *me* happy because I prefer that to being miserable.

Now, as the father of three small children and multiple pets[21], I'm not so crass as to think that all personal tragedy has an upside; I'm just saying that, then, I had very little to complain about of real note, and I suspect it is the same for many people. I just wasn't going to get too upset about a few poor marks – I'd done that once before in recent memory and it hadn't helped.

I had bigger fish to fry.

My first room in halls was about as far from the Founder's Building as it was geographically and aesthetically possible to be. Having rooms in the main building was a definite plus: practically, as you were closer to the lecture theatres, the union with its bars and live music; and socially, as the building was basically a French chateau and your rooms looked out on manicured quadrangles, deer parks and attractive Surrey woodland.

---

21 Or rather *owner* of this latter grouping: I have fathered no cats or dogs.

Through whatever lottery decided where you wound up, plebs like me found themselves in Cameron Hall at the far edge of campus, in what was basically a breeze-block bunker. *Prisoner Cell Block H* was a big part of post-pub viewing at the time and, excepting the meaty-forearmed lesbians, we lived in pretty much the same conditions.

Except not quite: Cameron had quite a lot to recommend itself. Firstly, my room in the freshers' year was on the ground floor and looked out on the very leafy oak woods you could only admire from a distance if you lived up on the hill. I just had to open my window each morning to feel like I'd woken up in an autumnal glade. In the third year it was arguably better: my room was on the first floor and, by some stroke of great fortune, it looked right into the girls' showers[22].

For some reason, they had used opaque sticky film on the bottom two-thirds of the window but not bothered with the upper part. The upshot was a clear view of the top half of girls showering each morning, from about the curve of a shoulder to the navel. Between the hours of 8am and midday I could lie in bed, my head propped up by my pillow, drink coffee and smoke, whilst watching youthful female forms at their peak of physical exquisiteness step gingerly into the shower, hunch shoulders against the cold then stretch as the water warmed, backs arched and breasts soaped. It was a kind of mental torture.

To be fair, after about a week I did begin to feel guilty and even considered telling someone. However, I'd left it too long – if I did tell Works & Maintenance to come and blank out the offending window, I'd essentially be blowing the whistle on myself for two weeks of perving. So, I suffered in silence

---

22   OK, so it's going to get a bit *Carry On* now. If girls' showers don't float your boat, skip the next two paragraphs.

until someone did find out and the window was replaced with something about as see-through as a blast door.

On the bright side, finally I could get some work done.

For the whole of that first semester we seemed to be having an Indian summer, and I loved to breath in the cold, sunny mornings through my open window and gaze blearily at the wood with its rusting leaves, clumps of bracken not-yet-turned and squirrels the size of small cats. I'm not kidding here – Christ only knows what the college was feeding them but they were also tame and would happily snatch bits of bread from your hand.

It wasn't until years later that I got into the habit of feeding squirrel to our first springer spaniel, Touts. I used to boil them (to be super clear, they were stone dead before I did this) along with a few handfuls of rice thrown into a huge casserole dish I plonked on the BBQ outside – assuming no-one who lived indoors would enjoy the smell of boiling rodent. However, upon lifting the lid once it had all cooked slowly, the aroma of boiled squirrel and rice was surprisingly pleasant. Had I known about that as an undergrad, when I had to make do with over-processed meat curling under the refectory lights…

But, for now, I was content to watch them and feed them the occasional corner of bread, bit of muffin or bowl of Frosties. Which explains why they were all overweight – and probably type 2 diabetic.

In that first year, our studies were a vague hindrance to the serious business of getting to know members of the opposite sex, which was an education in itself and far more important to us at this stage in our life – and useful, I daresay.

The world was here: studious girls, girls marking time, girls who were away from home for the first time, girls with no time. Ladettes and ladies, the mysterious and the maybes. Girls with soft arms, the exquisite geometry of form and no qualms. Girls with soft thighs, lingering looks and bright eyes; freckles,

130

flavoured lipsticks and sighs; smiling mouths that kissed and knew tricks and tasted of wine; girls with knowing looks who allowed us awkward boys to get close with subtle signs. Girls who knew they would allow this one brief rush of *letting go,* before decorum took hold and towed the line and learned to say no.

However, I was beginning to suspect that all this shagging wasn't healthy – in the moral sense, that is: I now had the aerobic fitness of Lance Armstrong. It's all very well to discover you have the libido and concentration span of a chimpanzee, but throw Catholic guilt into the mix and it all becomes troubling.

I started to make a conscious effort to spend a bit less time thinking about who I could seduce next, and I tried to knuckle down to reading in the library. But this just made it worse: libraries are basically cathedrals to sexual tension – they really ought to split the sexes in these places.

So, I turned to the next item on the list of hedonism. Demon drink.

Again, how I afforded it is anyone's guess. My parents, sort of understandably, deciding they had forked out enough for my education, gave me an allowance of just £1,800 a year – quite a bit less than the poorest students on a government grant. However, I still had some money left from when I was working on the building site, and beer in the union was cheap. Cheap but crap.

But it was cold and refreshing. You're not fussy after you've spent thirty minutes flaying around to *2-4-6-8 Motorway* or anything by Happy Mondays (because all their songs essentially sound the same if you're a bit pissed). Drinking pints is very different from anything else – I dig the volume.

And the ritual. I've always loved that first sip to test the temperature, followed by a satisfied gulp before you put the pint back down and admire the bubbles from two feet away. With wine, it's a taste-sip-getting-pleasantly-drunk combination. With beer, the trick is quantity and abandon. Throwing lots of liquid down your neck makes you feel a bit like a Viking and its attraction never wanes for me.

Once I'd got into my stride, I spent the latter half of the second year wrapping up what little actual work I'd roused myself to do in the Founder's Library by six, then going to the refectory for an early supper (that usually consisted of a jacket potato covered in own-brand baked beans), then two-day-old cheesecake. I'd all but stopped going to the union, having lost my taste for sweaty discussions about politics over beer in flimsy plastic pint beakers. The latter could be relied upon to cave in on the slightest pressure and your pint would turn into a half pint long before you'd fought your way back through the throng laying siege to the bar. The former was just boring.

My family debates as they breathe. It might be the Franco Hispanic influence, or it might be we just love the sound of our own voices, but from five years old I was given to understand that the best way to enjoy an argument is to win it at all costs – it's got nothing to do with the right or righteous. Anything went *chez nous*: you would ridicule your opponent (brother, sister, auntie, mother), mimicry was good because it riled, or talk over the top of their best points, finish their sentences for them – always in your favour – and (my own favourite, when someone is wrapping up on an especially good point) stare out of the window and say something random like, 'Next door's cat is pregnant. Again.' As if the argument is no longer your concern.

Sitting in the union, it quickly turned out that these techniques came as a thoroughly unpleasant surprise to most people. In our family, we can have a stand-up row, we can hurl insults and cheap furniture and ultimatums, then walk the dog together and no-one bears a grudge or mentions it again until the next meal. It wasn't all shouting, we also learned to be subtle: to seem to agree, then attack an exposed flank, to maim with humour, wear down with calm insistence, make up quotes by famous people. You name it.

132

However, when the person in front of you in a union debate has gone purple to the tips of their ears, 'Get over it, Cupcake' is not a winning play, and I learned that if I didn't want to hurt people's feelings irrevocably I either played by the rules – which was dull – or I kept right out of it, which was fine by me[23]. It was another stage in my personal development, and one of my better habits: I learned not to get into arguments just because I thought I was right or had a point to make. Keep it to yourself.

Present day
I'm back at Royal Holloway today, retracing my steps in time. My first disappointment is that the woods outside my old room window have been replaced with two more halls of residence. They were always threatening this when I was there but the cash, in the form of a couple of Constables and a Turner that hung in the college picture gallery, was locked in a trust which was tricky to unpick. Like all these things, it took just a bit of time and legal effort to break the trust, and the college was able to use the money to expand. All over my wood and the fields, in a messy tumble of halls and car parks. It's horrid. I'm pleased to say the Edwardian gardens are still largely intact, although brutal weeding and thinning out has robbed the borders of the damp air of jungle and made the paths look respectable. Still not a soul about.

---

23 As a rule, and allowing for heartfelt feelings and principled stands, I don't warm to people who call themselves any kind of 'ist' as it's usually just a cheap ploy to assert intellectual or moral superiority (with the exception of those people who look at fossils, who are dotty but nearly always charming and engaged). One positive aspect of my upbringing I seem to have clung onto is a distrust of posturing – especially when it is being done to assert moral high ground or (worse) drag you into a conversation you'd rather not have. Usually both. And university was teeming with communists, surrealists, misandrists, chauvinists, absurdists, activists, empiricists and even capitalists. Dull.

Windsor Great Park nearby hasn't changed a jot, thankfully. I'm feeling energetic, so I put on a pair of wellies and take the dog around the entire lake. *I used to run this and barely need to catch my breath*, I think ruefully. Cooper, our spaniel, jumps into the lake after a moorhen that scuttles off without too much fuss, as if dogs trying to eat it is something that just happens every day. Cooper gets out, moorhen-less, and looks at me regretfully, as if he has let me down.

I give a little involuntary shiver: here was pretty much the exact spot where one warm evening in June I crawled out of the lake and lay coughing and spluttering in a bad impression of someone being washed up on a sandy shore after a terrible storm at sea. In only very slightly different circumstances I could have ended up dead right here. I shiver again and pat the dog, although he's wet. It's always reassuring – to pat dogs.

I think back nearly thirty years to that evening when somebody had had the bright idea to hold a toga party by some Roman ruins in the park. When I say bright idea, you may infer I am being sarcastic – well, I'm not. I thought it was an excellent idea... *at the time*, and I enthusiastically donned a sheet, bought a four-pack and got a lift to the park in someone's car.

Most of the girls had sensibly secured their togas with belts and pins and things, but most had also elected to go braless, so there was just enough side boob and bare thigh to keep the boys happy. Someone had brought along huge wax candles and we lit a fire. With the ruins in flickering light and the lake stretched out in front of us under stars it was magical.

And then I decided to go for a swim.

I wasn't so drunk that I didn't remove my toga first but I was drunk enough not to care that everyone else turned back, sensibly, after fifty yards. Not me – I struck out across the lake with great bravado, quite alone.

I do remember it was lovely, though – the water was cold, but in a way that swimming pools never are: tingly and refreshing,

Charles, me and our Cairn Judy.

Downside Abbey. Class of '86.
I'm second row, second left, having brushed my hair.

For about three days in 1992 I was cool.

Great Auntie Mill in her heyday –
before she got lumbered with my welfare.

Major Francis Budd, Grandson and my '68 Daimler whose
bonnet flew off on the motorway going home.

Hortense wearing his
Légion d'honneur medal.

*Houseboat Mallard
in Chelsea.*

Peter Boizot (centre) with crack team of Cambridge graduates. And me.

Hélène putting on a brave face.

Hammering out a few deals.
Just another day in the office.

The only reason I made the documentary was so I could wear this.

...then having a lot of explaining to do.

Life in the Pyrenées with Cooper.

Playing at being a smallholder in Oxfordshire.

What I'd like to be doing most of the time.

What it is all for at the end of the day.

and I felt so full of energy that when I reached the other side, about three hundred yards away, I didn't stop to rest, but turned back and slipped into what I imagined to be a rakish crawl.

After a few minutes, however, I started to enjoy myself a bit less. The water seemed a lot colder now, especially as I got near the middle, and I started to shiver. Then, through a combination of too much beer, half-cooked meat and the cold, I began to feel sick. For some reason, I decided it would be better if I actually was sick, so I stopped and, treading water, tried to put my fingers down my throat. Naturally, not using one arm made me sink lower in the water than I should; having two fingers jammed in my mouth meant that lake water poured in; and the fact I was probably too drunk to react by closing my mouth meant I started choking and retching. I really was freezing now, feeling sick and, worst of all, I was suddenly very, very tired.

I looked behind me and tried to guess whether it was quicker to go back or keep going. Unfortunately, I did not have my glasses on, so it was impossible to tell whether one dark, blurry shoreline was nearer than another dark, blurry shoreline. My now slightly muddled and panicky brain reasoned that my momentum was forward, so I should continue in the direction I was going. As I started swimming again, I remember feeling faint, then a massive wave of nausea hit me again and I did puke. To this day, I am sure that's what saved my life. There's usually a couple of minutes after vomiting when you feel great, and I used that energy to swim as fast as I could. As it wore off, my arms began to get heavy once more and my stomach cramped every thirty seconds. Pretty soon, I was going to be sick again; I looked up and, to my dismay, the shoreline seemed impossibly far. It was at this point I properly began to panic: the stomach cramps were getting worse and I couldn't swim when they hit me, so instead I sort of doubled up in the water and hoped they would pass. I was freezing and incredibly tired and frankly couldn't see how I would make it. I thought about shouting for help, with what little energy I had left, but the middle-class part of me felt quite strongly that the thought of drowning was better than making a fuss. So, I swam on, just concentrating on one stroke at a time. I willed myself not to look up until I noticed the water turning warmer. When it did, I saw to my relief I only had thirty or so yards to cover – but, just then, the worst cramp so far hit me.

Dry retching, and flaying about, I tried not to sink any lower in the water than I already was as I was having trouble keeping my head up.

Finally, with ten yards to go, my feet finally found the soft, muddy bottom and I lurched out and fell onto the grass.

'You were ages. How was it?' A bloke I knew vaguely was sitting on the shore smoking a cigarette. He offered me a drag. I shook my head and tried to stop my teeth chattering, or laughing hysterically.

'Fine,' I said eventually. 'Bit cold.'

Later on, after my trip back down University Memory Lane, I go for some tea with a friend in Windsor and we take a walk up and down the Long Walk, which is actually quite a short walk – and only seems to take ages because there are no corners. I remember cycling down it as fast as I could go with a friend one afternoon. From the other direction a large black car approached, which was unusual because no cars are usually allowed on the road. We stopped to let it pass as the window at the back went down and the Queen Mother (for it was she) stuck her head out. 'What are you doing?'

'Cycling!' we both replied chirpily.

'Well, stop it!' she snapped and wound the window up.

I met her very briefly again, when she came to plant a small tree outside the science wing at university. On that occasion, she stopped in front of me once more, looked me up and down and said I looked very nice. Which was an improvement.

To be honest, what struck me on both occasions was how

exactly like *herself* she was. If this sounds odd, or obscure, I don't intend it to be – what I mean is, if I was expecting her to look younger, or shorter, more cheerful, more like Mrs Slocombe, less like Mrs Slocombe, or just in some way different from the hundreds, if not thousands, of times I'd seen her over the years in newspapers and on TV, then I was going to be disappointed. She was very consistent.[24]

---

24 I have form meeting prominent people in unlikely places. I was given an impromptu grilling once by Margaret Thatcher. It lasted the time it took to get from the ground floor in Selfridges to the 4th floor – say, six minutes, tops – but it was ample time to make me a) feel a bit stupid and b) re-evaluate what I was doing with my life.

Then my daughter once shared a merry-go-round ride with a newly elected David Cameron's daughter. It was about seven o'clock one Sunday morning in Oxfordshire, in his constituency, and the place was deserted: it was just me, our new Prime Minister and our children wanting to be waved at – so that's what we did, as we politely ignored one another in a way only the British can do.

Best of all, when my wife and I were newly married we spent a few months in Australia, trying to do all the things you are meant to do when you are there, but the weather was problematic. We spent two weeks in Sydney. It was cold and drizzly. One week on the Barrier Reef. It cycloned and all the beaches filled up with box jelly fish and people got stung and taken to hospital. Then we went to the desert and it was literally pouring. I've never seen weather like it: not even in Scotland.

In desperation, we bought cheap ponchos one afternoon and set about walking around the circumference of Ayers Rock (Uluru). Unsurprisingly the place was empty. There was just my wife, a park ranger, me… and Bill Clinton. Coming around a fold in the volcanic rockface, we virtually fell into his arms. We exchanged pleasantries, then parted, only to meet again about five minutes later. This time it called for a more personalised contact, so he asked where we were from and seemed pleased when I replied Henley-on-Thames: he told us he'd studied in Oxford and remembered Henley. We chatted some more, he asked me where I got my hat and then we took different forks in the path.

Ten minutes later we bumped into him *again*. By now we'd had enough of Bill Clinton and his big red face, and the park ranger was giving us suspicious looks, so we pretended not to see him.

By the start of the end of the Lent term, I was running out of money. My parents were loath to up my allowance, and Ken Livingstone, who was at that time running London, decided that if they weren't going to pay, then he wasn't either. It was a catch-22, whereby my parents earned too much for me to get a grant and, in its absence, they were only prepared to give me the minimum to stop me from starving to death.

Did I whinge and moan and think about giving up? Or did I roll my sleeves up and get on with making up the shortfall under my own initiative? The former, of course. Or, at least, at first.

So, I did my own fair share of kicking my toys around my bedroom and generally complaining about how hard done by I was that neither my parents nor a socialist administration were prepared to subsidise my drinking and shagging with a bit of education thrown in. Then I waited until I really had no money at all and had been reduced to boiling broccoli in a kettle one evening for supper.

Finally, with no other options open, I did what any self-respecting student would do... I got myself a job as a clown in a funfair[25].

Naturally.

This turned out to be not only beneficial to my bank balance but overall a welcome break from a campus life that was becoming a bit cloistered. The 'company' was basically run as a one-man endeavour in tax avoidance. The entire assets of the corporation were a couple of thousand shiny foil balloons (unfilled), helium canisters (dozens, rusty), a choice of cowboy or clown costume (the cowboy get-up I rejected as being a bit too Village People), and there was a crumpled-looking transit van someone had painted a few balloons on in flaky emulsion.

---

25 Not really that unusual – almost all student jobs either involve stupid clothes or a lack of clothes.

Barry, the owner-cum-chairman, was a walking advert for all that was terrible and truly magnificent about Thatcherite enterprise.

It was my first proper introduction to the cash economy when, at the end of the first day, Barry pulled out a wad of notes like a Hovis loaf and peeled off a hundred pounds for me. This was the equivalent to what I'd see in a week on the building site the year before and I made a mental note to keep an open mind from now on about how to earn a living.

Don't get me wrong, Barry worked his arse off and he expected you to do the same. He had a dozen sites all over South East England, and he drove to each one every morning to meet whoever was selling for him, fill enough balloons for the day and scoot off. He would come back in the afternoon, to grab the takings, pay you and bugger off. There was never any wastage as this was basically the early days of the cheap helium balloon and they would all sell, and there was something mildly threatening about Barry that stopped you from escaping with a couple of grand in cash before he got to your site. Watching *Snatch* thirty years later, I recognised the type as soon as the caravan door opened.

It was also my first introduction to showmanship as well. Having avoided anything that smacked of acting or performing arts throughout school, I found I quite liked making a spectacle of myself. I spent six hours a day marching up and down the fair holding two hundred balloons in my hand, pretending to fly off or walk into lamp posts. If messing about, making people happy doesn't necessarily reciprocate for you then, firstly, cheer the fuck up and, secondly, you have to admit it does make the day pass and beats working in a supermarket.

I loved it, and I was truly sorry – and not just from a financial perspective – when Barry told me, 'I'm knocking it on the head for a bit. See you around, son.'

Present day

Today, I have taken the dog to Roncesvalles, which is an hour's drive from our house, on the French–Spanish border. This is very far from Windsor and all this university stuff, but bear with me.

It's March and the weather is frightful. Last week it was nearly thirty degrees at home and I even started fiddling about with the pool: wondering whether it was time to clean out the dead hedgehogs, lurking salamander and three months of leaves that had somehow got through the two layers of pool cover and turned to vegetable mulch. Nothing is as unpleasant as the drowned hedgehogs that have a habit of disintegrating into a stinking mass of guts and bones as soon as they hit the fresh air. Currently my life can be divided into three equal measures: my family, my job and the bloody pool.

But the kids love it and I must say, the ten times of the year I actually stop caring for it like a sick relative who just won't die, the pool is lovely and you can slurp the drink of your choice whilst bobbing about looking at snow-covered mountains from our back garden. I am very lucky.

And snow-covered mountains is pretty much the order of the day today. The weather turned right after lunch when I embarked on my pilgrimage to the site where an Arthur-type hero, Roland, commanding Charlemagne's rearguard, was ambushed by Basques and wiped out.

On a fine day, the Pyrenées are gentler in this neck of the woods compared to where we are: all lush pastures, leafy overhangs and rolling hills. Gone are the granite peaks of the central range, jutting scapulas that look not-so-bad when covered with snow but seem stark and formidable in summer. I love the way they balance churches and small, fortified farms on the very edge of drops here: it gives a bit of drama to the landscape and offsets the safe, shire-like feel. I can only assume that in the eighth century Roland must have been asleep at the wheel, lulled into a false sense of security by his reassuring surroundings as he meandered through the leafy valleys and thought about what he was going to pick up in duty-free before he crossed back into France.

It was the same for me. I grabbed a very pleasant lunch in Saint-Jean-Pied-de-Port, about an hour from home (Basque omelette: potatoes, ham and Espelette; and a large glass of chilled local white), and sat in the sun watching the world go by, before driving up the pass towards Spain.

I'm now in a howling sodding gale and the dog is looking at me as if I am mad. I'm feeling a bit mad, if I'm honest, as it has become a point of honour to get to the spot where there is a chapel and visitor centre before we both die of exposure. As soon as I get there (and find the centre closed), I turn around and half walk, jog back down the mountain to where I've left the car. Cooper runs ahead.

I came here once before, years ago. I was with my parents on one of our New Year Odysseys to Spain in our cramped Renault 18. I didn't know much about Roland at the time, nor care about early medieval history, so I probably just sat in the back of the car and stared out of the window or tried to give my brother dead legs, whilst my father explained why we'd gone two hours out of our way to look at a spot much like any other for hundreds of miles around.

However, in 1987, it was my delight with *La Chanson de Roland* that bumped up the marks in my crucial first-year exams and got me through to the second year – which avoided me having to do a lot of explaining to my parents. We worked off the earliest Anglo-Norman edition, for those who are interested – the most complete version being discovered as the padding in a later book's cover in Oxford (of all places).

The subject matter is proof positive that chivalry and the joy of reading about knights bashing each other up is eternal and is the reason why we still love reading Tolkien and GRR

Martin. We were working off a written text, probably the work of just one brilliant author, whose sense of rhyme and rhythm was as good as any Renaissance poet, and half the fun was in saying the words out loud. For weeks I found myself repeating segments under my breath as I walked about campus, just for the shapes my mouth made and the sounds that came out. The words felt substantial and chewy, as if I were taking bites out of language.

And it was relevant: French national identity, religion and encroaching ideologies (the Basques were converted to Moors in the epic poem itself).

Thanks to *La Chanson de Roland*, I felt engaged with my degree in a way I hadn't been before. So, I spent a frantic two weeks revising for exams I now believed in and scraped a pass.

I was through, not just to the second year but, because there were no exams until finals, I would certainly stay the course (of the course). I also had the third year abroad to look forward to.

Right now, I'm looking forward to a cup of tea. Extremely doubtful that I'll get one worth the stopping in Basque country, I plough on, my clothes and the dog slightly steaming from the car heater. I'm down to the foothills now, out of the worst of the weather, and thinking nostalgically about the massive amount of enthusiasm for life I had in that first year – and rightly so. The university and environs had everything I needed to be happy: if I was in need of company, I could step out of my study; if inebriation was called for, I could find abandon in a crowded bar or quiet nook virtually any time of day and no-one would judge me; if I was short of money, I could earn it; if I didn't know something, I could learn it; girls were friendly, kisses cajoled or freely given; and if I craved quiet, there were books everywhere, with libraries, quadrangles and pretty fields to read them in.

In reality, we had very little. None of us owned houses, had spouses, children or jobs, or any of the things that tether us and make us happy as we grow older. And we were still on the good graces of the real grown-ups who decided if we passed muster and were fit to move on to the next stage of life armed with a sheet of paper that would make it all a bit easier.

Nevertheless, I had learned that I could use my brain to solve most problems, and those I couldn't solve immediately would wait.

I was learning not to fret over the unfrettable.

Chapter 9
Royal Holloway, Part 2

*And you don't even need to go to lectures to learn
stuff at university*

It's March 2018 and I'm standing outside New York Central
Library searching for something familiar, but nothing looks
remotely how I remember it, which is perplexing as this looks
like a solid, dependable type of building, one that you should be
able to rely on to not change much. I've been over in Brooklyn
for a week at a conference about translation (I know) and I
have given myself a day or two off either side to wander over
the Brooklyn Bridge, visit old haunts in Manhattan and drive
about the Hamptons in a rubbish car I hired at the hotel.

I couldn't do the latter when I was here all those years ago
– not just because at eighteen I still had no idea how to drive
a car but also, when I came to New York thirty years earlier, I
was stone broke. As in no money at all, in danger of starving
in a ditch were it not for the fact I at least had a roof over
my head, courtesy of two girls I knew from Oxford who were
out on a sort of fluky secretarial secondment that came with a
luxury apartment on 34th Street, between 9th and 10th.

Dominance of the London–New York route was, at the
time, hotly contested and flights were therefore incredibly
cheap. I had jumped on a plane with £20 in my pocket. Most
of that went on a fry-up as soon as I left the airport, but I

reasoned that being a long way away in America meant that Barclays Bank in Henley would not be able to let them know I had no money left. I would therefore be able to extract money with impunity from these new-ish machines in the wall.

On the list of stupid assumptions I have made in my life, this is high.

Quite perceptively, my school friends who had come out with me told me I was a moron and that I was on my own. The girls were slightly more understanding and pampered me in a sort of long-suffering way by cooking me a nice supper and telling me that they would at least make sure I wouldn't starve.

However, this was the end of the '80s in New York and the place was awash with yuppies spending money and falling in and out of limos, bars and waterbeds.

In short, I was buggered if I was going to be left out. Asking Lucy[26] if I could make an international call, I got up early and dialled the number I had for Barclays in Hart St, Henley. Amazingly I got through to a manager at the branch (those were the days).

I explained my situation in very broad terms – i.e. *I am in New York, I have no money, bad things may happen to me as a result... we've all seen Midnight Cowboy* – leaving out the bit about flying there of my own free will with the intention of fraudulently drawing funds I plainly did not have from their branch. Even more amazingly, the manager did not laugh and put the phone down; instead he gave me an address for Barclays on Wall Street and told me to go and pick up four hundred dollars there the next day – where they did indeed give me all that money. And a cup of tea.

Loyalty should be repaid in kind. As a group of companies we have put very large sums of money through the Henley-

<hr />

26 It was her parents who allowed us to use the prefab house for the party at Downside all those years ago.

on-Thames Barclays in the last twenty-five years, which goes some way to paying back earlier generosity in the face of my stupidity in 1987.

Back in the present day, I've walked into the library building and it's starting to look more familiar. I try and picture myself here three decades ago and I feel quite protective of this skinny man-boy, who spent so much of his two weeks in here, the staff were on nodding terms with him. He is prone to making rather rash decisions, but his heart was in the right place in those days: he wants to do well in his studies, he cares about people and doing the right thing (most of the time). The me, now, in New York is certainly more self-assured, but also more self-aware and cynical. The business clothes I'm standing in probably cost more than that whole first trip here. I find that thought a bit depressing, somehow.

Four hundred dollars thirty years ago was ample for two weeks' drinking and going out but didn't leave much for sightseeing. I walked everywhere during the day, to the extent I developed a sort of sideways limp, which would have made me feel even more like Dustin Hoffman in *Midnight Cowboy* if I were still broke.

I don't think there was an inch of Manhattan I didn't tread whilst I was there. In those days, New York was dirtier and definitely a lot more dangerous than it is now. I've been here a week and not once has my Early Warning System (developed over years of travelling about in insalubrious parts of the map) gone off. Back then, it went off like an ice cream van virtually every time I turned a corner.

My friends went home and I had a week on my own, so when I wasn't street walking (so to speak), I started going to the library whilst the girls were at work. Instead of using the time to read the long list of books I'd never got around to studying in my first year, I sat down and started to write.

This wasn't the first time I tried my hand at creative writing (outside of homework and exams), but it was the first time I wrote something that wasn't basically a diary.

I liked to think of my first effort for younger readers, *Makesh and the Grunepig*, as a post-modern *novelle* (it was about a dim but perseverant dog whose arch enemy was a highly sophisticated and charming wild boar). However, the word *novelle* probably just meant I was being lazy, and it was short. I never kept it, as far as I know, which is probably for the best.

During my first summer vacation, I mainly read twentieth-century texts such as Gide and Ionesco, which made me feel like hanging myself. I then threw a bit of Balzac in, which made me feel like buying a waistcoat and corrupting a seamstress.

Coming back to Blighty, my second year was not productive.

After my very nearly ill-fated holiday in New York, for the next three terms I only managed to hand in two essays and probably went to no more than half a dozen tutorials. Certainly no lectures. Given this seemed in no way to stop me getting a degree, I think it is fair to say that my French BA could have been completed in about half the time allocated, which is what I remind myself of when I am tempted to feel sorry for undergrads of most disciplines that are not directly vocational.

So, what did I do with my time in that second year?

Well (I would answer in all accuracy): I fell in love, then sorted out my dire finances. In that order.

For the first few weeks of term, I did get bored, then I decided to do something about it. At that age, my decision-making process still had a lot of work to do since, at first, the only solution I could come up with to counter boredom was to go out and drink more.

This should have been a disaster, but hiding from reality by concentrating on one's social life has always done well by me. For example, if I hadn't been whiling away an afternoon in Cameron Upper Bar nursing a beer I couldn't afford, I might never have been introduced to Elsbeth.

She was arty and very English in a way that reminded me of Jenny Agutter or Felicity Kendal but obviously loads younger. The fact that she sat down and started talking about her boyfriend was a bit of a problem because I'd already decided she was the one for me.

I've always fallen in love very easily. I think my only saving grace in this respect is I don't necessarily fall out of love with quite such illogical abandon: it takes quite a lot for me to decide that I was wrong about someone. This might be stubbornness – or it is more likely laziness, as the opposite of love nearly always requires the huge, boring effort of bearing a grudge, which I find takes up quite a lot of time and energy.

With Elsbeth, I knew from the off that the blow was terminal: everything about her was right. Up until then all the girls I had met had been somehow too unlike me for the connection to be made beyond being drawn to the exotic (difference) and the erotic (physical, obvs). I'd always liked girls' company but I preferred talking to men, on balance – I don't think I'm unusual in this respect (for a man or woman): it was just we had more in common and it was more relaxing because there was no agenda.

But Elsbeth was something else, and each time I met her after that day just enforced the idea I'd never met anyone I enjoyed being with more. I fancied her in a way that I had been attracted to Francie all those years ago: she was Virginia Woolf's more attractive sister (or Nicole Kidman's version). We talked in the same way about the same things, but disagreed on enough subjects to make conversations interesting and a challenge. She had a sense of humour that was nearly the same as mine, but drier.

But after several weeks, one thing I was beginning to notice was that being funny and getting on with someone like a house on fire did not lead to anything more than nice walks and the occasional curry.

There had to be something else I wasn't doing, but I was buggered if I knew what it was: Elsbeth was always pleased to see me and we sometimes bickered like we were already going out, except we weren't. She didn't love her boyfriend – I don't think she even liked him much – and I was the one who was there. If I complimented her she seemed pleased, and she made me meals, mended my beanbag with careful stitching... and never let me kiss her.

So, I did what most blokes do when faced with a challenging female there is no immediate solution to – I started going out with another girl. Chantal was like an *Elsbeth Light* – similar in looks, country girl and funny – but my heart wasn't in it. Her father was serving in the SAS, which I found alternately intriguing and disconcerting. However, the breakthrough with Elsbeth came in part thanks to her.

We had decided to go to Bath one weekend. Elsbeth, who was part of our group, was not coming; she had gone down to Cheltenham to split up once and for all with her boyfriend. For no other reason than convenience, Chantal and I spent the night at Elsbeth's house before we made an early start to go to Bath the next day and, because she was not there, we slept in Elsbeth's room.

Bath was fun but pretty much underlined, once and for all, that Chantal and I weren't ever going to be a long-term project.

The following week I bumped into Elsbeth somewhere on campus and she confirmed she was finally free of a sixth-form romance that had run its course. She then told me she had been lying in bed at home on the Sunday evening and had found herself thinking about me, then she realised the reason she was doing that was because her bed linen smelled of Robin.

I was mildly surprised she wasn't pissed off. If anything she looked thoughtful. She was off to see her grandmother in nearby Datchet and asked if I wanted to come along. Even I could tell the invitation was loaded.

And it was dicey.

As said, children warm to me for reasons I do not know, but old people generally do not like me. If her granny hated me, which was a strong possibility, then my chance to get in early and fill the gap in Elsbeth's love life would be blown. In this, I was assuming she loved her granny a great deal and would be watching like a hawk for her approval.

What I didn't know was that her granny was an evil witch who didn't like anyone – besides her overweight King Charles spaniel that smelled of decomposing carpet.

Also, like a lot of strong-willed people, Granny G delighted in being contrarian. If sweet old ladies were to frown upon me, she decided I cut the mustard. I even took her overweight and complaining dog around the park, which earned me an extra slice of Battenberg and a top-up at tea.

Showing I had the mettle to survive the granny was just what was needed.

Everything about our day was different, without being radically so: we talked in the same way, argued on the way home when the bus did not come and laughed a lot. But Elsbeth had changed. Her eyes were softer.

We went back to her house and went upstairs without saying anything.

I was so delighted at the change of events I had to concentrate quite hard for several days to wipe the smile off my face. Elsbeth was far, far better a girlfriend than I had expected – in truth, far, far better than I deserved.

I was much too busy being in love to go to lectures now but, on the plus side, I stopped going to the pub quite so much and started to eat proper meals and go to bed before 2am. I did also continue the writing hobby I had started in New York. My reading material had a lot to do with my early style, which was interesting as it was in French. However, there was so much stuff to get through that it threatened to cut into my free time, so I switched to using Penguin Classic translated versions. Reading French set texts in English made the process of ploughing through everything from eighteenth-century romantic poetry, to avant-garde plays written in the '50s, far quicker.

The translations were generally so good that, after a while, I stopped buying my course books in the original, if I could help it: I could get through a four-hundred-page Flaubert in translation in a couple of days, but the same book would take me two weeks in French. And anyway, my reading French was still essentially A-level standard, so all I was getting was meaning – nuance and tone were largely lost on me.

Subsequently, laziness has given me a lifelong respect for good translation and, as the proud owner of three translation companies, spanning twenty-six years, it also had a bearing on a large chunk of my future career.

So, I was in love, and doing a course that gave me lots of free time to make up stories. Life was very good.

Except I was broke. Yet again.

My parents' allowance in September had given me some breathing space but it only just about covered hall fees, and my overdraft facility was already creaking. In fact, my finances were feeling a bit like that moment in old submarine films when they are forced to dive deeper than they should (something to do with depth charges, usually): the hull starts to creak, pipes burst and, as a build-up for a lethal finale that never happens, rivets start popping like small corks... a single bead of sweat trickles down the captain's brow.

That was me when I got my bank statement, except the sweat was coming down in torrents – at that point there was a very real chance that something would give and I'd be swept out of university on a tide of red bills and bounced cheques. My parents made it clear that there would be no bailouts; and I'd been signing up to temping agencies everywhere I could, in the hope of picking up two or three days' work a week. But there was no work, and the cost of phoning these agencies from the payphone in halls every morning to check if they had anything for me was just making matters worse.

I was sitting in the refectory one lunchtime, wondering what to do about all this, when something occurred to me.

The refectory catered for roughly half the halls on campus – so, around three thousand hungry souls. However, it was always the same faces one saw eating there, day in, day out. As I sat there mulling it over, I guesstimated that there were probably only around five hundred regulars at any given mealtime and pretty much the same bunch. I also saw the same faces in the library and at the union. This observation was borne out when I'd gone around our hall of residence the previous summer canvassing votes to become hall secretary (a post that guaranteed a room in halls, so I didn't have to fork out for an expensive flat in Egham or Staines). Doing my rounds, I'd found myself meeting all sorts of students I'd never clapped eyes on in my life, and they lived barely fifty yards from where I spent most of my life. My take-home point was, there seemed to be quite a lot of people who rarely left their room, unless there was a fire or it was the end of term.

Well, I thought…

Barry the balloon entrepreneur had been an inspiration insofar as it was obvious to me that earning money for yourself not only had the potential to be far more lucrative than working for someone else, but also more enjoyable.

People still need to eat: even reclusive Maths students. I will make them delicious sandwiches and sell them for less than the college shop charges. They will get a better, healthier lunch and it will be delivered to their door, I said to myself.

This is where Elsbeth came in: she was pretty and, like a lot of pretty girls, I was starting to realise, she also had lots of pretty friends. The male undergrads who stayed in their rooms tended to be geekier than most and would therefore not only be very pleased to have someone lovely knock on their door, but delighted that they were offering them a freshly made lunch that meant they could spend even more time hiding.

My market research consisted of banging on around ten doors, more or less at random, and asking if they would buy a £1-only sandwich if someone offered them one. Assuming it was really tasty, of course they all said, why not?

I decided I'd done quite enough focus-grouping for one day and went to the supermarket where I invested the last of my cash in several iceberg lettuces, a pre-cooked roast chicken, cheddar, some proper butter and lots of sliced bread of various sorts.

The next day I set about making around thirty sandwiches in the hall kitchen, which took me an incredibly long time (about two hours), but by midday (barely half an hour after they had been made, and Elsbeth dispatched with a tray nicked from college) they had sold out.

The next day I quadrupled the ingredients, spent four hours making sandwiches (I was slowly getting quicker) and made £100 before *Neighbours* came on at 1pm.

This carried on for a couple of weeks, whereupon I realised I'd made enough money to cover my immediate debts – making sandwiches was hard work anyway – so I stopped.

Now, you could say that that was very lazy of me. And foolish. And you'd be right: I'd done all that work and established a client base. I pretty much had a going concern.

In my defence I just wasn't that greedy, and I also had an inkling that, if the enterprise became established, the Hall

Powers That Be, who had up until now left me and my tiny empire alone, might start taking an interest in my use of college facilities to run an illegal catering business.

In short, I wasn't going to push my luck.

Later in the year, when I began to run out of money again, I started a small gardening business, getting people's gardens ready for the summer, then went back into catering, but this time with a partner.

Saul and I 'borrowed' a shopping trolley from one of the supermarkets in Egham, then went to the college Works & Maintenance and managed to persuade them to lend us a hacksaw and some bricks. I still find it mildly surprising that they never asked us what we intended to do – we were obviously up to no good: any plan involving a hacksaw and an undergrad, by all that is reasonable, should raise anyone's suspicions. Then again, luckily for us, Saul had the sort of manner about him that meant people usually decided it would never be *all that* bad and *oh, well, what the hell.*

At that stage in life I already knew that talking to people in a way that made them feel good about themselves generally was the best way to get something done[27], but Saul was a real master because he managed to combine the charm with sheer front and huge reserves of energy.

We used the hacksaw to slice up the trolley into a handy grill, and the bricks made a good barbeque base.

Setting ourselves up on the grass behind the bar in our halls, we nabbed people leaving, provided they had enough money left to pay us 80p for a burger or sausage. After a while we needed a much bigger grill, so more shopping trolleys were retired from their primary use and given a second career. We recruited. We were just getting into the swing of things, offering cans of beer and crisps, when our friend Mark stepped in.

---

27 Both because it works and it's a pretty pleasant way to conduct oneself.

As a union official (like us, but technically he was senior – Hall King, or something socialist perhaps, like 'Overseer') he was here to tell us we couldn't just go on until there was a fire or someone died of food poisoning. However, we had identified a market and, with the help of Courage Brewery, he was arranging to have the whole area we were using, including Cameron Lower Bar with its Formica tables and plastic chairs, turned into a proper pub with outside tables, food and a nice late licence.

The Stumble Inn, as it is still known today, was an immediate success and one place on campus where you could go for a pint and a burger and feel like a proper grown-up in a proper grown-up pub.

I suppose Saul and I should have felt hard done by: we got nothing out of the deal with Courage and the revamped pub basically killed our business.

However, as said, we really weren't greedy: we'd both made quite a bit of cash in a few weeks – enough for the rest of the year (and before incessant frying of burgers started to feel like hard work), and I actually felt quite proud at how our humble pile of bricks and the hacksaw we returned with effusive thanks had morphed into the only real pub on campus.

The whole catering idea was initially mine, and I managed to get people more talented than me roped in, which has pretty much been my MO ever since. But, unlike Mark, I was never thinking big – in fact, I never have gone in for true empire building, even now. But I had learned that entrepreneurship was actually quite easy: all you needed was a reasonably good idea and the will to carry it through and invariably things sort of work out.

It is also interesting (to me, anyway) how the three of us have gone on to quite different paths in life – but entirely predictable ones given our roles in that early foray into doing stuff.

Mark became President of the Union, then went on and climbed the corporate ladder all the way up to being MD of a British blue chip. I did what I did/do and started lots of small companies that people who work for me run better and more decently than I ever could. And Saul shamed us all by using that incredible energy to make a career distributing aid to people who desperately need medical supplies and food in Somalia.

Meanwhile, back to Elsbeth – and oh, but it was exciting to be in love at twenty. When I looked at Elsbeth and she looked at me, then she'd say, 'I really love you, you know, Mr Bennett,' and I'd think happily about us in ten years' time.

As the summer drew to a close, it began to dawn on us both that my going to France for ten months as part of my four-year degree course was going to be painful.

Bordeaux at the time of my arrival was going through some sort of renaissance (after the renaissance it went through during the actual Renaissance). There had been some excellent vintages in the 1980s and the extra cash had been partially diverted into giving the whole place a good scrub. Up until then, I'd been used to the nineteenth-century stone facades of French towns that looked like they'd been caked in black mould and grime for gothic effect.

The centre of Bordeaux looked like it must have when it was newly built: almost white stone, gleaming lead plumbing and pristine cobbles the colour of assorted toffees.

Deciding that I didn't want to be a teaching assistant during my 'sandwich' year – when we were meant to be combining goals of fluency in French with some sort of life experience, before going back for the fourth year to sit our finals – I found a course in marketing and 'international business' that looked like nothing I had been doing for the last two years and so it got my vote. My father was very enthusiastic about what the business college in Bordeaux was offering and agreed to pay the tuition fees.

My course was full of bourgeois French kids: children of wine producers and booze brokers. It was tough to start with, partly because everyone kept their distance until they worked out that I was house-trained. So I was rather lonely for a bit.

Marketing as a discipline was interesting and I began to get into the logic of brand as an identity that sells – it's like a person you are meant to like. If I wanted a career 'in business'[28], it became clear that that was the way forward for me: that is to say, if I was to do anything interesting in a commercial world, I was attracted to the idea of an endeavour that had a strong sense of personality. Like in writing.

This was all very different from when I started the sandwich business – then, I thought commerce was all about triumph: having a better idea than the competition; inveigling the client base into parting with cash by ruses and cunning; in short, lining your pockets at the *expense* of clients and competition.

Being introduced to marketing as a theory – but one that could be shown to have provable results in the real world – felt like another door was opening. And it was something else I might like to do.

You know, we're incredibly lucky in this modern day and age: I suspect that there has never been so much choice – especially in the UK, where one seems to be able to wake up one morning and announce, 'Henceforth I shall be a plumber, or a vicar, or a plumbing vicar (a vicar who plumbs),' and no-one bats an eye as long as you're reasonably good at one

---

28 And by now the lure of becoming a Guards or cavalry officer was receding: the OTC was the same level of physical hardship as the CCF at school, without any of the fun stuff, and I hated having to go up to Russell Square in London every Tuesday to go on parade and get shouted at for not being able to iron my uniform.

or the other... or both. In France, it's tougher – you have to take exams and get a lot of bits of paper to prove you can do something (I was once asked in all seriousness by a French editor about what qualifications I had to write books about things that don't exist, as if somewhere in England there was a PhD in Making Stuff Up).

My only problem back then (if it can be perceived as that) was a potentially confusing stockpile of career choices. Some young people get a bit upset by this and feel they need to make the right choice first time. One of the only bits of advice my father gave me other than, '... duck!'[29] or 'Duck!'[30] was you don't really need to fix on a career until you are about thirty. Before that you should give yourself time to try things out, hunt around.

The fact is, I didn't want to choose, and although it took me until I was twenty-eight to suss out that I didn't necessarily have to, thankfully (instinctively) I didn't let the choice bother me too much. Back then, the army was still my first choice after I graduated – it was social and decent and I could shoot the stalk off an apple at fifty yards, so perhaps I could be a sniper, then nobody would care if I couldn't keep my shoes shiny or remember to brush my hair. I was also very fond of writing – it was the only thing that shut me up for more than five minutes – and yet business appealed increasingly. I especially liked the idea of taking something you were interested in and getting it to make some money.

Back in Bordeaux, my social life was finally picking up and I found myself being invited to lots of expensive houses that had their picture on wine labels.

I was also invited shooting one weekend.

---

29 As in 'Watch out!'
30 As in 'There is a water-born bird – shoot it immediately!'

Not knowing much about French shooting in those days, I rashly accepted.

This was to be *la chasse aux palombes* – migrating pigeons that move south towards Spain in huge flocks. I've seen over a thousand in one mass, preceded by a disconcerting *chuchotement*[31] of feathers beating frozen air.

However, shooting a pigeon whilst it is flying by is considered very bad form in France – this is the opposite of the UK, where you are generally considered a bit of a cad if you don't let the bird get some steam up before taking a pot at it. Around us in France, shooting a *palombe* on the wing will get you drummed out of Le Club des Chasseurs. This has nothing to do with shoes – for those of you whose French is rusty; in France, a *chasseur* translates as *man in green who gets dangerously pissed whilst armed to the teeth*.

Even twatted to the point you cannot stand up, there is still very little chance of going away empty-handed, as the French method requires almost no ability at firing a gun, save for remembering to stand at the right end of it when you pull the trigger.

I've been a few times since and it is one of those activities where you tell yourself, never again. Until the memory fades and, like childbirth, seaside holidays in north Wales or bungee jumping, you just remember the good bits before deciding, what the heck.

My first day of *la chasse aux palombes* went something like this:

Woke very early. Lift, in a pickup, to a wood. Scared I will never be heard from again. In the car, I am offered a hip flask. Bit early; but if I am to be raped by French rednecks and buried in a shallow grave, I might as well get a drink out of it. The plum *eau de vie* strips the first three layers of skin from the roof of my mouth and makes my teeth hurt.

---

31 Whispering

Arrive at spot in wood where we are met by more scary men wearing what look like green bin liners attached to their bodies with binder twine. They are carrying some of the oldest shotguns I have ever seen not on someone's mantelpiece. Am handed a generous lump of *saucisson*, some bread and more of that moonshine. Worryingly, I'm beginning to acclimatise to the taste. Someone lends me a rusty gun that weighs more than my leg.

Feeling less anxious, warm and slightly pissed, we make our way to the hide.

I look up at it. I blink.

It's hard to describe what I am seeing: those houses on stilts in Asian fishing villages are as close as I can get... except, instead of hovering above a blue-green lagoon, these are substantial huts that are about forty-seven feet up a tree, connected by a series of gantries that are basically homemade ladders lashed together with the same stuff they are using to stop their trousers falling down.

The men grin and nod at me encouragingly and I start to feel nervous again.

I am shown a ladder that goes up to the largest cabin on stilts and invited to climb it. I take another swig of the plum drink and race up – before I change my mind and dash off into the woods.

The interior is surprisingly well-equipped and, within ten minutes, a stove is lit and we're all very cosy. But not too cosy, thankfully.

Somebody produces some beer and I tuck in.

I've noticed that one of the hunters has stayed below, and I watch from a small window as he goes to a cage and brings out a live pigeon. He attaches his pet bird to a miniature platform.

'What's that?' I ask one of the guns.

'That's the *piège*,'(decoy), he replies.

'Oh,' I say, surprised and admiring, 'in England we use plastic pigeons for decoys.' He stares wordlessly at me as if I'd just said, *We English dangle our willies out of our trousers to attract birds*.

I smile weakly and get up to help myself to another beer. The plum stuff was incredibly strong, and on a mainly empty stomach, and I'm feeling properly pissed now.

By the looks of things so is everyone else and the atmosphere in the fuggish hut right up here in the tree is cheery, without there being much by way of actual talking. There is some grunting, whereupon most of the guys pull various packets of food out of their bags and trouser pockets.

Lunch or *branch* (brunch up a tree) is clearly a lot more important than shooting, so it's just me who watches the decoy pigeon's platform being raised on a sort of mini winch.

The pigeon, attached by leather jesses, looks out of sorts as it is hoisted slowly to the top of the canopy, that is at least another thirty feet above our heads. Can't say I blame it. Job done, the pigeon man goes back to the cage and brings another pigeon out. He repeats the process three or four times until we have a good spread of decoys about forty feet from the hut (no distance at all, in shooting terms). Then he climbs up the ladder, winks at me and asks about food.

Shooting still seems very much off the agenda (much to the decoys' relief, who are all up their trees doing the pigeon equivalent of saying 'Faaaarrckiing hell...' under their breaths as they wave about in the breeze a short distance from a lot of pissed men with guns).

Food seems to be coming along nicely and I'm poured a very large glass of red wine and offered some more *saucisson*, neither of which touches the sides as it goes down. I'm famished and now completely accepting of the fact that this is really just an elaborate drinking contest.

But the hot food, when it comes, is also delicious. These guys have produced a meal of marinated venison steaks and boar spare ribs with all the trimmings – sautéed potatoes, vegetable gratin and tomato salad – on a stove you'd normally use for making a cup of tea by the side of the A303.

The wine is excellent, too: rough, but in a good way, it cuts through the grease but goes down well because, underneath the tannins, it's perfectly balanced.

Unlike me.

We are mopping up juices with more bread and someone is getting out the cheese when there's a shout and everyone puts their plates down and picks up the nearest gun.

It seems the decoys have done their job and the air above the canopy of bare trees is full – utterly blue-grey – with pigeons. The flock must be made up of something like three hundred birds, and it wheels and turns above our heads almost like those swarms of swifts that roost under bridges in London.

Our decoys now are properly agitated. I can almost imagine one or two of the 'free' birds wheeling about overhead saying to the rest of them, 'Look, there's Dave, and he's sitting in a tree… Dave! Dave! Daaaaave!! Dave.Dave.Dave.Dave.Dave. Dave… Daaaaaaaaaavvvvvvve! … Ah, fuck it, let's go down and see what he's doing.' Whilst Decoy Dave is frantically trying to shoo them away:

'You really don't want to come down here – there's men and they're armed to the teeth.'

'Bollocks,' his friends say, 'you're probably just stuffing your face. We're coming down.'

And come down they did. Several hundred in the trees all around us.

Within seconds the sky was filled with lead as Frenchmen pick a spot in the trees above and let rip. There are so many birds, you can't miss, and what's more they keep flying up then coming back.

For about five minutes it's mayhem. It feels a bit like the final scene in *Zulu* and my ears are ringing when somebody finally calls time and we all stop and peer over the side of our airborne Wendy house.

At the base of the trees there must be over one hundred dead or flapping pigeons.

'*Très bon*,' they grunt and go back to their cheese course.

So, France was getting interesting and I was *still* in love.

In spite of all the new experiences, my life in those days was basically built around Elsbeth: when I saw a film, I'd wonder what she'd think of it; if I went somewhere I liked, I'd imagine going there with her at a later date, in the future – and the day would be brighter, warmer and, in every small aspect, more satisfying. During the course of my day, dozens of small events, observations and feelings would be stored and preserved for later when I would write them down in her daily letter. Once a week, we'd talk on the phone but, most of all, I basically lived for when I'd be seeing Elsbeth again.

The whole thing was a kind of torture, though. Love at that age could not be at a worse time: you have no control over your life, so there's a very high chance of having to go through a long-distance relationship because you've been sent somewhere; and you have no control over your feelings. I can't speak for Elsbeth, but emotionally I was probably not much beyond the sandpit and swings.

In the final few weeks of term, I had made friends with this guy who was hardly ever in class. Michel had treated the whole year at business college like a sabbatical and I don't think he even pitched up to the final exam. Incredibly laid back, to the point of being almost prone, he seemed to spend most of the time I was with him slouching about, basking in female adoration.

His parents had a beach house on the coast and it was all a bit reminiscent of the times we spent in the early '80s on the beach when I was growing up. Except this time the girls were twenty (and still largely naked). They had all the confidence that came from knowing their breasts and bottoms were flawless. Michel also opted to be naked when not in town... but not me.

After a few long, lazy days driving about in Michel's brine-rusted 2CV, picking up beer then wiling away the rest of the day drinking and reading on the porch of the summer house, I eventually got tired of catching sight of Michel's knob as he sauntered about with a cold beer in his hand. I began to yearn for hedgerows, greenery and chilly mornings, and girls in sensible dresses and cardigans.

I had a lot of thinking to do. This was to be my final year and, up until then, I'd just assumed I'd take up a commission with the Grenadier Guards. Now I wasn't so sure. A love of reading had morphed into a love of writing, and I also couldn't deny that the results-driven, money-making, swashbuckling world of entrepreneurship didn't appeal, too.

I went home a week early, to the soft folds of the English countryside and the gentle contours of Elsbeth.

Present day

Just last week I was back at Royal Holloway, sitting in my usual spot in the library thinking about students. In small doses, I like young people. When they are not being political, they are cheerful and I enjoy being around that vibe – I could choose to be irritated by their chirpiness but I won't because I think it's well-placed.

Thanks to NYC in 1986, I still prefer writing in libraries, which is why I am here today – they rarely have internet access and nor do they have fridges filled with nice cheese and slices of processed ham: my two favourite distractions.

I love this spot in the Founder's Library at Royal Holloway, wedged between two narrow rows of books (seventeenth-century French dramatists D-E on one side, S-Z the other); it forms a literary *carrel* and I can look out over the neatly mown quadrangle and let my mind wander.

I returned to Royal Holloway as a very minor college celebrity when my first book was published by Harriman, in order to explain to undergraduates how I became so marvellous. A couple of years later I started to go there and use the library for peace and quiet to write my first serious effort at so-called high fantasy, *Small Vampires*. It's only a shortish drive from Henley-on-Thames and I still go there when I want peace to write.

In 1986, the break from academia in Bordeaux had done me good: I came back and started enjoying lectures.

Mooching about one day for a place to sit, I discovered this lost corner on the ground floor where nobody seemed to go. I was very pleased with this discovery, it was just what I was after and so here I went every day for four hours.

From April to June 1990, whenever I looked up from my notes in my library spot, I could see the lipstick kiss that Rebecca Davis had left on the window pane for me.

Rebecca Davis.

When I attended Royal Holloway there were around six thousand students. Four thousand five hundred of those were female. If there was one femme fatale amongst them all, it had to be Rebecca.

Rebecca was a couple of years younger than me. I used to sit with her when I went to screenings of art nouveau cinema or if I fancied having a challenging discussion about Philip Larkin or Seamus Heaney. She had already had articles published in a few national broadsheets, and she looked like Kate Beckinsale would look if she dressed like Lady Gaga.

I thought that was pretty cool, but mostly I was content that she was not my problem. For Rebecca was trouble, and it was safest to appreciate her with a degree of detachment.

I knew several people who had fallen for her and the lure of the salon she had gathered together, made up of interesting, usually rich, students in an exclusive and aesthetically pleasing part of the Founder's Building. They all went about the place looking distracted and miserable, as if nothing meant anything unless they were sipping tea in her rooms, discussing Proust, whilst being treated to the sight of her perfect hands perching a book on perfect knees.

The salon-of-sorts was on the top floor and had a turret room on a split level. There were about six studies there, and throughout my time at Royal Holloway they were always allocated to a certain type of undergrad. Had it been Harry Potter, they would all have been in Slytherin.

As I say, I used to pop up from time to time but was content I could take it or leave it.

One day I was chatting to Rebecca in the main refectory and Elsbeth came up. I noticed Rebecca always took an interest in Elsbeth: they were both similar – Rebecca had the edge on looks but Elsbeth was more arty and, dare I say, charming, and I sensed that sort of rankled Rebecca. She could always spot the strong points in a person or whatever made them stand out, and would want to know the why and the wherefore of any talent. At best, it was a healthy interest in people and made her more interesting, at worst it was a competitive, bordering on acquisitive, jealousy.

Elsbeth, on a three-year History course, had already graduated when I got back from Bordeaux, so we were apart during the week whilst she worked in London for a private stockbroker. Rebecca wanted to know how our relationship had survived a year abroad and I casually mentioned we wrote every day.

Rebecca immediately locked onto this, like a cat seeing a bowl of milk through a window. I could tell she was genuinely intrigued: she got the whole idea of the investment in time and the fact that, with around two hundred letters each, we had produced something like a proper work; she also loved the romance. The letters seemed to tick all the boxes for her.

Elsbeth was lucky, she said, staring hard at me.

Perhaps stupidly – who am I kidding? – definitely stupidly, I started to see more of Rebecca after that. I think we both sort of engineered it. She became flirtatious but was always quick to say, 'But of course, you have Elsbeth.' Which would excuse the standing too close at the bar, staying late in her rooms drinking wine, the accidental touching… and looking up one day to see Rebecca smiling at me through the library window.

She motioned for me to come closer. So I did, half rising from my desk until our faces were very close either side of the glass. She was smiling at me and then she half closed her eyes and her lips parted. Instinctively, I leaned in, and she did so, too.

We kissed, our lips not touching through the glass… but that is still my kiss – my *Memento Amori*. Everything we knew about romance, everything we felt about each other went into that moment – separated by a few millimetres of clear pane.

When I read the final chapter of *One Fine Day*, the line

… and they kissed in the street as all around them people hurried home in the summer light, and it was the sweetest kiss that either of them would ever know.

made me think of that moment, as I leaned across my strewn notes and we bridged a gap though the cool glass with intention. The cleaners should have hung their heads in shame, too, for each time I looked up from my studies for the next few months, I could see the kiss, still hanging there, in Rebecca's fading lipstick.

A line had been crossed and we both knew it.

The affair, when started, was oddly unerotic. Rebecca was all about the chase, and although we kissed without a sheet of glass between us, and lay naked together, it meant less than what had gone before.

We were in the thick of finals now, not that I was aware. Luckily, I'd done enough groundwork that I would be more or less OK because my mind was definitely elsewhere.

Despite my intentions, I had become one of the mopers: the love-struck and oddly unrequited. I pined when she wasn't there, resented being in other girls' company, including Elsbeth's, and felt on edge when we were together.

On the bright side, I was too lovesick to get nervous about my exams; but, even so, after five weeks I'd had enough.

No-one told me that having an affair makes you miserable. I had kind of (naively) thought it would be the best of both worlds. Thrilling sex with one girl and a nice stable relationship with another.

In this I found I was absolutely and completely wrong, and I strongly suspect this is the case for most affairs. What I came to realise is that trying to have an intimate relationship with two people enhances nothing, especially not your happiness – *it dilutes*.

There's also rarely a real justification for infidelity: most of the time it's just about sex. Elsbeth and I were obviously not married but we had talked about it: in all seriousness once, when her period was late. So, what was happening with Rebecca felt like a real, proper affair and it made me feel guilty and shit – especially when Elsbeth came up one weekend and bumped into Rebecca who was wearing a jacket of mine.

Eventually I wrote Rebecca a letter about how I felt and she came to see me in my room. I think we both intended it to be a sort of dramatic end to a whirlwind romance: a valedictory letter, a rushed visit and a final embrace; but, like the affair, it sort of felt flat.

It is very much a reason (and not an excuse) that we wish and long so hard for someone to like us that when two come along at the same time, we find it almost impossible to pass up on the opportunity. Greed is *not* good – wanting more leads to less.

And that doesn't just go for human relations; it applies to money, too.

Chapter 10

London

However bad things are, they could be a lot worse.
Take heart in this

In fact, everything was getting a bit serious.

1992 was not a good time to graduate. The recession had started to bite and there were almost no graduate jobs out there. I hadn't worked for actual cash in the whole of my final year, the better to concentrate on my studies, and I was in hock to the hilt – over £10,000. This was before student loans came in, so my undergraduate overdraft was immediately converted to a 'Graduate Loan' and the bank gave me another £1,000 to tide me over – then informed me they were charging 29% interest. In those days, this meant nothing to me, but it was usurious in the extreme, at a time when mortgage interest rates (according to Google) were around 6%. Then again, whilst I was blissful in my ignorance at how much money the bank was making at my expense, knowing would not have helped – I had no other choice but to borrow heavily.

A few weeks before my finals, I'd finally – after years of going around the issue – decided the army was not for me. I wrote another long, rambling letter – this time to my commanding officer (to be), telling him I'd decided to be something of an entrepreneur; problem was, I didn't have the foggiest idea how to go about becoming one.

Instead, with my languages and my spectacularly mediocre marketing credentials, I applied for various brand management jobs. With no luck whatsoever.

Then, in June, I applied for a job as a trainee broker in the City. This was more like it, I thought. They offered me the job, but neglected to mention anything about a salary in their letter. I phoned a number, asked, and was told there was none. 'What?' I said, assuming I'd misheard.

'It's commission only,' replied the person on the phone from HR. They sounded like they were typing.

'Oh,' I said. 'OK.'[32]

My unpaid job was not due to start until September, so I took another unpaid job: I was to be a door-to-door salesman of aerial photos of people's houses. In Yorkshire. My career as an entrepreneur hadn't got off to the most promising of starts.

I'd just passed my driving test and used up part of my Barclay loan money (about £400) on buying my first car – a blue Lancia Delta, which I loved.

Lancia Deltas had won a few rallies in recent years and it *looked* fast, although the bite had gone out of the engine several years before and it was now all bark. The interior dash reminded me of the *Star Wars* X-Wing cockpit, and I transferred my cassette collection there, a toothbrush, umbrella and wellies[33].

I was set.

---

32 This was certainly a big feature of recessions in those days: huge interest rates and commission-only jobs. And people really did get made redundant and lose their house thirty days later. Thankfully the last recession, in the UK at least, did not end in mass redundancies and an epidemic of mortgage arrears that follow on from huge borrowing rates.

33 This skeleton pack of essentials is little changed today. I've added a dog lead and headache pills, but that's about it.

I left my parents' house for a hotel outside of Coventry at 5am one rainy morning with one of the worst hangovers of my life.

We'd all met up in London for a final goodbye to life at Royal Holloway before we sloped off to crap jobs, or our parents' sofa for six months of daytime TV. There was a frantic element to the drinking, and little joy. It felt like our last night of being students, because it was. Meanwhile, my parents had been annoyed about the army but had not even asked about my new job.

So, I gingerly made my way up the M1 in a dodgy car that at least I had bought myself[34], weaving between the lorries and the coaches in the rain, keeping an eye on the water temperature gauge, as I'd noticed the Lancia had a tendency to overheat.

The three days' door-to-door sales training was essentially about learning a script and then delivering it at a sort of frantic half shout, as if talking very loudly in people's faces would strip away all their reservations about having their door knocked on by a stranger. There were about fifty of us, all students, and the trainers had all been in our boots the previous summer. It was clear that, for a lucky few, you could make good money selling aerial pictures. Most of the trainers drove decent sports cars, bought expensive rounds and talked all the time about *The Close*.

Take away the required manner of our delivery, and the training was pretty good for the basics of any sales, and I'm grateful for that: simple, to the point and all you really need to know about selling anyone practically anything.[35]

We were attempting to sell people a picture of their home (in amongst about one hundred other houses) by knocking on their door and saying something like, 'Hello, have you ever seen your house at four thousand feet?'

---

34   The fact that my brother had been bought one as a gift at uni did rankle.
35   I didn't know it at the time, but we were paying for all this. Hotel costs, food and training would all come out of our first commission cheques.

This was designed to get their attention and it generally worked: people like their houses, and if you have a picture of where you live shoved under your nose, you are bound to want to at least glance at it.

Getting their attention was essential, because you'd need to hold it for at least six minutes whilst you: 1. described what you were selling; 2. answered their objections; 3. did the price build-up; and 4. closed.

1 and 2 had to be done with charm – no-one buys from anyone unless they like them, especially not someone who has banged on your door just when you are putting your feet up in front of the telly. So, it was up to us to make a good personal connection *very quickly* or you were wasting your time – even if they listened to the rest of the pitch, they'd just be weathering the storm until they could go back to watching Terry Wogan interviewing Cher again.

Number 3 (the price build-up) was easy enough, but I found you needed to speed things up here: they usually could tell you were nearly done and needed to be reassured they were getting a good deal, so it was time to tell them what they would normally pay, add some extras (better frame, scratch resistant glass, etc.) and then (really important) knock some more off.

Then *close*.

I'm quite sure whole books have been written about the art of the close (they are probably called things like *The Art of the Close*) but, in truth, closing is very simple: it's all about timing. In that respect, it is like a punchline and why I have a theory that natural comics make good salespeople, not just because they are funny, but because of this timing thing. On a perfect run, you would grab a customer's attention, charm them into liking you and make them what seemed like an exceedingly good offer on price: completely out of the ordinary and just for them. It was all about bringing them to a simmer in under five minutes, close to the boil about a minute after and, just at the very right moment, asking, 'So, do you want one picture or two – you know, for a gift?' And that's your boil moment. If you simply ask, 'Are you going to buy?' they will invariably say no, because it's easier to say no to a yes/no question. If you ask, 'How many do you want?' they will panic and back off, thinking they might find themselves being startled into buying five. I found the 'one or two' line very effective, not just because any choice meant a sale, but it was also very hard to say, 'None,' without sounding like a dick, and most people would rather avoid that.

In fact, if you could deliver the 'one or two?' line with a hint of irony, showing that you knew you were being a bit cheeky but felt comfortable enough with them to chance your arm, you'd often get a smile and, nearly as often, a sale – because you'd just brightened up their evening.

In fact, the trick with selling is to simply make people feel good about saying yes to you. If this all sounds like cynical manipulation, then remember that if approached cynically, with just the sale in mind, then ninety-nine times out of a hundred the pitch will come out wrong and you will present as needy or pushy, or both, by turns. If you approach it as humanly as possible, with empathy, your goal being to make a connection, then offer them something you genuinely think they will like, then it will work reasonably well – even if you don't make a sale, you'll part on friendly terms and everyone likes that. Let's face it, I was only asking them to part with the cost of a round of drinks and perhaps a pickled egg thrown in.

By *reasonably well*, I found out that 70% of the time you wouldn't get a chance to pitch – either the person was out; refused to answer the door; were not the owner; or just flat refused to hear you out – and 20% of the time you got most of your pitch out, but the person at the door would stop you (invariably before the price build-up) and politely but firmly tell you thanks but no. So, on a normal night I worked out that one door in ten would yield a full pitch, and this was where I figured you needed to convert something like 50% into a sale to stand a chance of making a living. Our commission was good, about £20 per picture, so eighty houses should make around four to six sales: £80-£120. As they kept saying, it's a numbers game (but not like *Countdown*).

The first week was no fun.

I was made to share a room with the daughter of a vicar, who loathed selling, viewed me with deep suspicion and slept fully clothed, including a jumper. So, I had to look at the wall whilst she took her coat off for bed, then decided to stay that way whilst she carped and moaned about how much she hated the job. Luckily, she left after a week, and I had the room to myself.

Personally, I found I absolutely loved the job. We could choose the hours we worked, which usually meant around 4pm-8pm, and the rest of the time was our own. We were living in a rented farmhouse near Halifax in West Yorks. and the house of six ex-students got along well enough for there to be a social life rather like the one we'd just left. I spent my days exploring the countryside around Halifax and even bits of the Peak District. Ownership of my first car gave me total freedom to roam and I was averaging about twenty to thirty picture sales a week, so I was covering my debts with enough left over for fuel, food and beer. The very stuff of life.

I also found I was becoming thick-skinned, so people saying dreadful things on the doorstep did not put me off my stride – whereas, to begin with, if someone shouted at me, the next couple of pitches would be off-kilter.

I decided to forget a career in marketing, or an ivory tower to write, like Chatterton – nope, sales and the open road was the life for me.

If I made money – or not – it was down to me. I loved the high of making a good sale – similar, I think, to putting on a good performance acting, and I felt the master of my own destiny for the first time in my life: I didn't have a boss to tell me when to turn up for work, how many hours to put in, or a tutor to confuse me. This was great.

Talking of which, my degree results came in: I got a 2:2, which was entirely what I deserved. I can't say I was surprised, either. However, briefly, it had been looking different: earlier in the year, six months concentrating on medieval French poetry and the collected works of Samuel Beckett had started to pay off, and my tutor surprised me one day by saying I should expect a First. I can't say I believed it myself, but I was just happy that I was too far over one end of the dial to worry about failing – which was a first in itself.

A few days later, the college admin office chap rang the cottage in Yorkshire. I would not be able to pick up my degree, he told me pompously, until I paid for the damage.

'What damage?' I asked, knowing exactly what damage (he was referring to).

'The very obvious charred hole in your carpet,' he replied in the same tone as I use on the children to convey I have better things I'd rather be doing than listening to their crap.

'Oh that,' I said breezily. 'But it wasn't me.' This sounded weak, but it was 100% true. At the end of term, a friend had thrown a firework into my room whilst I was drifting off to sleep. Having a Galactic Blaster go off in your room is a spectacularly swift and unpleasant way of becoming wide awake. Given the circs, I didn't feel I should be the one to pay for the damage, but Royal Holloway was adamant: no nice new carpet, no nice new degree certificate and I wouldn't get to wear a cape and meet Princess Anne.

Fuck 'em, I didn't care: I was a door-to-door salesman, seller of things you had no idea you wanted whilst your supper congealed. I was the master of my own destiny[36].

Yet, in spite of all this testosterone salesy stuff, I was still reading anything I could lay my hands on, and had gone back to penning long, romantic letters to Elsbeth every day. Plus Yorkshire kicked off a period of writing poetry whilst sitting on rocks overlooking dramatic views of grassland and gorse.

Now, this was really, *really* bad poetry, incidentally, which – in a way – is the best sort, if you are just writing for yourself. I came across some of it recently, in an old notebook[37]. Reading through it nearly thirty years later it was obvious I was on a bit of a Thomas Hardy kick: lots of lines about scarred moors (the sprouting heather sort), dark doors and troubled futures.

Not me at all, but I think this was probably just a very late adolescent phase. And I had a bad habit of rhyming words like 'blasted' with 'wasted'.

One day I was due to be working one of the leafier suburbs above Halifax. Earlier, a nice old lady in a bookshop had seen me hesitating over titles and suggested a book by someone called Terry Pratchett, who I had never heard of. I'd spent the rest of the day whipping through *Guards! Guards!* thinking things like *Ha-ha!* and *Where have you been all my life?*. I decided I could afford to take some time off; sales had been going well that week. I might do just an hour of door-to-door: it was a beautiful evening and there was a pub I'd seen on my way over, with a beer garden where I could carry on reading my new book by my new favourite author.

Most of the patches one worked were estates built between 1930 and 1960, but these were all big new-builds. Like most

---

36 To this day, the small strip of telexed paper bearing my name and '2/2 Lon French Single Hons' is the only physical proof of my degree that exists.

37 Don't worry, I'm not about to reproduce any of it here.

door-to-door salespeople I'd quickly learned that rich people are rich because they are loath to part with cash. Trying to close a sale to an apparently wealthy businessman near Huddersfield, he had come right out and asked me what my commission was. Stupidly I told him, and he said, 'Give me half your commission and I'll buy one of your pictures.' I looked at the raked gravel on his forecourt, the huge carport that housed a Jag, an American pickup and a jet ski, and at the outsized fountain dwarfing it all. Then, very deliberately, I fished about in my pocket and found a crumpled fiver, some coins and counted £10 in cash in a small pile onto his outstretched palm, expecting him to tell me he was joking at some point. He didn't. Prick.

So, I wasn't that hopeful as I crunched up a drive to a house that looked a bit like Southfork.

Nobody seemed about, but I rang the bell anyway.

Almost instantly I heard the alarming sound of claws trying to gain purchase on deep gravel and turned to see two heavily muscled Dobermans tearing around the side of the house, right at me.

Our stock of pictures and frames came in a large blue bag – thank God – and it was this that I instinctively put up to my face, then immediately lowered as I realised that various tender and cherished parts of my anatomy were exposed.

The lead dog was huge: with very little effort, he was able to raise himself to face height, the better to bark and snarl inches from my youthful cheeks that struggled not to have tears rolling down them at this point. The second dog contented itself with doing the same to my rapidly shrivelling testicles.

I've always liked dogs but these seemed very close to that point of reversal where Human To Be Pleased To See & Respected becomes Mortal Enemy To Tear Asunder.

I had a fairly good idea that running would turn me into quarry and that staring them down could be construed as an act of aggression, so I opted to feign a sort of frantic nonchalance, whistling and looking in the air or at my shoes.

It was how the owner found me half an hour later when my whistling had dried up and my humming was beginning to sound, to my ears, like a whimper.

'You're lucky!' he said, smiling as if it was all a huge joke. 'If you'd tried to run they'd have had you.'

'Yes, I thought so,' I said, trying to look as if this had just been a minor blip in my day, and not a near-death experience. 'Would you like to see your house at four thousand feet?' The man's face clouded.

'Would you like me to leave you alone with the dogs again?'

Sadly, a couple of days later, a lucky break brought Yorkshire to a sour conclusion for me.

I'd been over the other side of the county for a few days, working villages towards Wakefield. They were generally a bit run-down and most people were friendly but obviously had no money to spare. It was hard going and I was struggling to make one or two sales an evening – a couple of times I didn't sell anything at all. It was still in the days when village shops were the norm rather than mildly surprising bastions, and I'd taken to visiting them first and leaving a picture with the shop. I usually had to give away a chunk of commission but I'd made a few sales that way, so it was always worth it.

I forget the name of the village but, unusually for its size, it had a bookies. I went in and got talking to the owner, who mentioned that his brother-in-law worked for the Department of Transport and was involved in major work on the A1(M). He knew that they were looking for several hundred aerial photos and it might be something that my company would be able to help with.

He would talk to his brother-in-law and, if I came back in a couple of days, he would let me know.

I didn't get my hopes up, but I did return two days later and he bought a picture for his shop and told me his brother-in-law was definitely interested. He reckoned they would need about seven hundred low-level shots.

I couldn't believe my luck – the commission on just a hundred pictures was huge... but seven hundred and I could afford to pay off my loans... buy a flat... Sod that, I'd go to Rio (the place, not the nightclub in Sheffield). When I got back to the house, I rang head office and (stupidly, it turns out) gave them all the details of my man at the bookies.

... Aaaand... that was the last I heard of that. Naturally.

After a few days of radio silence I rang again. My area manager was off-hand to the point of rudeness. There was no way I would get commission on the sale.

'Why not?' I asked. 'It's my sale.'

His answer was to say nothing.

'I don't think that's right,' I added.

Still no answer.

Stonewalling is my least favourite way of discussing something, and these days their feet wouldn't touch the ground on the way to court. In those days, I was far too meek.

I went to see the guy at the bookies. He politely but firmly told me to piss off (he'd made his commission, and there was no way he was going to jeopardise that).

The next day, my stunningly ineffectual response was to hand in my notice and drive back to London.

Elsbeth already had a flat with friends, and my mother made it clear I was living in Fulham in the family home on borrowed time, so I used some of my aerial picture money as a deposit on a maisonette in Tooting and moved in with two old school friends.

It was fine, I told myself, I was due to start my brokering job in September; with a little frugality I could make ends meet until then. However, one evening in the pub I got talking to one of Elsbeth's City co-workers. He asked what I was up to and I told him I was soon to start training with a City firm. He pulled a face when I told him which one, so I prompted him as to why.

'Don't do it,' he said, 'they're not brokers; you'll just be selling pensions to your friends, your family and gullible old ladies.'

That worried me, so I did some more digging. It was a sweatshop. I rang someone else who worked for one of the larger banks and he confirmed they would make you go through your address book on the first day and sell life insurance to everyone you'd ever met.

I rang and cancelled my job.

That's fine, they said, oh, and that'll be £375 to cover the cost of the training I didn't have.

Fulham Council had no summer jobs, so I signed up with an agency called the Beauty Company that specialised in putting people to work on the shop floor in department stores around London.

I still genuinely don't know what I was thinking except that this was a deep recession and there really were no jobs.

It was thus that within a week I found myself transported from a freewheeling job in Yorkshire where I got to be pretty much my own boss and earn £300-£400 a week, to being paid £28 per day to live in Tooting and stand on the ground floor of Harrods in the ladies' makeup section for eight hours a day under glaring lights. And be bossed around by everyone. My decision not to join the army, where I could be an officer in a smart regiment on a good salary, was looking like a dreadful mistake.

Also, I was rapidly eating into my dwindling savings because I was going out every night getting monumentally pissed to take my mind off the boredom of having to stand in a white marble room until all the blood in my head felt like it had settled in my feet. Unlike the aerial pics, there was never any chance to sell to alleviate the boredom – you basically just had to stand there and ring up on the till a paltry two or three bottles of perfume or mascara a day.

More than anything it was the total inactivity that felt like slow dying: of standing for hour after hour in a horrid environment. And. Do. Nothing.

One day I turned up to work in an off-white shirt – most probably because it had been washed with my socks – and was told I'd either have to go home and get another one (and lose half a day's pay) or buy a shirt from the shop floor.

I spent the rest of the day fuming in a shirt that had cost me more than a day's wages.

Unfortunately, by Christmas I still hadn't figured out a way to leave that didn't involve starving to death.

I was finally coming to the conclusion most of us reach sooner or later (bit late in the day, admittedly) that life (or Life) is relentless, and that's about as philosophical on the subject as one can get on just a bit less than thirty quid a day. Stuff, I realised, just keeps coming. Things look up and then they don't: fortunes *wax* and *wane*. Stuck there on the shop floor, I decided here on in that I would call Fortune's bluff and tackle it (or It) head on – then all the bad things that happened to me would be of my own doing and I'd only have myself to blame.

To be fair, a lot of this had come from the confidence I'd gained in Yorkshire and I knew I had to make use of it before that self-belief trickled away under the glaring lights of Harrods Perfumery Department. As far as standing up for myself it hadn't been a success, but it did prove I could make money on my own; I didn't need a traditional job. I decided that I was not going back to Harrods in the New Year, or ever again.

I would take my chances.

Chapter 11
From Tooting Broadway to Soho

The grave risks of voting with your feet

Now, obviously, I didn't waste away in the manner of Chatterton, otherwise what you are now reading would be a long and surprisingly personal obituary. However, it was a bloody close-run thing.

I was ridiculously skint – I recall that at the time my food budget was around a tenner a week. Luckily, someone had given us[38] a large box of potatoes and curry powder. So, potato curry became my staple, to which I added meat I bought from the halal butchers on Tooting Broadway. This was cheap because it was basically the offcuts they kept for dog food. Having cooked it, I discovered I couldn't actually cut it into chunks small enough to chew and digest, so I invested £4.99 (half a week's food allowance) in a very sharp knife.

I wasn't sure where work would come from and for a few weeks I wandered around Tooting, and further afield to Merton and Croydon, in the freezing cold, wondering what to do.

As it was getting situation critical, my luck changed. As per.

I had signed up to a tutorial agency about three months before Christmas then promptly forgotten all about it. It had

---

38 The 'us' being two school friends who were flatmates – Downside in Tooting.

just blended into one of the hundred or so applications I made for jobs on my day off every week that came to nothing. Out of those hundred applications, I got about ten interviews but no job offers, aside from essentially the same job as the one I had just left except in a different shop – or selling, on commission only, products that were either: baffling (I remember a wheel lock that turned itself into a torch and/or truncheon for self-protection); impossible to sell (insurance); or illegal (counterfeit perfume on the street outside my former place of work, Harrods).

So, I was surprised – but not overly hopeful – when I got a call and was asked to go to somewhere near Croydon to help a small boy with his reading homework.

I had no teaching experience nor qualifications, and no-one had "police checked" me, which was pretty slapdash even for the early '90s. However, it paid £20 per hour, with £3 going to the agency, and I could charge travel, which seemed like a fortune, given my straightened circumstances.

Discovering the tutoring world was my turning point that year.

I remember, initially, fretting that I would be discovered as a fraud and thrown out on my ear, so I made a point of explaining before I went to someone's house that I was not a teacher, just a youthful and (by inference) hard-up graduate. As it turned out, most parents just wanted someone reasonably intelligent and enthusiastic to do the homework duties once or twice a week whilst they cooked supper or stayed late at work.

What I was teaching was easy and the variety suited me. The stock-in-trade was small children learning to read and do basic maths, but it didn't end there. I taught creative writing to slightly older children, English to A-level, and French up to degree level. Probably the second most common, at the time, was preparing children for the entrance exam to private prep schools in London. Then, as now, there was a paucity of places in fee-paying schools in London – particularly for boys – and most made kids take an exam, aged about ten, to check their verbal and mathematical reasoning.

They all claimed it was impossible to prepare for these exams but, after a bit, I found I could work out what each of the schools was after by talking to other mums and teachers, then it would be just a matter of practising similar questions with them ad nauseam.

Occasionally I would get something unusual: a rich Italian couple about my age wanted to be more 'cultured', so I spent several days with them being paid to go to galleries and or just sit around talking books; a pair of Saudi princes needed tuition (lazy, pampered – yet roguishly charming); a model, who liked to answer the door in anything from full evening wear to just a bra and knickers, wanted to learn French because her boyfriend came from Marseille. I even tutored children on the set of a feature film.

There were also the emotional ones who are hard to forget: kids with pushy parents who panicked and became tearful when they got a question wrong; a builder about my age who had spent his early years in young offenders' units and who I taught to read and write; a sensitive boy of about sixteen with anorexia and skin so thin it looked like it would tear.

And then there was Simon.

Simon was a very small, very grubby, distressingly jittery boy whose parents were both blind. I like to say they were loving parents but the feel of that house was wrong from the moment you stepped over the threshold: and it wasn't just the dirt and the smell of bad food – something intangible felt more off-kilter than that. The windows were never opened and there were often odd noises coming from upstairs, like another child or an animal. The first time it happened, I asked Simon what the noises were and he looked at the desk. 'It's a secret,' he said. I found out the name of his school and phoned them.

They noted my concerns and the family immediately stopped having me, so I guess my concerns were passed on.

I can't shake the feeling, after thirty years, that I made a terrible mistake by not following up.

But, on the whole, the tuition finally felt like I was doing some good. Unfortunately, it was taking a while to build up a client base and, whilst I was happy about work for the first time in ages, I was getting a bit desperate.

My flatmates were in a similar hand-to-mouth position[39] and Sunday lunch with random parents, or *spag bol* with Elsbeth, was often the only square meal of the week.

The Lancia Delta was also pretty much dead. I couldn't afford to repair it, so it limped from place to place, misfiring on only three cylinders and drinking fuel; the head gasket was also going and if I sat in traffic longer than ten minutes it over-heated.

However, anything was better than being back in Harrods, in my book.

One Sunday evening, Elsbeth and I were coming back from somewhere along the A4 in nose-to-tail traffic. Turning onto the North End Road, I was aware that the two girls in the Beetle behind were not paying much attention to the road, and sure enough they went into the back of me.

Problem was, I had been driving without insurance for a couple of weeks and knew this was a divine signal to take the bus from now on. My bumper was a bit bashed up, but nothing major, and the girls were delighted when I affected nonchalance and told them not to worry. I was going for rueful – it probably looked more like relief; no more driving for me until I had scraped the cash together to get insured. Now, just to get home... as quietly as possible.

---

39   In the sense we were frequently reduced to gnawing our knuckles for protein.

We had parked up in a bus layby and, as I opened my door to get back in, I wasn't paying much attention to my surroundings. That very instant, a large bus went past and hit my half-open door. I plastered myself against the bodywork and watched the outer edge of my car door gouge a metal groove in each and every panel along the bus's flank whilst taking off the rubber strip that flopped at my feet like a dead snake. As it got to the wheel arch of the bus, my door gave up the contest and sheared off at the hinges. I looked up to see the girls in the Beetle staring open-mouthed at me and my poor car, and I fancy I did smile ruefully then – there really wasn't much else I could do.

The sound was probably the worst thing – that is until the bus driver got out and started swearing. The detail was hard to follow, because he was very angry, but the gist was I had parked illegally and now his bus was fucked and I was going to pay. And I was a cunt – in his considered opinion. Anyone would have assumed he had built the bus with his bare hands. The thought of having to pay for several new bus panels and a fine for not being insured made me feel a bit unwell.

'Um, we're blocking the traffic,' I said, sounding as reasonable as possible. 'I'll reverse up so you can get into the layby, and we'll exchange details.'

The bus driver glared at me balefully, but got back in the bus.

Good, I thought.

As soon as he began to pull off, I lifted the severed door up and threw it in the boot. Then I got in my car, avoiding Elsbeth's incredulous looks, did a screeching U-turn and headed off to the wilds of Shepherd's Bush as fast as I could.

The next day I took the car to a breakers yard as far out of London as I dared drive with no driver's door or insurance, and sold it for £25 in scrap.

Thankfully, more regular tuition work eventually started to trickle in and things slowly began to improve financially, and about time too. By the spring I was on about three to four hours' tuition a day, in cash: I was slowly building up a small pile of £10 notes in my desk. It looked like quite a lot of money before too long, and it was the first time in a very long time I felt reasonably well-off.

It was also nice not to have to work in the mornings. A bit like the door-to-door selling, I read or wrote most mornings, had some lunch and went for a run. Tooting was a dump in those days, so not the nicest place to run about in. The only other people I saw regularly in the park were the actor, Ben Daniels, and our neighbour opposite, a young drug dealer. We had a fair amount in common we three: we were self-employed start-of-careerers who were evidently trying to get the most out of life with the least input, judging by the amount of mooning about in the park we all did. Of the three of us, the seventeen-year-old drug dealer was definitely the most successful at idle fucking about for the maximum financial return: in the few months I 'knew' him, he went from driving about in a rusty XR2 to an all-white 7-series BMW with a sky-blue leather interior.

As a career, the tutoring still felt temporary, but I had a plan: as soon as I had scraped £5,000 together, I was off to Malaysia, where I could live for £10 a day. This would give me a year to write my masterpiece. I reckoned I could get to my target by the end of the summer.

I told Elsbeth about this in excited tones and, unsurprisingly, she was less than pleased.

Typically, I was quite surprised she was focusing on the negatives (me, buggering off without her. Again). And none of the positives (me, pleasing myself. Again).

It seems incredible now, but I was genuinely baffled as to why she wasn't more enthusiastic, which just goes to show... well, quite a lot really.

But in spite of how I behaved, I did love Elsbeth, and I think that that was the moment I should have seriously asked her to marry me. But of course I didn't. Partly what was stopping me was money, but mainly I had a lot to prove to myself. I didn't even feel like I had got properly started, which is ironic because I *still* feel that way. But during those months in Tooting, my gut feeling was that however much we might have been in love, however romantic it would have felt to have gone to a church, said our vows in front of friends and family, and been twenty-two, married and making our way, I felt we could do it better tethered but not bonded. Not just yet.

But it was clear I'd lose her if I left, so I decided to shelve plans for Malaysia, and when a friend invited me to interview for a job subediting on a magazine he was working for I thought that I would give proper jobs one more go. So, I went.

Jazz Express, as far as I could work out, was a smallish jazz and blues music magazine based in Soho (the heart and soul of British jazz – though I didn't know that then).

I knew it was somehow linked to my favourite pizza chain, PizzaExpress, that much Gary had told me, but I'd been for so many duff interviews I kept my research to a minimum.

Up until then, jazz for me had been men in bow ties on fake paddle boats going up the Thames, or black and white footage of Louis Armstrong smiling and sweating profusely. I liked blues, though, and still cherished a tiepin that BB King had given me after a concert I went to in Croydon, of all places.

So – to recap – I liked pizza and I had no strong views on jazz.

The *Jazz Express* offices were above Kettner's restaurant in Romilly Street and, not having a clue where either was, I was running late as I dashed up the stairs and went through the first office door I came to.

I'd only intended to ask where the editor, Cat Bass, worked, but the two venerable-looking old men who were enjoying what looked very much like a glass of sherry (each, of course) wanted to know who I was, why I was there and did I also like sherry?

I hadn't had sherry since the infamous sherry parties at Downside, but I took a glass and, pretending to sip it, explained about the subbing job as best I could, then I talked about the army and the door-to-door selling and tutoring. The larger of the two men (who also owned the biggest eyebrows), who was sitting on the business side of the desk, eventually introduced himself as Peter Boizot, owner of PizzaExpress[40] and also the unimaginatively named *Jazz Express*. He picked up a phone and called an internal number. 'Hello Catherine, are you busy? I don't care… Would you come downstairs for a minute?'

A few moments later, I was being introduced to a girl about my age who was the editor.

'This is Robin,' said Peter, looking immensely pleased with himself, as if he'd just invented me; 'he'd be a hopeless subeditor and I'm not sure we can afford one – don't you have Gary?'

'Um, yes we do…' Cat started.

'Good, he can just try a bit harder. I think Robin here would be an excellent business manager – not just at PB Publications; he could look into Peroni and the Festival. We'll pay him £1,000 a month. I'm sure he'll be full of ideas.' Peter trained his giant eyebrows on me. 'When can you start?'

'Monday,' I said, feeling pleased and excited, as you do when your life seems to have shifted into a more interesting gear.

I spent exactly a year working for Peter. It was my apprenticeship in the very satisfying business of turning an idea into money. At the time of my joining, Peter was in deep trouble: the recession hit PizzaExpress hard, he was mired in debt and it was getting worse every day. It didn't stop Peter continuing to do just as he pleased.

---

40   And founder, I was later to discover.

From the off, it was obvious he had simply combined some of his interests – eating, jazz and drinking – into core businesses: pizzas, *Jazz Express*/Soho Jazz Festival and Peroni beer, amongst a host of other things he did, like sponsoring the UK hockey team and buying Peterborough United Football Club.

Soho was still an interesting place to be... just: Jeffrey Bernard was certainly unwell, but he still managed to drag himself to The Coach & Horses next door to our office each day, and could be relied upon to be civil to you if you went in with a pretty girl; Boizot mixed in a wide circle of people so it wasn't in the least unusual to walk into his office and find Princess Margaret sitting there, or the pornographer, Paul Raymond. The latter was our landlord in Soho and I usually made myself scarce when he was around. Apart from once getting stared at furiously by Johnny Rotten (in someone's house in Kensington), I never met anyone quite as intimidating. However, I've just looked at some pictures of him online and he looks quite normal, so I can only assume, like John Lydon, he just didn't like me.

The money I earned wasn't really that good, but I hardly spent anything on food or drink because we ate for free at Kettner's at lunchtime and there was always an invitation for something in Soho where food and drink was put on.

This was either something music-related (so you had to listen to jazz in return for free stuff) or media launches: anything from books to films or a new restaurant. I got quite good at gatecrashing events at the Groucho and rubbing shoulders with minor celebrities whilst filling my jacket pockets with sausage rolls[41].

___

41 It's a regrettable feature of the modern canapé, with its fiddly bits of fennel and lumpfish toppings, etc., that you can't scoop up a handful and put them in your trousers for the journey home. Sausage rolls were ideal scavenging food: compact, transportable and could last for days. Mini cheese sandwiches will eventually curl and harden into a sausage roll – so are, arguably, even better!

Out of this tribe, the easiest to talk to were the writers: Auberon Waugh was clever but grumpy, but at least he'd talk to you like an equal – provided you didn't say anything really daft; Julian Barnes was jolly and boyish; Alan Bennett and Stephen Fry competed for being approachable and avuncular. I always found musicians to be a bit twitchy and neurotic, and actors/ TV 'personalities' would ignore you with a vengeance unless you might be important; one exception being Emma Freud, who breezed into some party at the French House one evening, talked breathlessly *at* me for about five minutes, like we were old friends, and left – but not before I fell hopelessly in love with her.

Sadly, *Jazz Express* – like its parent company – was perpetually in deep financial trouble. Every few months, Boizot would look at the figures, his eyebrows bouncing up and down on his forehead like mating caterpillars, and threaten to shut it down. This was mainly because the expense of it was borne by PizzaExpress and, unsurprisingly, the general management hated us as a bunch of graduate fops who were part of Peter's vanity project and thus a huge waste of money.

So, the first thing I persuaded Peter to do was separate *Jazz Express* from PizzaExpress. We got our own bank account and I took a look at the paltry income streams. Right away, I noticed that half the subscribers (about 1,000 jazz enthusiasts) had not paid a subscription in quite some time but were still getting a copy of the magazine each month, and there were hundreds more whose subscriptions had lapsed but had never been chased.

It took me a while to figure out how to make labels on the ancient MacPlus I was given but, eventually, I printed a load of reminder letters and franked them on the exclusive PizzaExpress franking machine – making sure it was late, so there were no witnesses.

Not long afterwards, we had a couple of grand in subscription money in our bank account. This was extremely satisfying. Then I managed to get rid of the old printing firm we had used for years, which was basically robbing us blind, for a much cheaper outfit in Wales.

About a week later, Peter called me downstairs. He was looking at our bank statement and wanted to know where all the money had come from. I explained about the subscribers and the lower overheads, but I could see he wasn't happy about something. 'And you paid these cheques in yourself?'

'Yes?' I said, wondering why that was relevant.

'Waste of money!' he exploded, going very red and banging the desk. 'We don't pay you a fortune to walk about the place – get one of the waiters to do it in future!'

And that pretty much summed up my relationship with Peter. About a third of the time he was praising me to the skies: we went to a funeral together one day and I spoke for a long time to Humphrey Lyttelton, the aristocratic journalist and trumpet player. I knew enough, even in those days, to twig he was a big deal – our eldest elder statesman and a very nice man to boot. Peter was enthusiastic as we walked back to his chauffeur-driven Rolls. 'I'm pleased to see you talking to people; would you like some lunch?'

For another third of my working day, I think he kept me about as a sort of court jester: he laughed at my jokes, pretended to take my ideas seriously and then did just as he pleased. I played up to it to an extent: I used to do things like replace his handset with a banana after I noticed he'd always answer the phone without looking.

For the final third of my day, I got yelled at in that booming voice of his.

This was understandable because of all the mistakes I made, which must have been galling, especially as they cost Peter money.

However, after a few months it began to dawn on me that I'd misjudged the situation in a more fundamental way. The fact of the matter was that the more I got a handle on things, the less he liked it; not that he was jealous of my success – far from it – one of the best things about Peter was the fact he wanted to give young people a chance, even when it was costly to him personally. It was more, I think, that *Jazz Express* was his Fuck You to the group as a whole – a sort of *look at my hobby as it drains money – you can't do anything about it... because I'm in charge.*

I could sort of cope with this were it not for the editor, Cat, who must have read a book called *Management by Sulking*. To my mind, everything I did (whilst not always successful) at least made some kind of sense. *Jazz Express* desperately needed money: I negotiated a deal with WHSmith to stock it there, and hit the phones to sell advertising. This was fine until I sold Coke space for their logo on the front of the magazine. Cat seethed for a week. She liked her front covers pristine, with no hint of commercialism. I could understand she wanted the magazine to look as good as possible, but felt annoyed we were being high-handed when we couldn't afford it.

In hindsight, she was right and had read the situation better than me – Peter would always bail us out. Thus, we could afford to be high-handed and lose money. Basically, they didn't need me.

One thing Cat and I agreed on was the profile of the people we interviewed each month. Peter basically wanted us to fill it full of his jazz friends, most of whom nobody had ever heard. Instead, we started contacting people like Jamiroquai, Candy Dulfer (Prince's hot saxophonist, and a Grammy award winner in her own right), Jools Holland and David Bowie. The latter, in particular, had never been asked about his jazz credentials in all his born days, and we got interviews and lots of free stuff from his management. The front cover we did of Jamiroquai was a brilliant piece of acid jazz design and timed perfectly, just as he was breaking worldwide. He came to lunch and talked a lot of crap, mainly directed at his group of admirers who came to lunch too and gobbled up half a ton of margheritas – but he gave a great photoshoot in that daft hat of his. We sold out of that issue and it looked like we were on a roll.

Then Peter stepped in: he strongly objected to the direction the magazine was going, he grumbled; so we were back to reviewing unknown bands with names like Bobby Bunker and his Jazz Maestros, Davey Dave Davies and The Norfolk Swingers, and trying to sell £25 spot ads for record shops that never made any money and usually didn't pay us anyway.

All things considered, it wasn't a bad magazine: some of the writers – especially Larry Adler and Miles Kington – were top flight, but a lot of it was tawdry and almost impossible to read. After eight months, I decided that, much as I liked free food and knowing some famous people a little bit, trying to make something commercial that didn't want to be was depressing, and so I started to take myself off to the stockroom to read Terry Pratchett books or hide in The Coach & Horses alongside a perennially hungover Jeffrey Bernard, who glared at me over his twenty or so vodka tonics because I didn't have a discernible pair of breasts.

Boizot had been an inspiration but it was obvious that I was never going to be happy being told what to do and having no real say. I realised what I already knew in Harrods: that a job, even a loose-fitting one, was not for me. Peter and I were alike in that respect. I loved the fact he could be as idiosyncratic as he liked, could come up with the most outrageous solutions, run on his own time when everyone else was tearing their hair out, and almost always come out on top. This wasn't business genius so much as knowing that, when you are completely in charge, there are a great many ways to skin a cat.

However, it was in pulling off his greatest coup that I think he also made his biggest mistake.

His money problems were becoming too severe to ignore and so he hatched a plan to float PizzaExpress off the back of a defunct computer company that was listed but no longer trading.

And the City loved the idea of PizzaExpress. After all, they ate there at weekends.

Almost overnight he went from being broke to being worth over £50 million. This is incredible, like winning the lottery several times over. In all respects it was a triumph… except in the one that was key to his personality: he no longer controlled the company.

Peter hated the new set-up and promptly disappeared from view – to mope, basically. This left control to the new major shareholders, two bankers: Luke Johnson and Hugh Osmond. Neither had Boizot's style or personality and, from the little I saw of them, they didn't seem to have real creative acumen either, just a knowledge of the rules of acquisition and plunder.

They briefly latched on to me whilst they thought I had Peter's ear, and I remember batting with Luke at a PizzaExpress cricket match in which he made a mistake running between the wickets – an error of judgement – that got me (not him) run out. He didn't apologise, and I decided on the spot that working with them would be worse than working for Peter. It sounds like something someone in a PG Wodehouse novel would say, but you can tell a lot about a man by the way he plays any sport – cricket, in particular. There are so many rules that are more like guidelines that allow for a player's sense of fair play or gentlemanliness. Mr Johnson could have assumed responsibility for his error in calling a run he couldn't make, and fallen on his sword, but he wanted to carry on batting, so he didn't. He had a choice: either I got out or he did. Naturally, in his mind, it would always be me.

This isn't just bad sportsmanship – it was an error of judgement, too, as he had invited me to curry favour, but his personality had got the better of him, as I notice it still does.

So, in June, a year to the day after I started at *Jazz Express*, I handed in my notice, and started a job a few weeks later with the Fulham and Hammersmith Council, gardening again. I was to be looking after Shepherd's Bush Green.

But this time I had a plan.

Chapter 12
Shepherd's Bush

Going backwards to go forwards is basically taking a run-up...

A school friend of mine lives close to the BBC studios in White City and I recently stayed the night at his.

The following morning, me and my hangover have taken a wander through the Westgate Shopping Centre and out onto Shepherd's Bush Green.

These days it's got a nice play area for kids, nice shops, nice pubs and lots of nice shrubs. It's nice.

Shepherd's Green is clean.

Used not to be. In 'my' day, there was nothing for kids – it was basically an outdoor hub for the homeless and one of the first places people seemed to choose if they found themselves sleeping rough. I spent five months working there: strimming the borders, emptying bins, picking up litter, and then the phone to tell the police about the dead bodies as the winter drew in[42]. There were also two shootings. After the second

---

42 The pattern was nearly always the same. A man (ninety-nine times out of a hundred, I am bound to say) would turn up on the green one day, usually dressed for the weather, usually clean-shaven. Billy, who I worked with, told me they were invariably kicked out during a family split. As the days went by, they became grubbier, moved about less, and they nearly all seemed to swap whatever decent coat they had for

one, I was approached by a scary man in a leather coat as I sat in a café off the green and warned not to talk to the police. People were keeping an eye on me.

In those days, Shepherd's Bush Green was not nice.

But I did become quite fond of it, and I did my bit by making it cleaner – outwardly, at least. I had my orange Rascal van and I felt quite proprietorial as I went about tidying things up into black plastic bin liners and cutting back the spindly, exhaust-choked shrubs. It's a shame I've come back here to look at it in June because between March and April there is a carpet of daffodils on the south side that I planted. I spent several weeks putting in two thousand bulbs – we had ordered double that, but everyone back at the depot helped themselves, same as they did with the fuel for the mowers.

Once in a while, when I tended the green, I'd look up and stare east at the leafy hill of Notting Hill Gate, beyond which was Hyde Park and London's West End, where I'd had a much more glamorous but ultimately unfulfilling lifestyle just a few weeks previously. Oddly, all the parties, the launches and the feeling of being in with the media felt like another life after just a few weeks.

I'd moved out of Tooting by then and, in a moment of inspiration, I put a notice on a tree outside some boats moored on Cheyne Walk in Chelsea. Within a week I was bobbing about on the top floor of an attractive blue houseboat called *Mallard*. My room was small but it was dry and warm, and the view in the mornings, across the Thames, was fabulous. A nice old lady called Steph lived downstairs some of the time when

---

something thin and made of plastic sheeting. Most of them drank to stave off cold and boredom, and if they didn't pull themselves together quite quickly the next thing to go, after their sensible clothing, was their health. If they were too depressed or disturbed to look after themselves or look for help from one of the charities, there was a good chance of finding them dead on the green – especially if there had been a frost.

she wasn't in France. She had edited the children's Scratch and Sniff books in the '70s and was arty and just a bit mumsy. I paid her £80 a week, which left me enough money to run the elderly Triumph Herald[43] I'd bought for £100 and still buy beer.

Sounds OK, but there was a massive downside. I would have liked to have moved in with Elsbeth – now I knew what I wanted to do with my life (I'm coming to the specifics of that), I felt ready. However, there had been a change – she'd gone away on a summer holiday without me that year and come back a colder more distant version of herself.

I sensed it the very day she got back. I wasn't being particularly sensitive: normally, when we'd been away from one another we could wait to meet up. I still enjoyed talking to Elsbeth more than anyone else I could think of and, having finally given up her job in the City for teacher training (long holidays), she'd been away for a while. I was missing her. She rang to say she was in Battersea but that she was tired – she'd see me the next day. Nothing wrong in that but her tone set off alarm bells: she sounded like another person, who had borrowed Elsbeth's voice and a bit of her personality. The cold, unfriendly bit. Something was up.

It sounds like a massive overreaction but it was so unlike her, so unlike us, I immediately thought *she's fallen out of love with me* and, as soon as I thought that I then thought *how can I possibly know that, she just said she was tired*. But I knew, in my marrow, I was right. Knowing what I do about relationships now, I have learned that if you are very close to someone the small things are genuinely significant – even if, to an outsider, they seem utterly inconsequential.

---

43 This was the start of a series of very cheap cars I bought for under £200 and ran into the ground. I found I could usually get 10,000 miles out of them, using the AA for servicing and repairs. Later, I tried the same with motorbikes and nearly killed myself.

By the next day when we did meet, although I'd managed to convince myself I'd imagined it, ten seconds in, Elsbeth's company made it obvious I had not. She sat as far across the table from me as she could and looked bored. So, I did what you do when you are young and too impulsive for your own good: I told her how much I loved her and how I thought we should get married that year.

Dead silence. This wasn't just an absence of a response from Elsbeth, it felt like an absence of everything, as if a black hole had just popped into existence between us, cutting all connection: sucking in all sound, time... and light.

Even as I said it, I knew it was really badly timed. I was six months too late and six months too early: given whatever had happened on her holiday that had made her change, I should have kept quiet until I knew what it was. I should have let her be, let her come back to me if she wanted. I could have affected nonchalance, or pretended not to notice. But the relationship was too important for this kind of emotional mucking about.

Over the next week, she made it clear she wanted to spend more time with people on her course I did not know, and she now had regular bouts of being capricious or cold. Even sex felt oddly impersonal. It felt shit, but there was just enough of the old relationship, a few flashes of tenderness, to keep me hopeful that she would come around.

Most of the time, I put it to the back of my mind and concentrated, instead, on the positives. I knew I'd made the right decision with my life by leaving *Jazz Express*, even when one of the managers at PizzaExpress Head Office – a guy I knew reasonably well – stared right through me in my litter-picker clothes as he walked across Shepherd's Bush Green one day.

London Tutors (home tuition and supply teaching) was my first proper business and seemed the most logical continuation of what I had been doing before I worked for Peter. I wanted to make money but it covered moral bases, too.

I had managed to save exactly no cash at all working for *Jazz Express* and, in hindsight – with no financial cushion or experience – the whole venture seems pretty daft. However, I didn't know it at the time, but by sheer luck London Tutors was practically the best business I could have chosen.

First of all, it was a growth area: not only were there lots of parents who were desperate to get their children into highly competitive private schools, but there was also a huge groundswell of middle-class folk who, a generation before, would have sent their children to a private school but could not afford it now. What they could afford, though, was a few hours' tuition a week.

Secondly, I now know that the best business ideas are rarely the most outrageous or original: they are usually in established markets… with tweaks. I knew how the industry worked and I was sure I could do better, simply by putting it on a more professional footing[44].

Finally, if you have no money, then start a clean business that requires no stock and the lowest start-up investment risk.

Essentially, I needed something that only required a phone and a computer and had a decent chance of making money in its first three months. It would be a race against time to get money through the door, but doable.

I was able to get a £3,000 loan that would buy six months' office space and £1,000 of advertising in the *Yellow Pages*, and my grandfather loaned me £1,000 to buy an Amstrad computer. On 8th January 1992 I started the business.

Just at the precise moment the rest of my world fell apart.

I was getting settled into Chelsea nicely by now (as if that's hard). Cheyne Walk, where the boat was moored, seemed to be

---

44 Most home tuition agencies were run from people's front rooms, part-time, and were basically one home tutor farming out a few jobs they could not do to a handful of other tutors.

packed with artistic pedigree, to the extent it's hard to imagine you could have made it as a writer, painter or performer if you hadn't, at one time, lived there[45].

It was the Sunday after the Monday that London Tutors was officially founded that, out of the blue, my parents announced they were coming to see me. It was only ten minutes' drive down the road but it was very rarely I saw them unless I went round to Sunday lunch. However, my father has always loved boats, so I assumed it was to take a look at mine.

Unfortunately, they had come not to admire boats but to tell me my father had lost all his money. All *our* money really, too, as he'd spent my grandparents' legacy and my great-grandparents'. A couple of years previously he had left his superbly well-paid and secure job in Remy Martin and bought a fish production plant. In Scotland. In hindsight, it was a terrible decision, but at the time it sort of made sense: he'd spent twenty-five years making other people a lot of money and he finally had the opportunity and the cash to do something for himself. Unfortunately, he over-invested in a company he was trying to run at arm's length. At the same time, the money he put in was woefully short for the amount of cash you need to start a brand – Galloway Seafoods, as he named it.

The business was also loaned to the hilt and the family home in Fulham was security. 'So, it's just a matter of time before the house is repossessed and they lose everything,' my brother muttered ominously.

The money side of things was disquieting because, by now, we had got used to our parents being financially very secure,

---

45 Cheyne Walk residents have included: Rossetti, Hilaire Belloc, Bram Stoker, TS Eliot, Elizabeth Gaskell, Mick Jagger, Keith Richards, Ralph Vaughan Williams, Bertrand Russell, George Melly, Whistler, Joe Strummer, Henry James, Pugin, Laurence Olivier, Somerset Maugham, Ian Fleming, Sylvia Pankhurst… The list of wider Chelsea alumni is longer than this but you get the picture.

and the idea that you could go from being so wealthy to losing everything in the space of a year was upsetting and, frankly, pretty disconcerting. Oddly, it was family pride – honour, if you will – that stung us the most. Instantaneously, this punt I was taking on London Tutors became something vital: it felt as if it was up to me alone to prove the Bennetts had it in them. The desire to save one's parents and save the day is not limited to children's books. I was going to make it all better. I was going to do my best.

However, only eight weeks after my father announced they were bankrupt, it was also looking like I was going to lose everything (admittedly very little). My career as an entrepreneur seemed to be over before it had started.

I was running out of cash.

My £3,000 loan had been spent, and whilst I had a bit coming in from my own private tuition, to buy food and other basics, it was not nearly enough to pay for an office and rent on the boat.

The main problem seemed to be me not getting the average value of a tutee right. I'd assumed about £60 commission per booking when – in reality – it was more like £20. Some of this was down to dishonesty (the tutor simply lying about their hours and keeping the agency cut, or parents doing a private deal with the tutor after one or two lessons), but it also had a lot to do with naïve business planning[46].

Supply teaching in schools had been slow to take off and language tuition in companies was the only thing that looked like it was a success.

The upshot, though, was that I was simply spread too thin and not earning enough.

Then Elsbeth sacked me.

---

46 I've learned, over the years, to halve any forecast in revenue, double costs and triple the time it takes to get things done and you might be pleasantly surprised – although you'll usually be in the ballpark. This is not an exaggeration.

Funnily enough, recently I had thought Elsbeth and I had turned a corner. For a few weeks our relationship had seemed better, but perhaps I was just getting used to this new distance and the fact that, when we were with friends, she had switched from being my cheerleader to being my main detractor.

Over that final year we were together, I had become used to Elsbeth positioning herself to be at odds with whatever I said or did. London Tutors was the main bone of contention: without a teaching qualification, according to her, I had no business running a teaching agency; it was also grubby – this *making money from learning*.

The fact is, I just don't think she liked me very much anymore, and it wasn't until twenty-five years later that I understood the anger and frustration. At the time, I was in a towering rage that she had told our friends she was leaving me before she told me, when we'd always said we'd be open with each other if it wasn't working. I had to go round one day when she was out and pick up my spare clothes, records and the books she did not want, under the tight-lipped supervision of a flatmate I had never met. She made it feel like I was a liability in those first few weeks we split, not to be trusted and certainly not to be alone with, and I hated that because it wasn't true; I'd just had my heart broken, that was all.

Then one day, in about 2014, I was cleaning out a cavity in the mezzanine floor of the office in Henley when I came across the box file of her letters.

I sat down and read around forty in one sitting and at the end of it the penny finally dropped.

She had really loved me. Once. The letters showed me something I had completely failed to see between the ages of nineteen and twenty-three: she had given her heart with a maturity and honesty that made me feel ashamed all those years later. At the time, to say I was blithe is an understatement. I had taken her love as my due because I was so amazing – why wouldn't she love me? In her letters it was clear she had given me her complete trust and her future, if I would take it. In return, I had taken her love lightly and, after five years, she'd finally had enough.

I would contact her and apologise but, by one of those quirks, a few years later she fell in love with and married one of my best friends from school. So, some kind of autopsy and grovelling apology would just be inappropriate – and irrelevant – because at twenty-three, I think we were young enough for this to have been a different life. The school friend she married is far nicer, far less selfish and we still see one another. Elsbeth gets on with my wife, Hélène, I get on with my school friend, our children get on with each other. It all turned out OK.

But at the time, Elsbeth going felt like the small turd on top of the giant humble pie I was trying to keep down. To recap in a very short space of time: the person I loved had left me; my business was failing before it had got off the ground; my parents were having cars and furniture taken away by bailiffs. And bankruptcy caused them to separate.

Then this fairly minor thing (in the Grand Scheme of Crap Things) happened, but it felt like a last straw.

I had bought a motorbike when I started the business, the better to make meetings on time and not rely on the Tube, which was getting too expensive for my dwindling purse, anyway. It was a monstrous trial bike: heavy, ugly and it was missing its rear exhaust, so it sounded like a drag racer. Unfortunately, I had also not learned from my Lancia–bus contretemps, and when the bike's insurance ran out I didn't bother getting it re-insured. Or MOT'd – because that would involve a service I could not afford.

Early one morning, my mind probably dwelling on the list of bad things that had been happening to me in a very short space of time, I was hauled to one side by the police whilst going along the Thames Embankment. The bike was in such a state, sir – they informed me – it could not move another inch. It would have to be left on the side of the road for collection by trained professionals. They took my details. I would be hearing from them via the Crown Prosecution Service, as this was too serious a matter to be dealt with by points and a roadside fine. I was also to hand my (non-existent) insurance documents in to the nearest police station in five days, for inspection.

My only means of transport was being impounded and I was looking at a conviction and a fine I wouldn't be able to pay because I was going bust, just like my dad. The one person I wanted to phone for comfort I couldn't because she didn't love me anymore.

I leaned against the cold stone of the Embankment and looked out across the choppy, grey water.

And I felt very sorry for myself indeed.

The last two years had been a series of very bad decisions: from Guards officer, to door-to-door sales, to working in a shop, unsuccessfully trying to stick to a real job, then being a council worker and now about to go bust before I'd had an ounce of tangible success. Before the week was out, I'd be back in a department store counting the minutes until my tea break. Each move I'd made looked very much like one step down on a ladder, and I only had myself to blame.

The wind got up and, out of the corner of my eye, I could see the policeman giving me an odd look. I don't think he booked many people who wandered off, whilst he was filling in the forms, in order to philosophise with themselves.

It wouldn't mend my broken heart, but as I walked back along the Embankment to the boat I knew I really had no choice: I had to get something good out of this terrible fuck-up. And that meant I had to find a way to make the business work. Fast.

And that was probably the biggest factor ensuring I did.

Chapter 13

Chelsea

In which I learn that perseverance is the hidden agenda of necessity and the engine room of luck

Nowadays, I spend most of my time (when not writing books hardly anybody reads) curating cash. On the face of it, managing investments is a nice job – you've made the money, now you're trying to hold onto it – but it's a bit soulless. Then there are the remaining businesses I did not sell or wind down when we moved to France.

For these, I tend to get wheeled out only when things either go very well or very badly. So, delegating responsibility works OK for me about 95% of the time[47]. In between times, I do what every other businessman does, which is: watch cashflows, fret about invoices, staff, the economy and carry boxes about[48].

The rest of the day – about half of it – I'm pretty much retired and free to waste energy on things that really shouldn't concern me.

---

47   You can guarantee that once or twice a year something will horrendously balls up and the chances are you'll be the last to know. This will nearly always cost money to sort. Business is relentless, because it is life.

48   It's a fact of life that however important you become, you will still need to pick up boxes of stationery on a depressingly regular basis and carry them from A to B. I bet Elon Musk still has to. In fact, I feel quite good about that.

I'll give you an example: just recently, we arrived back from our travels to find our perfectly flat wooden flooring in France had gone rogue. It now undulated like waves in a small harbour.

After previous incidents, that I would call 'learning experiences', but Hélène talks about as national catastrophes on a par with the Eiffel Tower disappearing into a sinkhole, I solemnly gave my word I would never touch another power tool as long as we both drew breath.

Nevertheless, as soon as H had gone to the shops, I changed my trousers and went to the barn with a great sense of optimism, to hunt out a jigsaw I bought when I built a kitchen (badly) in our Clapham flat in about 1997.

The problem was simple: the floor had expanded in the heat and was too 'long'.

I would make it shorter.

It was a win-win – we'd be back to non-corrugated flooring, and everyone would be so impressed I could revert to my old ways of taking a lump hammer and gaffer tape to any DIY problem around the house.

Turns out jigsaws have a shelf life. Since I had last used ours it had got used to its retirement. Seconds after I turned it on, flames with sparks started coming out of the plastic casing as I flayed about with it in my hand. Briefly, I looked like Zeus.

Coming to my senses, I turned it off at the wall and spent the next five minutes getting my breathing and pulse back to normal before deciding that it was only a minor blip and I would press on.

Old school, I thought when I noticed the plane; *back to basics*. From woodwork lessons at school, I remembered the calming effect planing wood has on a person and, sure enough, within five minutes I was even thinking of a career change: I would turn my back on Mammon, lead a simple and good life. I would *carpent* (= repent + woodwork).

Time passed and my soul healed.

When I finally blew off all the shavings, I saw that my work had done the trick: the bit of flooring in my hand was noticeably thinner. Hang on, it was much thinner.

The cold dark shadow of foreboding fell across the worktable and I walked slowly back to the house with a rising sense of dread.

I think now is the time to tell you about our underlay.

Underlay, in my experience, is usually a neutral colour: russet, Sherwood green or taupe. For some reason, ours is made of a sort of super shiny material cute female aliens on '70s episodes of *Star Trek* always wear. Captain Kirk was always a sucker for gold lamé.

The underlay now shone through the floor with the intensity of the sun. It was as if I had just chiselled away the planking to discover a hidden world – a happier place of light and colour below our feet.

Perhaps that's how I would sell it to H?

Bollocks, I thought, reality flooding in, *that won't even work on the children. Nothing for it, I will have to cover my tracks.*

Mastek will be my friend.

… so, this all seems a long way from the end of the last chapter when I was looking at no business, no girlfriend and no family life. However, it is relevant insofar as when it was all going to hell in a handcart I did wonder if my parents had been right all along: am I sloppy – more to the point, did I not give enough of a fuck about anything to do anything worthwhile… in their words, was I not a bit *lightweight*?

This wasn't just a throwaway line that has stuck with me, I often had this, growing up: I was told, a lot, that I couldn't be bothered – and that bothered me. A lot. Especially when my life was unravelling in 1992.

Rightly or wrongly, I never bought into this version of me. I never thought of myself as particularly lazy – in my mind I was always doing things – nor slovenly, if what I was doing was interesting. But I do like to cut corners and I'm easily distracted, both of which is evidenced by all four of my first four cars ending up unsaleable wrecks.

One thing I most definitely am, which I rarely get accused of, is stubborn. And over-competitive: as I said in the first chapter, I think the jokes and the easy-going manner were an unconscious way of masking this as a child. I've also always had something else going for me.

Dumb luck.

Now, I know we're all supposed to make our own luck, that it's just a numbers game etc., etc.... but I've known people slog for years and get nowhere; and sometimes, quite frankly, you just get lucky; and some people, much more than others (however unjust that may seem), are simply luckier.

In many respects that has been me. I guess my only worry is when my luck might run out.

Right then, though, back in 1992, I was due for a change in circumstances and it came not a moment too soon, when it was most sorely needed – a bit like at the end of a movie.

First of all, the motorbike, whose state of decrepitude was about to wind me up in court, needed sorting.

For the insurance, I went and got a cover note the next day. Unfortunately, this would not solve my problems: the cover note was dated the 11th of the month and the infraction had occurred on the 10th. They would spot this and know I was driving without insurance. So, I did something even more reckless, considering the shit I was already in: I forged the temporary cover note – as it had been written by hand, I spent a couple of quid buying black biros that matched the original ink and added a cross bar to the '11' (between the 'ones') to make it into a plausible 4, albeit slightly lopsided.

Never having had to hand in my documents at a police station, I had no idea what this would entail. I was banking on the fact I would probably be faced with a busy person who didn't care. However, I sketched out my plan to my friends in the pub, and they exchanged concerned glances before reminding me that falsifying documents was a huge risk and likely to end up with me getting nicked. You don't have the sort of face that gets on well in prison, they said; nice things will not happen to you, one of them added darkly. As if he knew.

So, I very nearly didn't go through with it the next day. It *was* a risk. But my gut instinct kicked in: I was due a change of luck and now was the time to test my theory about myself. If I came clean I was certain to get into trouble and my life would get worse. If I pinned my hopes on my rather crappy forgery skills not being picked up, I still had a chance of getting away with this. The point being, always go for the option where there's still a chance.

And it worked.

When I took it down to the police station, the clerk glanced at it, ticked a box or two and asked for my signature. The whole process lasted about a minute but, as I left the station, it felt momentous, like I had finally turned a corner.

There was still the matter of the summons. There I was helped by Michael, the ex-husband of the lady who owned the boat, and a thoroughly charming alcoholic. I had always got on well with Michael and he'd introduced me to lots of other very charming alcoholics dotted around Chelsea.

When the bailiff came round to the boat to issue the summons, he was greeted by a very affable, possibly tipsy man who told them (on instinct – no prompting from me; I'd never mentioned it) that I had moved away. Boats and pissed people do not make for the impression of fixed living, and the person issuing the papers believed Michael. And that, dear reader, was the last I heard of that.

Then there was the more nagging problem of going bust.

A day or two after the cover note forging incident (and probably about three weeks before I had to tell the people who ran the business units that I would be closing down, and my landlady that I could not afford to pay rent), I got a call from a client in Battersea. We had sent an Italian teacher around a few times to teach the staff how to order food, exchange pleasantries with potential clients and decipher purchase orders in Italian.

'Turns out learning a language is really hard,' said the office manager to me when he rang.

'Yup,' I couldn't dispute that, 'but it's worth the effort,' I added chirpily, assuming that the next thing to come out of his mouth would be: *We're going to stop your lessons and just use a guidebook in future.*

'I suppose so,' he said, meaning, *I don't agree with you, but I can't be bothered to argue the point.* I could hear him shuffling bits of paper. 'So, we've got some contracts and we thought we might as well just ask you if you can get them translated. You do do that, don't you?'

I paused for a millisecond as my financial situation flashed before my eyes.

'Of course,' I said. 'All the time.'

The next day, I pulled the *Yellow Pages* off the shelf in the office and hit the phones: Translation – now, why hadn't I thought of that?

And it was odd, but throughout a four-year degree in Modern Languages no-one had ever mentioned translation as a possible career path. These days it's a path that has turned into a veritable concourse for people studying languages, and it's getting bigger: the amount of data we produce almost doubles every year and a large chunk needs translating. Master's degrees in translation are sprouting up all over the place, and internships, where people can get real experience in translation, not filing and traipsing about after a project manager, proliferate.

A few people on my course studied interpreting in Paris during their year off, so I had an idea to phone up people working in hotels, hospitals and marketing companies and plug spoken, rather than written, translation, which I assumed was a lesser field.[49]

After speaking to reception in a few hotels and getting nowhere, I went to 'M' in the *Yellow Pages* and phoned the first marketing company I saw which was based in Chelsea.

'Hello,' I said, trying to sound cheerful, clever and grave all at once, 'do you ever need interpreters?'

'Not really...' came the response.

'Oh,' I said, already looking at the next company on the page in SW3.

'... but we've just been given the contract to launch the *Jurassic Park* video next year – it's going into thirteen different territories initially and we're looking for a good translation agency. If you're that, your call couldn't have come at a better time.'

Later that morning, I phoned St Mary's Hospital. They were pleased I rang, too, and wanted to see me the following week.

Now, since then, I have made literally thousands of calls to prospective clients and, back in the old days of fax machines, I would spend my lunch hours with a sandwich in one hand and an A4 flyer in the other, faxing companies in the *Yellow Pages* I thought might want to buy translation services. Like the door-to-door selling it's a numbers game and the trick is to work out what those numbers are. Those days, on average, you needed to make one hundred calls (two days' work) to

49   I was completely and utterly wrong about this.

get a client. Therefore, to get two major leads in a morning is vastly fluky[50].

Thus, I had two meetings to go to. However, foot in the door or not, I realised my biggest problem was my age and the fact that I looked about five years younger in those days. Good now, bad then.

With the marketing firm in Chelsea where I pitched for the *Jurassic Park* work, I was fortunate enough to be pitching to people only two or three years older than me. For the meeting at St Mary's Hospital, the manager in the documentation department came right out and asked, as I walked through the door (jokingly, I hope), if my dad was parking the car.

To get around this, I dusted off the title I had at *Jazz Express* – Business Manager – which gave the impression I was a recently employed salesperson-cum-marketeer with a company that was going places, and not the callow owner of a one-man band with a single rickety desk and phone.

My next problem was that I knew absolutely sod all about the translation industry. I knew a lot about translation, thanks to my degree, and what constituted the good and the bad from an intellectual – rather than commercial – point of view, but I needed to work out how to sell the services, what to charge, how to hire translators (what to pay them) and set up a process for doing projects that made money, and I needed to do it quite quickly.

---

50 I still feel that the quickest way to get something done is to pick up the phone. Even in these times of Google businesses, with their metatagging, adwording, optimisation and – what sometimes feels to me is best described as Shouting into the Void – Twitter. Obviously social feeds work for some people – especially if you're Donald Trump or Lady Gaga's cat – but most of the time, if you are an average person with a normal life, no-one cares except your friends and family. That's what Facebook is for.

However, back then – pre-internet – it really was the only way to drum up translation business. Well, that and the nuisance faxing, which had its fair share of success, amazingly.

This was because, when I went to see the *Jurassic Park* people, instead of asking me questions, then getting a quote and generally taking their time about the process, they told me they wanted to start the following week, and then, as I went out the door, they handed me a strapline *Coming Soon* to translate into thirteen languages for the next couple of days.

'Does that mean I have the job?' I thought I was just there to chat. In fact, most of the meeting had been about the film and very little had been said about foreign words.

'Yes,' they said, beginning to look doubtful.

'Great,' I said before their doubts found a voice; thinking, *Actually, shit.*

As soon as I got back to the office I wondered where I was going to find someone French, German, Italian, Spanish, Swedish, Estonian, Finnish, Japanese, Latvian, Lithuanian, Romanian, Norwegian and Dutch at very short notice.

I had a think and phoned the Job Centre in Clapham Junction, and surprisingly that was how we found our first translators and how I carried out our first proper translation.

It was barely a business yet, but the work (and the name, *Jurassic Park*) coming in allowed me to go back to Barclays and get another £2,000, which bought me some breathing space.

Shortly after we started working in translation, I was walking about the West End one day and saw a very respectable brass sign on a door. It said something like *MST Translations* or *Worldcomm Translations* and had an engraved globe with what looked like an arrow shooting around it – a bit generic but the signage looked top flight. The building was one of those large Georgian affairs you get around Manchester Square, and it gave the impression of dull but secure corporate respectability. I wasn't up to much that day so, on a whim, I rang the bell and was buzzed up without being asked what my business was.

I climbed the stairs and was greeted by the sight of five guys barely older than me playing office cricket in amongst antique furniture piled with paper and computing equipment.

As soon as they worked out I wasn't anyone especially important, I was roped in to playing wicketkeeper, and the chap who seemed to be more or less in charge explained between balls that they had started the translation company five years previously on the back of a contract with the EU but were winding up now as the money had gone out of translation and, in any case, they'd already made enough to more or less retire.

I decided not to hear the bit about the industry being on the ropes and entirely focus on the idea that I could make piles of money and get to play cricket in a giant office. I explained that I'd just started out and asked very humbly (for me) if I could ask them some questions. If I bought him lunch he would tell me everything he could but, he was apologetic, you'll struggle to make over 80% margin these days.

We went to a restaurant in St Christopher's Place and two hours later I felt like a new man.

As far as I was concerned, 80% margin was pretty bloody good (and clearly I had been charging the *Jurassic* people far too little, which went a long way to explaining why they handed me the job on a plate). The important thing was I now had the basic figures in my head, how a project was run, where to find translators and, crucially, where to find clients. If it hadn't been for banging on a door, there's a good chance I could have stabbed about in the dark for months, earned too little and become disheartened and given up. I still had a lot to learn but I had the nitty gritties, and I am hugely grateful to a chap to whom I owe so much whose name I've forgotten.

About nine months after I started, I had two businesses: London Tutors and Aktuel Translations – both in profit but only just. London Tutors was still taking too little for the hours put in, and I no longer had the time to teach four hours a day – one or two at best. Aktuel made good money but the work was sporadic; *Jurassic Park* was taking longer to come through and was smaller than expected: £25,000 worth of work quite quickly boiled down to £10,000 – about £4,000 profit.

I was getting fed up of starting each month not knowing if I would make it through to the next.

I didn't so much know it at the time as feel it: our figures weren't bad for a start-up but I needed something steadier, something surer to even out the cashflow. I now know what every business studies student probably learns in their first term: steady, positive cashflow is king. However, four years studying theatrical techniques in eighteenth-century Dramatic Comedy or the Christian Existentialism of Gabriel Marcel hadn't been much of a help in that respect.

Solving the problem of how to even out my cashflow came from an unlikely source given how bad my previous experience of the industry had been.

Department stores had been one of the sales targets of mine in the last year, but I hadn't had much luck. I was also learning that, generally in business, 90% of one's endeavours are abject failures: even when you get some successes, most of what you do will seem like a complete waste of time in hindsight.

I've spoken about work coming in (and it might sound easy) but I've left out the entire dull days of phone calls where you don't get through, or people are not interested or are very rude. I've also left out the supposedly great ideas you work on for weeks that come to nothing, and the meetings you go to only to realise that the person in front of you is wasting your time or is too junior to make any sort of decision. And days when the only computer you have won't work, or something personal crops up, a lead comes through when you're on holiday and there's no internet because you are in Cornwall.

Or you are sick. In fact, hardly anything you do when it's just you seems productive. Worst of all is when you do think up a good plan, put it into action and it works – i.e. work comes in. This feels great... then someone in the delivery of that plan (in the case of translation, usually a translator or proofreader) makes a mistake or lets you down and you lose the client.

Department stores looked like a damp squib until I got a call one day from Selfridges to say that they were looking for someone to put together a team of linguists whose job it would be to make friends with foreign customers. Each would have to be trilingual and they would have the title, *Ambassador*. I thought it was a terrible name but they were suggesting a healthy fee for my time, which meant I should keep my opinions to myself. It did also mean I had to be in the store for twelve hours a week, but they said they would give me an office in the Marketing Department.

The contract would give me an all-important £2,500 bedrock a month, with similar coming in from London Tutors; ad hoc translation projects therefore were the icing on the cake. The pressure was off, but I knew I had to justify the time spent in Selfridges by keeping up with selling translation or the work would drop off and running these *ambassadors* would be all I had. Growing a business is a discipline of habit, more than anything.

Selfridges probably would have been pissed off to know I spent quite a lot of my twelve hours a week in the tiny fifth-floor office taking care of London Tutors and Aktuel, but I had put together a good team for them who needed very little actual managing, and when they foisted looking after the Catalogue Desk and the guy who stands outside in a top hat on me, for no extra money, I felt justified.

I knew that the project had a shelf life – partly because someone in HR had let slip that my ambassadors were earning more than department managers, so the knives were out, and partly because it turned out that foreign visitors were every bit as reticent about speaking to people in shops as the British.

Pretty soon, the ambassadors became walking information desks, and then the Information Desk was made my responsibility (for no extra money, again). My 'staff' in Selfridges was now about thirty people, but I persuaded HR to let me borrow an experienced manager, a lady in her early fifties who ran everything for me as only a lady of a certain age who has worked in retail all her life can do. Thus, I was still free to keep up to speed with London Tutors and Aktuel Translations or sit and write poetry in the nearby Wallace Collection. Mainly about my still-broken heart.

Present day

I'm back in the Wallace Collection today, a five-minute walk from Selfridges. I am sitting on my old bench in the Great Gallery where I used to spend hours scribbling in a book, trying not to think about the shop floor with its intense lighting, overly accurate mirrors and constant babbling noise of thousands of people talking slightly more loudly than they would in their own homes.

Even then, I noticed that shoppers interact after a slightly antagonistic fashion – everyone is under each other's feet or in their way. Here, in the Wallace Collection, nothing has changed, and it's easy to feel the same way as I did over twenty years ago. The timelessness just adds to the sense of peace and polish, of old masters, meandering feet and meditation. Yet time for me flew here, as it always does when I write, or does for anyone when they are enjoying themselves, I suppose. On the shop floor, that I avoided at all costs, time seeped away slowly… along with your soul.

The only times when I liked the store, when I felt we had come to terms with one another, was after 7pm: when all the shoppers had gone away and this Cathedral to Wanting Things felt like it slumbered. Walking through the empty departments with their lights now dimmed at the end of a long day, I felt quite fond of the place and almost proprietorial.

Walking through it now, looking (in vain) for anything I recognise outside of the façade, I feel exactly the same as I did then during store hours. I want to find a quiet corner. Even better, I want to leave immediately and sit in a field and feel the breeze on my face. But there were moments in my time here when I enjoyed moving around the departments, talking to the familiar faces, getting to know new people who worked there who looked interesting. There was about six thousand staff when I was there but it still managed to feel like a village at times. It even had its own dentist, chiropodist... and priest.

Being back here today, whiling away an hour I have to kill before drinks at the RAC, I don't think I've changed a bit in this respect: there's still this conflict between the small boy who was smacked by his granny because he would not shut up and the one who is happy to watch and write or read in peace.

I doubt if it will ever be resolved, but that thought is whisked away by the freezing wind as I now leave the store, and by a memory of a phone call I got on my brick of a mobile phone in this very spot twenty-five years ago.

It was from my mother.

'Your father and I had an argument this morning; he's stormed off. Do you know where he is?'

'No,' I said. He'd 'left home' before, but the arguments had become titanic in the last few months. Even by their standards. To go home for supper was to experience life in a giant pressure cooker.

I mainly remember watching my father being subjected to a series of harangues and sniping, presumably designed to shame him into being rich again. Disappointingly, both my sisters who still lived at home seemed happy to join in.

My father, for his part, just sat through it all and looked murderous.

My grandfather, who could no longer look after himself, was living in the drawing room which had been converted to a sort of care home for one. It was a middle-class Charlie Bucket domestic nightmare.

One evening, right after my mother had tipped most of the contents of a bottle of chilli sauce on my father's food for something he'd done, or hadn't, I piped up. Just when we should have been rallying, I pointed out, we were splitting apart; also, I didn't think it was fair that we all reaped the benefits of my father's salary when things were doing well, but everyone piled in against him when it all went tits up. I thought I sounded reasonable. I thought it might bring everyone to their senses.

Ha ha!

At the time, I took from the look on everyone's faces that they viewed my outburst as my remit. Looking back, however, it was the start of a process of me realising that my parents weren't that fussed when it came to Robin and all things Robin. A few years later, not long before he died, my grandfather – my mother's father – spelled it out as gently as he could. 'It used to upset your granny and me,' he said, 'because you were a nice little boy… but Jane[51] was an unhappy child and she is an unhappy woman, and she'll never change.' He looked at me as intently as you can with cataracts. 'You mustn't forget, you are loved.'

Anyway, a few days after my mother's call and it was obvious my father wasn't coming back. Worryingly, no-one knew where he was.

With my father now gone, we were running out of options. The house still had a large mortgage and it could be

---

51 My mother.

repossessed at any time. Suddenly, as the son with a business (money), I was in favour. Temporarily, at least.

I moved the office to the top floor of my parents' house, moved off the boat and back home, so there were two lots of rent coming in, and my mother agreed to answer the phones for London Tutors for a monthly salary – an arrangement that looked sound as she liked talking to other mums about their children. The business was becoming healthier and I was able to help financially, but our family was sick in many more ways than financially and I didn't know what to do about that, so I just kept on at what I had some control over; if I could make that work – at least we'd have a roof over our heads to be unhappy in.

Grandpa Bennett was ailing and had been moved to Charing Cross Hospital in Fulham. I went to see him a day before he died: it was sort of heartbreaking to see a countryman cooped up in this huge urban hamster cage of a hospital to die. Personally, I'd try and arrange things so I died outdoors – weather permitting and as long as I had strong drugs about my person. I certainly wouldn't want to go like Grandpa Bennett: in a city he hardly ever visited his whole life and in an environment that must have seemed as confusing as it was unpleasant. I've been in and out of hospitals (children-related stuff) a lot in the last decade and I can say they have improved. In the 1990s, they seemed to be at a bit of a low point: Charing Cross was filthy, and whenever I went to visit there was no-one (no staff) around. It was just this huge mishmash of a place with sticky floors and grimy corners and, in the case of my grandfather, people dying in a rather boring, soulless way.

Death is friendless. By its very nature, we're on our own for this final step into the unknown – be it towards the light or into the void, whatever you believe doesn't change the facts. But the manner of our passing deserves little significance; it's how we get there and with whom, and how we deal with life, not death.

More to the point, I feel that we have been given the tools to look after each other, which is so much more important. We have infinite love but finite cruelty; I honestly believe that.

Going back all those years to when everything seemed so precarious, I definitely wasn't enjoying being a grown-up. Not only because life seemed to be a very insecure thing: success, just getting by, and total ruin were all too close together for comfort. More fundamentally, though, my heart was still broken: I missed being in love and I absolutely fucking hated dating.

After Elsbeth decided I wasn't husband material, I went out with Rebecca for a bit, but the romance had somehow left the relationship – now it wasn't an affair and we'd probably both grown up a bit – which taught me that going back was never a good idea. So, *forward*! I thought, and I started asking girls out for the first time. I say first time as previously I'd never actually been on a date – going out and romance had just kind of happened by proximity. Now I had the deeply uncomfortable duty of having to come up with a good reason to ask someone out. I learned that mumbling something about 'going for a drink' or eating in PizzaExpress wasn't the romantic call to arms girls were after, unless they were desperate. Instead I found that there had to be tickets involved or some kind of event that could reasonably be seen to be up their street.

In the main, though, I don't think anyone likes the whole dating thing: there's a false insouciance to it and creeping thoughts like *what if I'm very unattractive* which mar the whole experience. It's such a horrible concoction of being about everything important about ourselves: our looks, job, dress sense, conversational prowess, whilst pretending just to be about a meal out and a glass or two of wine.

This was all pre dating sites, and I don't know if it's any easier for the right-swipe generation these days: i.e. whether knowing that someone already fancies you and you have something in common makes it any easier. I suspect it doesn't, I suspect it's still pretty awful. So, in 1994 I was beginning to feel nostalgic for childhood, where you could be friends with someone on the basis of the type of bucket they had brought with them to the beach or if they owned a Stretch Armstrong, not if you were prepared to give them oral sex and put up with their family at Christmas for the next forty years.

Then I met Hélène.

By that time, I was heartily sick of meals out with virtual strangers and learning that a one-night stand generally peaks the moment you get to see each other naked and goes downhill from there.

Love and comedy are all about timing and the timing was right for me to fall in love again. This is where luck comes in: that the moment you are ready, you meet the right person. Or perhaps the right person is just a person you meet at the right time – we're all pretty much lovable, in our own way.

So, there I was, making a rare appearance on the shop floor. I was taking a group of Japanese businessmen from Hush Puppies around Selfridges and they wanted to look at the china and porcelain department in the basement. A very pretty blonde girl who was on the Wedgwood site came over and started chatting. She was from Lyons and had done roughly the same business studies 'BTS' as me in France. Her English wasn't brilliant, so we switched to French, which I hadn't spoken in a while, but it felt good and somehow easier than speaking to someone attractive and interesting in my own language.

Oddly, I kept seeing her after that – not just in the store but around the West End, which seemed like a sign – albeit a very small one but somehow significant as London is a very big place.

One day I was crossing the street near Haymarket when she did her trick of popping up again. She was just in front of me, carrying a small green rucksack and sauntering in a way that suggested she had no particular destination in mind. I was going to meet friends in a pub nearby and I remember thinking, *Oh, there's that girl from Selfridges… she's the kind of girl you would marry.*

I caught up with her and asked if she'd like to go for a drink with me and my friends. Standing in the pub twenty minutes later, I reflected that this was much more like it as 'dating' went. Mainly because it didn't feel like a date at all: I'd turned up with this girl no-one knew, but it was one of those evenings when everyone seemed to have dragged along a flatmate or work colleague, so I don't think Hélène felt she was on show. It was a perfect way to demonstrate to her I was reasonably normal and had nice friends and for us to get to know one another without there being an interval of a week between a proposed date, getting ready for the actual date when you're knackered and just want to stay at home and watch TV, then the tricky one-to-one over medium-priced dining.

Or maybe it would have been alright with Hélène in whatever the circumstances. The first thing I noticed about her personality was calmness and normality. Coming from my family, I like calm, I love normal.

Reflecting back, twenty-five years since we first met, on what attracts people to life partners, I think what we all most require is kind, consistent and sane. I won't say want, as it's obvious that people *want* all sorts of things from a prospective spouse: danger, large salary, like-mindedness, humour, right timing life-cycle-wise, norks. None of these can be overblown (ha ha), but the thing I thought when we were starting to see one another was that with someone this kind and calm not a lot can go fundamentally wrong.

Hélène wasn't flashy. On the other hand, I was. Cringingly so. On our first real date, I took her to a private white-tie dinner on the Saturday, followed by high tea and polo on

Smith's Lawn in Windsor, then back to Chelsea for dinner. In my 1968 Daimler.

Coming out of the restaurant, I'm surprised I didn't just hurl a kitchen sink at her head for good measure.

Something else I loved about Hélène in those early days (still do, incidentally) was her being one of the first people I'd ever met who was physically braver than me: she seemed more than happy to go first when it came to jumping off, climbing up or grabbing hold of things in dangerous situations.

And she liked walks!

This is sort of essential. I know people nearly always list 'Reading, cinema and walks' in their online profiles. This suggests long, cultural strolls in open countryside reciting aloud from Coleridge, followed by a critically well-received foreign film in a boutique playhouse. However, in my experience, closer to what they actually mean, is *I like to go to the cinema, in Reading, and I am prepared to walk from the car park if there is a bag of cheesy nachos and two hours of Magic Mike at the end of it.* And there's nothing wrong with that, apart from being honest.

Sharing interests works for us. We work from home, and every few days, when the kids are at school, Hélène and I will put on wellies and take the dog out for a two-hour yomp and a chat and it will be the highlight of the week.

Simple pleasures, shared views, kindness. Nice. Normal. As said, with a family like mine – and without overthinking it – these are the things I am fortunate enough to know I should value.

After a year going out – and one of the easiest decisions I've ever had to make – I planned to ask Hélène to marry me. But in a typically ostentatious place: Kenwood House, on Hampstead Heath, during a champagne picnic whilst watching light opera open air. I'm heartily glad I didn't now, as I think she would have said 'No', or – way worse – 'I'll think about it.'

The reason I didn't was because it suddenly felt wrong. Being relatively stupid, I've learned to trust my instinct over reason.

In the end, the very next day, I asked her in the pub whilst my friend John was in the loo.

And she said yes[52].

Ten months later, standing a bit nervously at the end of the aisle in the Holy Redeemer Catholic Church, Chelsea, whilst the musicians fiddled with their instruments and my family chatted *at* each other behind me, I reflected that, yawning sense of trepidation aside, things were looking up.

I was only a few hundred yards from where I'd decided I needed to turn things around just three years previously – looking out over a cold, grey Thames as a policeman impounded my motorbike: almost broke, broken family, broken-hearted.

And now I was marrying the girl I loved deeply and, what's more, it felt completely right. The big car carrying Hélène drew up and my parents were yet to arrive at the church, but I wasn't surprised, so it didn't bother me. Anyway, there was good news on that score: the day of our wedding was also the day my father came back home and stayed[53]. But not just that: I

---

52 She denies it to this day but, for the record, she said yes twice, in quick succession, in case I hadn't heard the first time, or I was going to change my mind.

53 For the curious, after he had done a runner a year or so before, he had eventually turned up in Manchester of all places. I've no idea why he chose this city he had no ties to. I do know that he was thrown out of the hostel he was staying in for going into the woods and lighting fires to cook dead things on. After a year, I went to see him and persuaded him that my fledgling business needed his acumen (it did) and to come home and help take Aktuel Translations to the next level. True to form, once he had moved back home, it was made clear that the upstairs office was no longer mine to rent.

could also pay for it. We'd had our biggest order of translation to date and work was steady. But not just that: it was a rite of passage as well as marriage. I do not know if this is the same for other people, but the day we got married felt like the first day of my adult life. It still felt a bit like play-acting (the British penchant for dressing up at weddings adds to that), but the make-believe was heartily sincere and that's all it took.

It had been a tempestuous few years, but it really did feel like a Happily Ever After.

Still does.

Chapter 14

Clapham to Melbourne…
and back

Life is relentless and not without remorse

So, things were going very badly, then they were going very well.

I was newly married, the family was back together and the business was flourishing. A rainy honeymoon in Turkey, mainly spent on coaches full of very hairy men smoking, did nothing whatsoever to dent my mood. Two weeks after our honeymoon, I took a cheque for over £40,000 for a single project and it was the start of a roll that was to continue for the next four years.

By 2000, I can honestly say that I had more money than I knew what to do with. I'd switched offices to an attractive courtyard in Battersea and turned the whole thing into what I knew best: a telesales outfit. There was me, someone from Reed accounts and a bunch of people on telesales going through every *Yellow Pages* we could lay our hands on, phoning people from film companies, marketing agencies, manufacturing blue chips, publishers, lawyers, defence companies, PR agencies, hospitals, hotels, drinks companies, government departments, bodies of the EU. We threw the net as far and wide as we could and it seemed that in almost every industry you could think of there was a need for translation, provided a company had an international clientele or ambitions abroad.

We'd phone them up, send them our prices, which we knew were lower than almost everyone's we could think of, and get the work if there was any to go around. Translation agencies had been working at huge margins for years and agencies were generally complacent as far as I could see.

The explosion of the internet at this time helped. To begin with, we had to use local translators and much of the work we did had to be transferred to 'floppy' disks and then couriered over to the client. One of my dullest jobs at the time was going through the monthly courier bill, logging off jobs against lists of postal codes they gave us, for hundreds of jobs.

Then, almost overnight, you could recruit specialist translators online anywhere in the world for a fraction of the cost of, say, someone Chinese living in London, and then return translations via email.

In short, we were lucky to be getting going just when the internet became a viable business tool, and we used it to keep our costs down and recruit translators who were generally better for being based in their mother-tongue country.

Luckily for us, the rest of the industry was sluggish to reduce their costs accordingly and clients did not seem to mind too much being phoned up if we were proposing a service that was cheaper and usually an improvement.

This meant for rapid growth but I was managing the lion's share of the projects myself – for about three years we were able to pull off the holy trinity in any tertiary industry: we were good, cheap *and* quick. But that can never last. By 2000, it was taking its toll. I took on my first dedicated project manager about this time but I was still working thirteen hours a day, and at weekends; and, to be frank, we weren't recruiting more project managers, so we were starting to be not as good as we sold ourselves.

From nostalgia, or perhaps hedging my entrepreneurial bets, I was also trying to keep London Tutors going, although it was time-consuming and the margins relatively pitiful.

On the translation front – like many fast-growth start-ups, I've come to learn – I was still sort of making it up as I went along: accepting jobs last minute, using untested translators and hoping to pick up the pieces during proofing. The problem is a proofreader cannot make a silk purse out of a sow's ear, and a bad translation is usually irredeemable. I've learned (and this doesn't just go for translation), that if something is fundamentally crap, no amount of polishing will bring it up to standard – most of the time, tear it down and start again. In those days, there were still a lot of hobbyist translators who worked between jobs like teaching, acting, parenting and journalism but didn't really care about standards, as standards in our industry had been low for years. So, who cared – most clients couldn't tell the difference.

In around 2000, master's degrees in Translation started to proliferate, and by about 2003 they were quite good. Nowadays, translation is a respected career path for graduates in Modern Languages and the translators we use generally appreciate the relationship between Translator–Proofreader–Bureau and End Client. In those days, a lot of translators would barely stomach agencies (which they suspected were making piles of money off their hard work – rightly) and they hated it and complained like fun if they were proofed critically.

I was also still thinking up other ventures. There was writing (there had always been that), but we also dabbled in software, CD/DVD production, life insurance, and I made my first attempt to start a publishing house.

But even on five hours a night, I'd run out of time and, if I'm honest, I was increasingly unhappy: I got up early and wrote in the mornings from 6am until 9am. Then 9-5 in the office, where I seemed to spend most of my day either firefighting projects that had been done too quickly by translators whose standards were up and down, or telling people how the photocopier worked.

Then, in the evenings, I'd try and book tutors, check timesheets and be newly married.

The money was a sort of proof that I was doing things right, but I wasn't sure if I could stomach another meal at Bibendum or round home improvements on our flat in Battersea that seemed to get a makeover every six months.

I took on an assistant and tried to scale back but we were still growing and it was all starting to feel like a train I couldn't jump off. Something was going to give – either me or the business was going to fuck up on a huge scale at any point soon and we'd derail.

At this time, my cousin Melanie, who lived near us in Clapham, worked for a publishing company in London. As a key member of staff, she had been invited to a business meeting in New York. Going on a jolly to NYC in your twenties has got to be right up there on one's list of Cool Things To Do.

But, for reasons I still don't fully understand, someone flew a plane into the building where she had her first meeting on the morning of 9th September. She was on the 106th floor when the plane struck the North Tower, between floors 93 and 99.

'A plane has hit one of the World Trade Center towers,' said Pierrick, my lead project manager, as I walked into the office.

'They think it's Al-Qaeda,' said someone else and then had to explain what that was.

We had a small TV in the office which I turned on as the second plane flew into the South Tower. I didn't know Melanie was in New York at the time but the second plane immediately confirmed this wasn't an accident and I think everyone knew right then that we were watching something life-changing. However, what has stayed with me more than anything from those first few hours was the sight of the South Tower collapsing: it just seemed so unexpected, so unlikely and, quite obviously, so momentous. I think the perception that we in the free world are safe and loved by the rest of the planet was wrecked that day. In many ways, none of our lives have been the same since.

In the months following 9/11, including Melanie's memorial service in Portsmouth – a harrowing funeral without a coffin – we weren't alone in deciding that life was probably too short for the minor stuff: in my case, chasing after money as an end in itself.

H and decided to go to Australia right after Christmas. I'd still be in touch with the office every day, but they'd have to manage without me.

A lot has been written about Australia in recent years and I don't think I could do better than Bill Bryson, so I won't try. I will say that what Australia meant to me at the time – apart from escaping this monster I had created – was a good way of avoiding the English winter whilst feeling like I was still in England. Everything, from the little old ladies at bus stops, the Victorian parks with their banks of roses and bandstands, the terraced houses, the comfort food in the supermarkets and the way people spoke a bit like they did at home, lessened the feeling of being on another planet, which would be easy in this vast country with its ridiculous heat, in-your-face geology and outlandish, untrustworthy fauna.

We did all the usual things you do in Australia: we swam; checked the house and car incessantly for spiders; drank lots of very cold beer; walked about in rainforests, grasslands, dustlands, knobbly lands, shopping malls and parks; we got tans for the first time in our lives in January; met the president of the USA behind a big rock[54]; ate more prawns than I'd had in my whole life combined; hired battered 4x4s; felt sick on a wide variety of boats; and drank more beer.

I also got clarity.

It was great, and when we got back three months later we found we had no desire to live in London and work all the time. I also found that the business was cockeyed and ailing. Ninety days was all it took.

It was still turning over a healthy amount of money but our profits were dismal and I couldn't immediately work out why: granted, this was partly because our biggest client, a technical writing firm in Paris, was winding down and the tractor manual project we had been translating for three years was down to small jobs of a few hundred euros. It was also true that after 9/11 we lost almost all our US clients overnight. I had opened a small office in Miami that was little more than a phone-answering service, but I had had big plans. John Deere in Ohio was starting to use us regularly, then the Twin Towers were hit and one of their attorneys told me in confidence they were no longer using foreign companies – at least he'd taken the time to explain, the rest of them just stopped answering our emails. Also, globally, from 2000-2003, there was a general slowdown in most economies – except Russian and the UK – but I was fast realising we were as much influenced by what happened outside home as global currency exchanges, war, you name it – translation, as an industry, is an excellent economic barometer of the wider world[55].

But this still didn't explain things fully.

Hélène and I rented our flat out in London and moved to a beautiful cottage near Henley-on-Thames that felt like a homecoming. I spent six months commuting into an office

---

54   See page 137
55   This was to become useful in a few years, but right now it seemed just another pain in the ass.

that was becoming quite a miserable place to be. Looking back at my notebooks for that period, most of my time was spent chasing debts and wondering where the next reasonable chunk of work was coming from. We were back to hand-to-mouth and I only had myself to blame.

The immediate problem was that the office and the staff were costing too much and we weren't selling ourselves out of the problem. This was useful information, too. Up until then, I'd assumed that selling was the answer to all business difficulties: it is, provided there is a market; if there isn't (and there wasn't, right then) it's just an expensive waste of time. And depressing.

Translation (or most service businesses, for that matter) can scale down if it has to. Luckily, in the end, I only had to sack one person, who was heartily glad to go anyway, the rest I simply did not replace when they left, and soon we were down to two full-time staff (including me): no sales, no PA and just a part-time bookkeeper who'd started asking for payment at the end of every day, which tells you all you need to know about our prospects at the time.

Once the staff had gone and I didn't have to worry about anyone's rent, except my own and Pierrick's – who had been a stalwart throughout – I felt much calmer and did what we should have done a long time before: I trawled through the figures.

Not much scrutiny showed that we were charging too little and offering too much, so I politely but firmly told a few clients who were just an emotional drain to fuck off, and upped our minimum charge to a rate that was profitable.

In the same week, I found a much cheaper office in Hart St in Henley-on-Thames and, on moving there, all our computers refused to work properly ever again. I put all the tables, the inexplicably broken computers, the posters, dozens of yards of network cable and the boxes of old letterhead in the cellar at home and bought two new computers and a huge desk from IKEA. It felt OK, like a new beginning.

We were turning over quite a lot less than a quarter of what we had been two years before, but we were back in profit and everything was easily manageable. My new office had a long garden with nice things growing in it, like strawberries; and, out of London, I could breath.

It was during the office move that I finally found out why the margins had been so bad. I was decanting old box files from the old office to the attic at home when I idly opened one of the project folders and glanced at the invoice on top...

Half an hour later I was sitting on the floor in the spare room feeling somewhat tearful: the penny had finally dropped; I'd been incredibly stupid. In my defence, I was so taken with letting the bookkeeper and project managers get on with the financial side of things, I had got into the habit of only looking at growth as a goal.

I had known that our smaller jobs hardly made any money; what now became clear was that a lot of our really big ones were also unprofitable. One of our other major clients at the time was the European Commission. The charging structure was very complex but, in a nutshell, we had the freedom to bid for each piece of work. There was an unofficial maximum and minimum rate bracket that was a good guide, but I normally ignored that and set our rate at around 60% net margin, which left enough for proofing, project management, tax and a respectable profit. However, it seemed that for the last six months someone had got it into their heads to always charge our lowest rate, regardless of language, complexity, deadline or if it meant we worked at a loss. It basically added up to hundreds of jobs, thousands of hours and a huge loss. There and then I vowed I would never lose control of the money ever again[56]. I would continue to delegate other stuff, but never that.

---

56 All in all, it was a time for lessons learned.

We were down to our last £10K and I had no savings left: this seemed extraordinary – a year previously, I had been throwing money around the best restaurants in London, hiring huge serviced apartments in Australia with pools and flying Business Class everywhere.

But we were still there and clawing our way back. Most importantly, I was happy at work for the first time in ages[57].

Around this time, I sat down and wrote the first book I ever had traditionally published. *Start-up Smart*[58] focused on starting businesses for a pittance – it was initially called *How to Start a Business for less than £5000*: I knew a lot about that but it was a few years before I worked out how to make that business stable and, in any case, in 2001 no-one was interested in that sort of business.

It had to wait until 2008 before it found a respectable publisher, when the crash hit and suddenly people were interested in low-cost models. Back in 2002 it was all about huge launches off the back of venture capital and a sale five years later to a blue chip. Undoubtedly, this is a much better way to make lots of money but that has never been of great interest to me. Because I thought it up and watched it develop from a conversation in the pub to something that makes money (hopefully), I've always been far more interested in holding onto the businesses I have created. I'm a business squirrel. I also feel quite strongly that debt is one of the main reasons companies fail (ditto, marriages). Debt is bad.

In my general life, things were much better as well – looking back, I'm quite surprised we took as long as we did to move out of London.

---

57 Perversely, I've noticed my mood improves at work when I've got problems coming out of my ears. This is the opposite to the rest of my life.

58 *Pub., Harriman House 2008.*

I settled into life in the country like putting on a favourite pair of wellies[59]. I'd managed to persuade Hélène to let me have a dog and I'd found a lovely springer spaniel we called Touts, who I walked religiously between midday and 2pm. This was the start of taking life easier: I'd work until 5pm, absurdly early by previous standards, and go to the pub for a cheeky pint, then home. In the evening Touts and I poached rabbits and pigeons from the local area. Comp Farm, where we lived, was on an estate owned by Lord Phillimore. From our back garden, we could see rolling fields that gave way to Phillimore's private cricket pitch and the wood at the side of the house. As said, it was only ten minutes' drive to Henley, ditto Reading, but it felt like a private paradise of woods, fields and hedge – we couldn't even see the lights from our neighbour's house at night.

Touts turned out to be an amazingly gifted gundog, which had nothing to do with my abilities as a gundog trainer. I joined a local shoot on the Phillimore land, the little brother to the swanky one on the estate. It had three hundred acres of just about decent driven shooting land and more rough shooting on my doorstep than I could possibly want. Touts became my constant, versatile companion. She could stalk rabbits with me, hanging back a few yards as I crept up on them with an air rifle, then race past me to retrieve them when shot; but she was also capable of sitting on a peg and picking up birds at the end of a drive, just like a proper posh dog; or she could work a beating line to put up pheasants then sit loyally with me in the pub for hours afterwards. I've had two gundogs since – both springers – and they are excellent: brave, devoted, quick to learn and they don't bite the children. However, neither were as naturally gifted as Touts, who would often mark, then pick birds up in the order I shot them after a drive.

---

59   … which is a ridiculous simile as similes go: almost no-one except the occasional German pervert has a 'favourite' pair of wellies – 99.9% of welly owners have one pair at a time.

But she was also the product of inbreeding. Almost from the off she suffered from mysterious stomach problems, and every few months she would develop ulcers in her mouth, run a massively high temperature and vomit everywhere. The vet was flummoxed (ditto my father-in-law, also a vet, who loved Touts almost as much as I did). On top of the stomach problem, it turned out her bones were also too fragile for her musculature; one day, whilst running across a field, her elbow joint simply exploded. To fix the leg, rather than amputate, cost the price of a new kitchen, but I happily paid for a brilliant vet to pick out all the shards of bone and cement a metal joint in her leg. The surgeon had worked a miracle and was worth every penny. Within a few months she was back to doing what she loved: out with me and a gun, working someone else's hedgerow for our supper. We both loved poaching.

However, when she was aged just four, I woke up one morning and went downstairs. I could see Touts wasn't well, but she caught a rabbit when she went out that morning and I almost didn't take her to the vet. Then she was sick, so I dropped her off on my way to work and got on with my day.

At about 11am, the vet phoned to say she was very ill and she was going to operate, if only so she could try and figure out what was wrong. I agreed and went back to work but distractedly. I had a bad feeling about this. An hour later, the vet phoned to say that Touts had died on the operating table: her lungs had just disintegrated.

I very rarely cry and never in public, but cry I did, like a baby, all over my bookkeeper, who was sweet and understanding in a way that I sometimes think only the English can be when it comes to dogs.

I still think of Touts every day I shoot and quite a few in between, and part of me will always grieve for her.

It is a drizzly November night in 2004, dark and unpleasantly damp, and we've been in the 'birthing suite' since early evening. It's now 2am.

Once you get married, you start to think about whether or not to have babies. Everyone does. What your decision is, is up to you. Obviously. But whatever you think you decided *before* you got married, you can bet that there will be a rethink once the honeymoon credit card bill has been paid off.

Hélène went for children right away and, because I like children a very great deal, I went along with it. Other people's children are great, I reasoned, and ours will be greater…

For most men, births are like turning up at your older sister's sixteenth birthday party uninvited. Times ten. No-one can deny your basic right to be there but frankly you're going to feel awkward and you almost certainly won't know what to do with your hands. Unlike your sister's party, though, there won't be any sixth-formers to look at and your partner will thank you for handing around drinks and cheesy Wotsits.

All birthing suites look like cheap hotel rooms – however, you're the only one in any position to notice this because everyone else is far too busy getting on with their job or thrashing about in agony.

Tonight, although I'm no expert – this being my first time watching anyone, let alone my wife, have a baby – it looks very much like we're approaching the endgame. Hélène looks terrible, but not so terrible that I should be worried. She looks like every other birthing mother I have ever seen in films and *National Geographic*: she looks in pain and very tired. But there's nothing I can do except hold her hand.

I'm not squeamish, so I take a look at the sharp end in the same way I look over mechanics' shoulders when they are fixing my car and nod as if I know what the hell is going on.

Actually, it's pretty easy to know what's going on. There's a bit of blood, but not too much, and a lot of clear liquid. In amongst the dilated, tufted mess, I can make out the top of a small head: grey and puckered.

Crikey, this is it!

I go back to the noisier but less gory end.

'You're nearly there!' I say. Hélène half smiles and squeezes my hand. She's two-thirds in her own world, but she must know it's almost over. I look at Judy, our midwife, for confirmation. She is frowning.

'What is it?' I ask.

'The toco belt,' she says, half to herself; 'I think it's been picking up mum, not baby.' She's looking at the belly monitor Hélène has been wearing for the last hour or so that is meant to monitor the baby's heart, then she looks over at the screen. 'I'm sure it's alright, but we'll need to attach an electrode to baby's head, to make sure we're getting his heartbeat and not mum's.'

'OK,' I say.

Then Hélène goes into another big contraction and I'm distracted by that and by telling her how well she is doing as Judy attaches what looks like a large pin to the baby's head, whose crown of matted hair is even more visible than it was two minutes ago.

'There,' says the midwife, all business. 'Right, let's see.' She goes over to the monitor and puts the other end of the cable into the slot. Once again, television and film tell me what to expect, as we both turn to the screen.

A single green line: an unbroken, unequivocal statement moves across the screen and the world stops revolving.

'It's flatlining,' she says. But what she really means is, *your baby is dead.*

This was seven years and six months after we were married.

Hélène's first miscarriage, seven years earlier, passed unnoticed by everyone but us. We were away with friends for the weekend in Norfolk and it was upsetting, but that's fine we told each other, it's nature's way of telling you the foetus isn't viable, etc. Then the second, third and fourth felt like Fate was upping the ante each time, but we coped. However, by degrees the pressure – not to conceive, but stay pregnant – mounted. Hélène got very thin, raising an unspoken worry that the anorexia she had suffered as a teenager was coming back. I kept jolly, because that's the only thing I'm much good at, but sometimes that seemed misplaced and even callous. We started seeing specialists in London but appointments on the NHS were a long time coming, and when they did they were rushed affairs in odd little rooms that felt temporary. It's fine, the consultants all said, scribbling notes, not really looking at either of us, you *will* have a baby.

Then Hélène got pregnant again and, at nearly three months, she started to gain weight, look happy and it sort of *felt* OK this time. The consultants had been right all along. Suddenly my optimism seemed brave and well-founded. 'That's why I married you,' said Hélène one evening, looking at me in a way you only get looked at when someone loves you very much.

She went into St George's Hospital in Tooting in the morning for a ten-week scan and I went to work. By lunchtime I hadn't heard anything, but it was busy at work and this was before mobiles were everywhere, so I assumed she was taking her time coming home. Shopping for baby things.

At about 3pm I remember that a new computer arrived and I was fiddling about with that when it began to dawn on me that something was wrong.

I went straight to the hospital, found maternity and eventually came across Hélène lying on a bed in an empty corridor. She was crying. She also wasn't sure what was going on, except the scan had shown the baby was dead and she had been given something to induce a miscarriage, which hurt.

I went in search of someone and eventually found a young Italian doctor who was watching TV in a sort of common room. He came back to where Hélène was and looked at her chart.

Yes, she was going into surgery to remove the foetus but there had been a nasty road accident nearby and her place in theatre had been bumped to deal with people coming in.

He arranged for Hélène to be taken somewhere less grim but I wasn't allowed to stay. Surgery wouldn't be for at least another two hours, so I left the hospital and wandered around Tooting. Feeling blank.

When I got back, the maternity wing was locked up for the night, so it took me a while to get in. When I got to the waiting area outside surgery, Hélène was being wheeled out. This time I was allowed to stay as she was put in a room and given a cup of tea and some buttered toast by a busy nurse. It's small kindnesses like that you remember: no-one had to give us anything, but they did; I'm sure my staying was breaking any number of rules, too, but we were young and both a little shell-shocked and it must have shown on our faces, so they were kind; as was the Italian doctor – clearly on his break – but he took time to help and did so with grace. The small kindnesses are one of the myriad reasons why the NHS deserves to be cut some slack.

I slept in a chair next to her bed until she woke around 4am and told me to go home.

When I got home I couldn't drop off again, so I sat at the kitchen table and wrote the following lines of deliberately childish verse.

I found a star, the Brightest Star
In the month of May
And this star, the Brightest Star
Said that she would stay.

We sought a star, the Tiniest Star
Amongst the thousands in the sky
But this star, like a tear lies still
So still in the orbit of mine eye.

And sometimes now
When I lie awake
I hear a passing at my door
Another star, the Wisest Star
Whispers, 'Nevermore

… nevermore.'

This was one time when writing was more of a comfort than anything else I could think of doing: alcohol, talking it through, even weeping would not have helped much, but writing did.

Miscarriage is tricky because it's a million miles away from losing a 'real' child. But seven miscarriages in total was a kind of regular grief, especially this last time, so late in the day. I couldn't wipe my mind of the fact that a foetus at twelve weeks is basically a miniature human: arms, legs, features, brain, heart – everything is there.

I got up from the table, made a cup of coffee and watched London wake up, before going back to the hospital to take Hélène home.

After that, Hélène stopped conceiving at all.

In a way this was better, as the routine of no period, the hopeful bump, then the disappointment was becoming a bit unbearable. We went back to St George's for tests (both of us). Everything seemed to be working but Hélène was ovulating so rarely and her ovaries were polycystic, which basically reduced our chances to almost nil. We tried ovulation drugs but they didn't work. We weren't going to have children, we were told, no point even going on IVF.

We grieved, but very privately, because it's hard to grieve openly for something that has never been, even if that absence feels like a loss.

I can't remember who brought the subject up first but we both agreed that the next option was to adopt.

'There are no little babies for adoption!' we were told at the first meeting by a shouty social worker. 'You cannot adopt outside your ethnic group, you cannot smoke, drink too much, grow certain types of flowers in your garden. You are advised to allow the biological parents access or at least the biological grandparents, you are *strongly* advised to be prepared to take a disabled child or older siblings.'

We weren't saints, we just wanted a baby, but after several childless years we were beginning to feel worn down.

'I feel like Geppetto,' I said during one session. The social worker gave me a practised sympathetic look.

'I know, you just want a child to care for.'

'… without strings,' I said.

After that, Hélène didn't let me say anything to social workers unless I ran it past her first.

After two more years, involving scores of meetings, evenings spent in classes in chilly rented halls, relief fostering and time spent feeling that, as adopters, we basically had to accept what we were given, I suggested to Hélène we give fertility treatment one more go. We wouldn't stop the adoption process – but they'd made us feel like second best, more childminders than parents: we were the needy and the grieving, so we would bend to their will because they represented our last chance to have what we yearned for, even if it wasn't what we really wanted but the best we thought we could do.

Then a friend of mine recommended a specialist in Harley Street.

'He's expensive,' said James, 'but he's good.'

Dr Ryan is one of the tallest people I have ever met. And also one of the thinnest – but with a giant Adam's Apple, like a large piece of Lego had got lodged in his throat at a jaunty angle and now it bounced up and down his thorax comically whenever he spoke. It gave him a very deep voice. The voice of a man who could father children. I don't know why I found this reassuring, but I did.

'I've no doubt whatsoever you will get pregnant!' he boomed, glaring at both of us after Hélène had been examined.

'OK,' we said meekly.

'I'm prescribing you this!' He shoved a white box across a very large desk. Hélène read the label.

'I've already been on a course of Clomid,' she said.

'Not in these quantities you haven't, the NHS would never allow it... but it will work!'

Two days later, Hélène phoned me at work.

'Can you come home?' she said. 'Something is wrong; I can't stand up.'

When I came through the door, she was sitting in the kitchen, looking a bit wan but otherwise OK.

'What happened?' I asked, feeling a bit like this was a wasted trip, although Hélène was never one to be dramatic.

'The pills made me feel dizzy, but I phoned Dr Ryan, who said it was normal. I'll get used to them.' We both agreed, without having to say anything, that it was worth the risk.

And Hélène did fall pregnant and, this time, it stuck.

Except a week before her first scan we were offered a little two-year-old girl with moderate to severe learning difficulties.

We had the best excuse in the world to say no, but neither Hélène nor I felt we could. We'd come this far adopting, we would see it through – baby or not.

I met our social worker – rather oddly at the local pool in Henley – and told her the good news about Hélène's pregnancy.

'However,' I said magnanimously, 'we're still prepared to take the little girl. We *want* to.'

'Well, you can't,' said the social worker bluntly. 'We wouldn't allow that.'

I'd like to say I didn't feel a tiny bit relieved, but I did. I think we both did. And then we both felt guilty about that.

Having a full-term pregnancy felt like we'd won the lottery. Hélène's body changed; she looked like she had eaten the telly at seven months, and people started to open doors for her and smile. It was like being in a cool club that made us feel normal and blessed all at the same time.

Five years of trying and seven miscarriages. Two more years of the self-diminishing process of adoption and lots of drugs…

… and now we are back in 2004, at the end of the road, in the delivery suite at the John Radcliffe Hospital. And a screen that is pronouncing an end to it all.

Judy looks at the dead monitor and presses a button. Our cosy nativity scene turns into a controlled panic as several people rush into the room.

I am buffeted to the side but hardly notice because all I can do is look at the unwavering green line.

'What do you suggest?' the doctor asks our midwife. She looks at him incredulously.

'How should I know – you're the specialist!'

By now Hélène knew something was wrong. The room had erupted with people all doing jobs but looking like they wished they were somewhere else because, I'm guessing, when a baby flatlines, at some point someone has to tell the mother that it has all been for nothing.

I'm pretty robust by anyone's standards, but here I was about to step forward and tip into an abyss. The sensation that I was about to fall was real enough for me to feel sick.

In a second, right after I took hold of Hélène's hand and told her our baby was dead, I would step off that edge and nothing would matter very much ever again. I knew that. It's come to this, I thought: all our wanting, all the disappointments, all of these events leading towards this, just at the moment when it looked like we'd done it. The green line I couldn't take my eyes off ran like a long line of intense sadness that would go on and on and on... now and forever.

'Just a minute,' said the midwife, frowning. She went over to the machine, pulled the cable out of its socket and put it in the one next to it.

We all turned and stared.

Bip, went the monitor, and the line jumped like a ball in a 1970s' computer game... *Bip*... our baby's heartbeat, as my own went FUCKING *BOOM*!

Bip... it sounded positively jaunty. I kissed Hélène – probably harder than I should have. It was such a simple mistake and it was the best mistake ever. My hands and feet felt oddly numb and floaty but, in an instant, the world seemed like the most amazing place.

I'd just had the very worst and the very best moments of my life in the space of under two minutes.

Chapter 15

Oxfordshire

Coming home when you don't belong

Turns out that every book on parenting I'd skimmed through, every antenatal class, magazine article and piece of friendly advice had been absolutely right: babies are hard work. Not impossible but I spent a lot of the first three months at home and the dog got walked a huge amount: we bought a 4x4 pushchair that cost more than my first car and we wandered about the Oxfordshire countryside in all weathers, because being out with the rain on his face was the only thing that stopped Jude (who was named after the midwife) crying.

Looking back, now with three kids, it's laughable that we expended so much physical and emotional energy on one child: I don't think Victor or Hortense took up half of the time put together. I wrote a book about it, *Alpha Dad*; but, in a nutshell, the one bit of advice we should have taken on board is if the baby cries there's not always an immediate fix and they are not about to die: babies sometimes just cry. Plus, there's two of you and one of them: split the tasks.

Being at home more, I did decide that I was going to have a proper crack at writing something big – a magnum opus[60]!

---

60   Work of art, not posh ice cream.

I'd had an idea forming, and the long walks began to gel the idea into a world. The previous summer we had gone to Romania and I'd written the following lines in my notebook:

A Small Vampire is about the size of a dragonfly. They travel widely, and you've almost certainly seen several and indeed been bitten by one or two right in your own back garden. You most probably thought that it was a mosquito, or a horsefly, and then forgot about the bite because it didn't itch or go red. But if you looked very carefully, you would have seen not one tiny pinprick bite mark, but TWO. I put this in capitals because it is important. The TWO holes represent one for each of the sharp little teeth of the Small Vampire.

It had originally been intended as the start of a story for younger children, but as I started to flesh out their world it became more complex and geopolitical: something for teens or cross-over, which was good timing because this age range was exploding. The Small Vampires Trilogy was also my first foray into high fantasy (describing a world with little or nothing of our world, the Real). It was also fun to bring vampires into English folklore and wrap it up in a grail quest (Grail-blood-Vampires – geddit?). I also wanted jokes.

I sent the first book to a couple of agents and Patrick Walsh from Conville and Walsh got back to me. I was quite naïve about what an agent got up to, but Patrick, who had worked on the original *Harry Potter* whilst at Christopher Little, took hold of *Mousch the Crooked* (Volume One, that eventually became Volume Two, of the Small Vampires Trilogy) and made me re-write it. Then he line-edited the result and sent it to publishers.

At the outset, it seemed like our hard work had paid off, not only was I a far better writer for having had things like characterisation, plotting and through line explained to me, but the result felt saleable. Barry Cunningham, from Chicken House, invited me for lunch in Soho and I started to get quite excited at that point.

Barry is credited with discovering *Harry Potter*, when many other publishers had discarded it as too long, too difficult – and boys did not read anymore. JK Rowling has famously said, 'If it wasn't for Barry Cunningham, Harry Potter would still be in the cupboard under the stairs.'

I knew none of this when I took the train to London to meet in a restaurant in Soho. I subsequently found out he was credited with bringing Cornelia Funke to an English-speaking market (she sells almost as much as Rowling in Germany, Austria and Switzerland) and had cut his teeth working with the likes of Roald Dahl and Spike Milligan. In short, what he doesn't know about selling children's books probably isn't worth knowing.

Harriman House had just offered me a publishing deal for my book on entrepreneurship and now I was going to be a famous children's author too, with a famous children's publisher. I would be a man for all seasons – writing successful books about making money on the one hand, and elves on the other.

In many respects, Barry epitomises my relationship with the world of children's publishing: I'm pretty sure he is fond of me but I don't think I'll ever be considered more than a gifted amateur.

Barry has taught me more about the heart and soul of writing for children than anyone, and I am immensely grateful for the trouble and effort he has gone to on my behalf over the years. I am grateful, too, to his former editor, Imogen Cooper, for carrying on Patrick's work, and I would credit her with getting me as far as I think I will ever go as a writer.

So, how far is that?

Well, not very, apparently.

To be frank, I feel a bit like the Tim Henman of publishing.

On a commercial level, I've put my acumen to good use and done what a lot of self-published authors have not achieved and that's to get proper distribution and sales representation. Monster Books sells over fifteen of my titles (more if you count translation). I've been shortlisted for and won a few awards and most children that eventually get around to reading my books like them – but if you look at the sales that is not very many. I'm a bit long in the tooth to want to be famous, but I would like more children to read my books, if I'm honest.

On the other hand, writing is not just another venture for me, another income stream – the best way to describe it is a compulsion: it's not essential to my survival, but it is a large part of what makes life worthwhile and fun.

Writing, if it is done for the correct reasons (and I hope I do do it for the correct reasons) is for other people, to entertain. I take it very seriously and I count myself as a trained writer. So, when I sit down and write, I am doing it for an audience: it's a solitary and, on the face of it, selfish activity but with a selfless goal. Its success is measured in the number of fellow human beings you touch, which is why I sometimes wish I was more successful.

But, all said and done, I've got fuck all to complain about in the wider sphere: when Hélène became pregnant after all the miscarriages and the certainty it would never happen, when Judith the midwife plugged the monitor in to the right socket, when children I've just met are nice to me and old friends call, I remember to stop moaning – I'm super-duper lucky.

When I made my next decent amount of money (about the time Jude was born) it was much less slog and much more swashbuckling. Perfect. And it all happened because my neighbour in London had his nose broken by my tenant.

By 2004, the business had been growing steadily and we were back to a level where I was no longer fretting about £100 gas bills, but, personally, I felt a bit short-changed: I'd been doing this for ten years and I had very little to show for it – in fact, I was a lot poorer in assets and salary than most of my friends who'd simply left university and got proper jobs. We'd had one flat in an ex-council building since 1997, and a rental property we bought a few years later when I had cash. At the time (around 1999), I sort of fancied the idea of using all my spare money to buy two-bed flats in South West London and becoming a property mogul. I'd been sharing an office with a property developer and in those days, at least, it looked easy.

As it happens, being a landlord is a horrible job. With only two flats to deal with, I still worried when they were empty, ran about the place when tenants phoned to say they had a leaky shower, and I grumbled every April that, after tax and time, they weren't that profitable. In fact, I've never made much from property: interestingly (well, a bit interestingly, anyway), a few years ago I wrote another book for Harriman called *Kicking the Property Ladder*. It took the idea that if I'd bought an average house in the Midlands in 1981 and someone had taken the same amount of money and rented, putting money otherwise spent on home improvements into shares, who would be better off. Pretty much every way I did the calculation, it came up almost exactly even.

The book was NOT well-received in some quarters.

We love property in the UK (too much in my view: all linked to my views on debt, which we're also far too fond of) and I might as well have written a treatise on electrocuting very small kittens for all the good it did my reputation.

Because of the title, the book was seen as an attack on property ownership (it really wasn't) and people went for me online having not read it. I took this to heart because I'd made efforts to be even-handed whilst writing it and do my research.

Know thyself is an important bit of advice and I now knew that I do not like controversy. It's a bit sad, but I like to be liked.

Going back to landlording, one of the problems with renting out flats is the time between tenants that can effectively wipe out your profits in a couple of months. To get around this I started to rent to the MOD. They paid less than the going rate but would not sever the rental agreement if the flat was empty for a period.

The majority of our tenants at that point were NCOs and Warrant Officers... and the SAS as it turned out. Once the MOD got involved, I never had much to do with our tenants – they tended to come and go but, for the most part, they were excellent occupants who would fix things themselves and leave the place spotless.

Our neighbour was the opposite. Richard was a complete disaster who had all the tics and habits of someone very disturbed. About the time of us buying the flat he lost his job, spiralled into drinking, then lost his wife, then got into drugs. He played loud music, stole our post and generally was a menace. The first time I met him, I decided, on the spot, to do what anyone sane would do and be polite but keep my distance.

Then he moved out and I assumed he had gone back to the Seychelles where, he told me once – and I don't know if this is true – his dad was Prime Minister.

Early one morning, though, his solicitor phoned me up and told me that my tenant (an SAS signalman) had punched him in the face the night before[61].

Being punched in the face by someone in the SAS is obviously a very different experience to having anyone else do it. I went to see Richard to find out what had happened

---

61   Richard, not the solicitor.

but I had trouble concentrating on what he said because the tip of his nose was trying to push out from underneath his cheekbone.

I went round to my tenant next. 'So, you punched Richard,' I said.

'Not really,' he replied.

We both looked at his hands, which had scraped knuckles, and thought our own private thoughts.

It seemed that Richard had returned from the Seychelles and had struck up a friendship of sorts with my tenant, who obviously hadn't spotted that our neighbour was a fruit loop.

Richard took friendliness as a green light to go round any time of day and, when my tenant refused to answer the door, he tried to kick it down, whereupon the door flew open and he quite literally had his nose flattened. The SAS signalman then phoned the police, explained he was a member of her Majesty's Special Forces and that he'd had a break-in. The police were round like a shot and promptly arrested a weakly protesting Richard and threw him in gaol overnight.

I had to work quite hard with Richard's solicitor to get the whole thing swept under the carpet, simply because I couldn't be bothered to deal with a court case between two idiots. Luckily, Richard's solicitor agreed and then I went for a pint.

By the next morning I had decided I no longer wanted to be a landlord and I put both flats on the market as soon as their agreements had run out.

The flats were one of the easiest things I've ever sold and suddenly we had a lot of cash in the bank and I felt quite rich again. And a bit reckless.

Aside from buying the world's most expensive, front-loaded pension, I'd had very little to do with investing outside of my own ventures. *Now's the time*, I thought, so I started to look around. By day one, I was quite intrigued and wondered why I had never got into this before – there were so many ways of making money and everything seemed to be on the up. By day two, I was in a muddle – and right there was my first lesson in trading: the harder you look at a thing, the less sure it seems. Yes, there are loads of vehicles out there for investing but look at any for long enough and you can think of several good reasons not to buy into them.

Everyone told me to diversify: in those days (not so much now) it was considered sensible to base it on your age: so, at forty, you should have 40% of your allocation in bonds, 60% in stocks; at thirty, a 30/70 split, etc. There were even plenty of funds that would do this for me for a 2% fee.

Ah, fuck it, I said after a week of fruitless deliberating and losing patience, and I put the lot into gold.

By gold, I mean I went large and bought the real, physical stuff. I went down to a bullion dealer in Trafalgar Square and came out with my pockets literally sagging with Britannias and Victorian sovereigns.

This was reckless but not as reckless as the investment itself. Gold had been in the doldrums since the '80s, and the only people who generally hoarded it – apart from Middle Earth dwarves – were elderly spinsters through inheritance, and drug dealers, because physical gold could be traded with no reference to HMRC[62]. The, supposedly very brainy, Gordon Brown had recently sold off our gold reserves as it seemed pointless to hold such a useless thing in such staggering quantities.

True to form, I got lucky, and gold tripled in value in a very short space of time, whereupon I sold half of it. In that period there were dips but I found they were easy enough to predict (most pundits would say gold is going down, so I'd sell some, and they were nearly always right; then I'd wait a bit and when

---

62   i.e. tax free.

the consensus seemed to be that the dollar or gold was going back up, I bought in again.)

In hindsight, it was completely stupid to do what I did, but I'd hit upon an investment that was massively undervalued and a period where first China fuelled huge demand for gold, then the dollar went up and then the crash happened in 2008... and everybody runs for gold when the market goes wonky.

I've traded almost everything since then, from individual shares to government debt, defensive funds, bonkers funds, bonds, art, even wine – but nothing compared to that first investment and the profits which more or less set Hélène and I up as a family.

I seem to have found my comfort spot when starting new ventures, too. I still very much favour starting small and growing organically, so I rarely, if ever, invest more than £30K in anything new – usually substantially less. Most of the trick is just getting up and doing what you said you would do the night before. Comp Farm Kennels, one of my smallest ventures, was a case in point – simply because it produced the largest return. When Hélène fell pregnant (properly pregnant) she was working in a school for autistic kids. One day she was kicked in the stomach by one of the pupils and we both decided it was too risky for her to carry on, but losing her salary was not great timing and she was bored at home. We had the idea to run a small kennel that morning and, around lunchtime, paid £10.95 plus VAT for an ad in the *Henley Standard*, advertising dog sitting in our home, with our dog, cosy fire and loads of green space. I think I got someone in the office to write a letter of welcome and a bit about it not being a formal kennel. And that was it, really. In its first year it made £9,000 profit and in the second £17,000.

It's not big money and lots of business people would scoff at this – it's not how we make our fortunes. However, the key for me is return on investment and time. The ad was cheap, we never had to repeat it and we already had a dog that needed walking. In a sense, for an £11.70 investment and no more than, say, an hour a week extra admin, we made enough for Hélène to justify leaving her job – or, looking at it another way, that's around two hundred hours' work at £130ph.

Chapter 16
The incident with the stag

Plus ça change

I'm in the Grampians in Scotland, it's late August but it's bloody freezing. The outside air temperature is made a lot worse by the fact I am currently crawling through a small, bitterly cold stream. I am staying as low as I can because the gully the stream is in isn't very deep and there's a stag, about two hundred yards away, that we've been stalking unsuccessfully all day.

Whoever imagines stalking deer to be glamorous hasn't been stalking deer. I also think this will be my last time. I get why culling is necessary, and the couple of times I've been stalking before I've been impressed at the respect the gamekeepers have for their quarry and the fact that every bit of the animal is used, even the bones and sinew. But I find it hard to kill something so large and beautiful: then again, I reason, why should size and beauty matter? Surely an earwig has as much right to life as a thoroughbred horse? But, like all purely rational arguments, that doesn't hit the spot – for me, at least: shooting a stag always makes me feel a bit shit for days, even if the last one I shot had hardly any teeth and a jaw so abscessed it would have starved sooner or later, without culling.

Today we have covered about fifteen kilometres across boggy heather, gritting our teeth, wordlessly jumping from tussock to tussock as we remain downwind and below the contours of the hills that keep us under the radar of the group of stags we spotted with the long telescope earlier that morning.

Our middle boy, Victor, has come along. He's eleven and he shot his first grouse yesterday, but I think I'm more proud of the fact that he's covered the tricky terrain today without one word of complaint.

His grandfather – my father – would think the world of him, but from the birth of our children he made little or no effort to get to know his grandchildren. I can't remember the last time one of them received a birthday card. It makes me sad and incensed in roughly equal measure but you can't make people do what they don't want to do, so I just try not to think about it.

By the time we reach the end of the gully and sneak our heads over a small circle of heather, we're praying the deer haven't already moved off – as they've done a couple of times already. Otherwise you have to repeat the process of going down into the valley and looking for a way up with cover, which would mean another hour or so hard walking, then crawling about.

But they are still there, about one hundred and eighty yards away. The ghillie, a young chap from Cumbria, ducks down and we put our heads together. He whispers that it's a risky shot, we're right on the march (border) with Balmoral but there's an old stag who needs taking out, to the right of the group. He's a distant shot and sitting down, so we'll have to wait until he gets up, but he's the best we'll get.

It's a long wait and the rifle in my shoulder is shaking because it really is ridiculously cold for late summer. I am beginning to cramp up.

When the stag eventually stands, all the physical effort and concentration of the day focuses in on the moment I get him in my sights and squeeze the trigger. A stag's heart is about the size of a largish grapefruit. Ideally, I need to hit an area about twenty centimetres in diameter where his front leg joins his torso. At one hundred and eighty yards, cold and tired, it's a tricky shot, made harder by the fact that I need to take it quickly as my target's body language tells me he's about to move off at a canter. But the truth is, there is always a risk when you pull the trigger, always a chance you'll just injure him. They have to be culled, but a clean kill is really the only humane result.

'It's a kill shot,' the ghillie confirms after I've fired. Nevertheless, the stag has bolted.

'He'll not go more than a few yards, but that's bad,' the ghillie looks worried; 'he's on Balmoral land. How do you feel about poaching?'

'Completely fine,' I say, and I realise, right then, that however far we move away from our parents, or think we do, we don't.

We've left Victor a few hundred yards behind us. The ghillie throws me the keys to the Land Rover. 'Take it round to Loch Muick and as far up into the treeline as you can go without getting bogged down!' he shouts over his shoulder, trying to run and unpack a harness at the same time. 'I'll drag him down the hill and we'll load him up as quickly as possible.' I run the quarter of a mile to the Landy. As I drove around to the spot, I can see a grouse-shooting party coming off the hill on Balmoral land. 'That's Prince Charles,' I hear on the radio. 'They will be coming past you in just a few minutes.' By now, I'm not tired at all and enjoying myself immensely.

I reverse the 4x4 off the track and up through the trees: it's steep but quite dry. I stop just as I see the ghillie cresting the hill – and he's got the stag harnessed up. I jump out of the Landy, run up the hill and help get the stag the last few hundred yards. We haul the carcass into the back, just as an advance party of squaddies comes past. 'That's the Prince's security detail,' the ghillie says, grinning but looking mightily relieved. 'We only just made it.'

I think, *Poor Victor*, when we pick him up, he probably feels a bit like I did all those years ago when I went to the Thames with my father one very cold morning, he shot a goose he shouldn't have, blew a hole in the canoe and I was abandoned on an island.

Plus ça change.

Epilogue

Of sorts

So, I'm about done now: flicking back, I do worry that writing a book about *me* was a bad idea. All this navel-gazing felt a little too much at times, and I'm looking forward to going back to making up stories about things that don't exist. On the whole, though, I think it's been worth it.

Broadly, I know that this up and down life is, well, *life* – possibly I take more risks than most, play things closer to the wire – what makes me do it?

I'm ambitious, and I wonder if that's because we were always slightly peripheral: at school and where we lived – especially the former because we were (relatively) poor in a privileged environment. It does give you a fire in the belly to get on and do things. However, I'm more inclined, after writing this book (and re-reading it), to think my ambition is more fundamental than that, or at least it goes back further: I think it mainly comes from the hyperactivity, this desire to be doing something all the time. It's only got direction because I'm a grown-up and I need to earn a living.

I am lucky as hell: I have a wife and children, a dog, a cat and lots of friends who all seem to like me or are good at pretending. I am wealthy by almost anyone's standards and I'm not exactly overworked: if being able to be a bit feckless is an achievement, then I'm an overachiever.

To come back to my goddaughter's list, what would I write to her when *she's* fifty – or to me now, for that matter? I'd say something like this:

Electrical things should be left well alone… right up until the front door closes and no-one can stop you fiddling. To tinker is human.

Before you leap into a project, by all means think about the whys, the wherefores and – above all – the consequences. Then go ahead anyway because nothing makes you feel more alive than doing things for the hell of it.

If someone is telling a joke, or an anecdote, sit and listen to it patiently. Do not do as I do, namely: fidget or be fully preoccupied by how to tell a better story the moment they pause for breath.

Kindness is the most conventional, yet somehow highest, form of love. It should be practised for no other reason than we're all in it together.

Teach your children not to be fearful. And to trust to luck.

There are twenty-four hours in a day: so, basically, there's plenty of time to be happy with what you've got.

Connect with your fellows at every opportunity.

If you don't know what to do about a problem, ask. Good people to buttonhole are: taxi drivers, people called Tom and five-year-olds dressed up as superheroes. All of the above always know what to do.

Fact is, sometimes those in charge of being nicest to you aren't. However, if you stick to the above, there will always be someone on your side.

When the world seems to be precarious and cruel, remember that the game is never up, there's everything to play for.

And it will all be OK.

Appendices

During the editing process it was clear that I had gone off track. Often. In the interests of maintaining narrative 'flow' I was cruelly forced to jettison certain sections – usually anecdotal or flights of fancy. And the book is better for that (I thank you, Karl French and Alex Campbell).

However, I remain quite fond of some parts of the whole I did remove from their original place in the book and so I came up with the idea to include them here, in the form of outtakes or bloopers. I'm calling it 'Appendices', to make it sound literary.

On language

I know dolphins, poodles and chimpanzees are very clever –
when compared, say, to a chicken or our cat Denis (who is a
simpleton) – but almost everything they have accomplished
is limited to survival. There is absolutely no practical reason
why we need to have so many words to describe *light*, *love* or
longing, or penises, but we do. *Mangata* in Swahili means the
road-like reflection of the moon on water, or the single word
ubuntu in Nguni Bantu (Zulu) means, 'I find my worth in
you'. Closer to home, but no less exotic, *feuillemorte* in French
describes the colour of a faded leaf. *Murr-ma* means to search
for something with your feet, in Wagiman (dead Australian
language).

Innocent fun can be had making up words. Not that
innocent, though – it annoys the purists, especially Académie
française, which tends to give birth to kittens when language
won't do what it's told. But this elasticity of language around
the globe is not as low brow as the academics make out – I
think it should be celebrated; the sheer flexibility of words in
the eyes of the beholder, the simple pleasure of shaping new
meanings and fashioning the tools to describe those aspects
of EXPERIENCE – the common condition – that have, as yet,
gone undescribed, uncatalogued and, thus, suffered in silence.
So, *agudo* (Spanish) could describe distracted driving, whilst
looking for a place to pee. *Bobdebouwer* (Dutch) is for one
who likes grouting. *Flamboiement* (French) can be put into
service as the collective noun for cataloguers ('a flamboyance
of librarians').

And talking about low brows: according to current thinking, the Homo Neanderthal (not that you'd call him that to his face) could not only rip us into small pieces with their bare hands but they were actually smarter than us.

However, crucially, language is how Homo sapiens came to rule the world, allowing for the fact we are stupid and a bit weedy.

The theory is rather brilliant and completely plays to my prejudices, which is the only reason I'm writing about it now. In a nutshell, Homo sapiens gained the upper hand through teamwork facilitated by cognitive language. By that, Homo sapiens took language beyond saying, 'Look, Ugg, danger!' to, 'Last week, Ugg was eaten by a mammoth by the river. He is stupid.' The first phrase is merely very basic factual information, no more sophisticated than a dog barking because it's seen the postman. The second, however, has detailed information – on Ugg: it fixes place, time (in the past), cause of demise and his mental capacity; it also has important information for the wellbeing of the group, i.e. *be careful about going down to the river, there's hairy elephants about*. There's even a joke at someone else's expense.

The *someone else's expense* is vitally important and explains why we developed cognitive speech in the first place – and also why we spend so much time on Facebook – and it is this: Homo sapiens are very nosey.

But gossiping and taking the piss out of our friends is the point. It is precisely our fascination in what our fellow humans get up to, however trivial, that enabled us to become the massively social creatures who worked as small teams of hunters, then larger groups that turned into villages.

However, beyond that, to be able to form the societies which made up cities, then countries… then empires, and all in a hugely short space of time (about thirty thousand years, which is a blink of an eye when you think how long it took us to get a decent fire lit), we needed something else.

We needed stories.

Myth and magic became cult, then formalised religion; shared anecdote became culture, then country. Religions have good stories to tell about where they come from and why they deserve our loyalty, countries have them and so do corporations (called brand) – in fact, no successful human endeavour can do without them. Stories are what make us work together behind a common cause.

You can harness huge numbers of people you have never met behind a strong plot. Before that the only way to get people to follow you was to be known to them personally and have a really big club, so it was limited in number.

Until I meet a horse that can eloquently express the way open water looks just before a storm or how they imagine it must be to die and live again in some sort of afterlife, then I'm going to go around feeling pretty superior to the animal kingdom in this respect. Dogs are cool.

On drinking

Whilst at university, I reached the conclusion that saying, 'I got trashed last night,' lacked verve – my level of inebriation needed imagination: it merited codification.

So, I sat down and did just that. The following guide to inebriation has been honed over the years, but I was a keen student and I had most of the basics off pat by nineteen.

Level One (relaxed):
These days, after work, I like to do something outside that is physical: wood-related in the winter, grass-related in the summer. Just enough to work up a sweat. Then I storm into the kitchen whilst Hélène is making supper and the kids are doing homework, and neck a very cold beer out of the fridge. Screw caps save time.

I'm then quite happy to drink water or milk at supper and perhaps a small class of red to go with the cheese course, but I don't really count that as drinking: red wine with cheese is a necessity – like ketchup with chips, or tea with digestives.

I never get tired of the immediate rush from a cold, reasonably alcoholic drink – beer is good, champagne much better, not whisky or anything neat: for me, neat liquor aperitifs are the fastest way to a hangover before you're properly drunk. Gin & Tonic is a capital alternative but it must be at least a double measure. On special occasions, a James Bond Martini hits the spot, but it is about the most alcoholic thing on the planet and the main reason why Fleming became a shambling inebriate in later life.

A Level One is perfect most nights each week and requires an empty stomach to start with.

Level Two (jolly):
This is all about laying the foundations of a good evening after the initial Level One buzz: it is not about getting pissed. We're still in learner territory – mistakes will be made along the way but stick with it!

WARNING!
If you stop after Level One it takes a breather of several hours before you can start the process again so as to achieve the same speedy buzz you have just so irresponsibly squandered. Incidentally, if you do refuse all top-ups after one drink, wait half an hour, then perhaps grudgingly accept another drink, sip, wait... and so on, it means you're basically French: you'll never get drunk, but you *will* get bored and start discussing philosophy or have an affair with the neighbour. I know this because I am forced to drink this way every year at Christmas with the in-laws who, in all other respects, I love and admire. We customarily arrive at an aged relative's house in Roanne (France's equivalent to Reading, but without the easy access to London). This is 11am, on the dot, and we are served one glass of champagne, which is usually a little on the small side if I'm honest. Between 11am and midday you might get a top-up, then not another thing until 1pm, when you sit down for lunch. There are bottles at the table but always just out of reach: to refill means asking, which signals to everyone that the wine may go, so everyone grabs a tot as it gets passed down to you. On arrival, there is enough for half a glass, including dregs. Truncated drinking of this ilk, plus rich food, leads to a nagging hangover by 3pm.

Therefore, don't stop drinking at any point between a Level One or Two *but* don't rush a Level Two, either. The best analogy is using your internal gears to break slowly: for, just as dangerous (and more common), is that the first kick is so good, the taste just so hits the spot, you go and guzzle like a sixth-former in Magaluf. The obvious result is you'll get pissed too fast. On a good day, your evening will merely end in a *Cinderella* (standing up abruptly in the pub, muttering something unintelligible and rushing for the door). On a bad day, you'll stick around too long and lose all dignity as you stumble from one conversation to another, smelling of vomit.

This is most certainly not what a true gent is aiming for.

The best Level Two is achieved with good food; at its apex you should be feeling energetic without being jumpy, happy without mania, and the conversation flows if you are all on the same page intake-wise. Let's face it, when tucking into food, the only drink here is wine, red at that. I could write a book about why I like wine but it's like writing a book about sex: I don't think I've got anything to say on the subject that hasn't already been expressed – better – by a great many people who know more about it than me.

By the way, I think a Level Two is perfectly achievable a couple of nights a week if you happen to lead a good and blameless life. Or at Sunday lunch.

In fact, a special footnote should be reserved for Sunday lunch, so here it is[63].

---

63   These days, I'd say I am a reasonable man: I rarely, if ever, get angry for no reason. I listen to others, take on board sound argument and I don't hold any extreme views that I am aware of (I know this is all relative – but that's how reasonable I am!). However, I do like, nay insist, on Sunday lunch whenever possible (around forty times a year, on average). There's an approach to drinking on a Sunday and, with the benefit of thirty years' experience here, I will explain what works for me.

First up, you can't just roll out of bed on Sunday morning and start drinking. You need to have earned a good Sunday lunch: so, church (deal with it) and a morning slashing and burning somewhere in the garden is a good way to start; children need ferrying to clubs; dogs

Level Three (proper pissed):

The evening draws to a close… your stomach is full, all the best one-liners have been used up, waiters are hovering. It's time for quiet reflection, gentle humour, for thoughtful anecdotes. It's time for brown drinks.

I fucking love Armagnac.

Not cognac, which is too rounded, not enough bite: I like the burn as it goes down. Armagnac, as the French say, is a *digestif*, i.e. it helps one digest a meal, and this is 100% accurate. There's something a bit too refined about the VSOPs, the XOs, and the etceteras: they've had the rough edges knocked off, traces of *terroir* removed… the ride is smooth, like an expensive car, except one with a bit too much leather and veneer. But I'm not much of a whisky drinker, for all that. Whatever its detractors say, alcohol is a subtle thing – whisky does not agree with me; in fact many grain alcohols don't, e.g. vodka. It's a question of taste, of course, but also internal workings. Booze is biology.

I love this part of the evening; a Level Three is usually when the professionals – or at least the gifted amateurs – get going.

Finding a comfortable chair, a dog and a fire is quite a nice thing to do now. If you have paced yourself right, this is the

---

walked; papers need to be bought; admin administrated. Personally, I prefer doing something physical and a tad uncomfortable (wet, cold, tiring), then go back home and shower, shave and put on something dry and comfortable.

It's essential to spend some time choosing a wine that will go with the meat, opening it to breathe and decanting (if required, dependent on age/vintage), etc. A Sunday lunch aperitif doesn't start until Hélène is ready to stop cooking and settle down. I love drinking with my wife.

Champagne is best of all, but Hélène won't let me open a bottle unless there's a reason to celebrate (I have some leeway here to be creative but excuses like *I've just fixed the chainsaw*; *It's the last Sunday of the month, by Jove!*; *You look radiant* have all been tried and thrown out), so often it's beer or gin & tonic. Actually, when it's really hot, I almost prefer a good gin & tonic to champagne.

time to get things off your chest. If you've got it wrong, you'll be half asleep, slurring your words and just talking shit.

But *in vino veritas,* this is the time of day your closest friends will collectively sigh, push themselves back in their chair and stretch out their legs. I love the communing nature of drinking, where inhibitions went hours ago; what this is, though, is somehow more profound: good booze (and good food) fed to you in just the right quantities frees you up. We like booze because, all too often, alcohol brings out the best in us, so: I dance better when pissed; sing almost in tune; and tell more interesting stories. Uninhibited people think freed-up thoughts and those come with insight.

Something else can occur here: the conversation ranges and our thoughts travel until we come to a sort of event horizon: the laws of space and time warp. The mysticism afoot is time travel. Seemingly a few minutes go by and you look at your watch to discover that 11pm, when dinner finished, has turned into 2am and you've barely got started. At the time you never think much about it: people normally look at their watch and say, 'Gosh, is that the time?' in mock horror, then look pleased with themselves. And as well they should. Try and think of any other scenario where three whole hours can pass by so rapidly, so remarkably pleasantly and so mysteriously. *In vino tempus intinerantur.*

Most evenings, the moment has come to retire gracefully or have just one last snifter. Very rarely has the evening got more to give. If it does, then these are the small handful of episodes in your life when you can watch the sun come up and still remember who you were with, what was said and how the shadows softened and the sky went from black to grey, then pink. This is the time to be with someone you love, or – better still – someone you are falling in love with.

Level Four (speed pissed):

Is to throw caution to the wind and get twatted as fast as possible and stay drunk for as long as possible by continuing to drink anything you can lay your hands on. A Level Four is for when you are too stupid (young) to know any better or you just don't care (usually because something very good or very bad has just happened in your life outside of the pub).

Eventually, all good evenings have to come to an end. There is often a price to pay, as we all know before the hangover: copious vomiting, loss of basics (wallet, shoes, mobile, kebab) meaning a long walk home that stops being fun after six miles, room spin and strange dreams.

The best Level Four I ever saw was Flintoff being interviewed outside Number Ten after the famous England Ashes win in 2005. The man had been drinking for thirteen hours and was a) still standing and b) incoherent but happy.

The 'best' Level Four I ever experienced was at my twenty-first, when I had drunk a lot of cheap wine at the party my parents grudgingly put on for me, followed by very bad cider in the local pub and then a showstopper which consisted of half a pint of Guinness, then a line of doubles (vodka, gin, etc.) to almost fill a pint glass, save for the final addition of a Baileys to curdle the concoction. Which I then drank. I then had another pint.

I woke up several hours later with my body in my parents' kitchen and my head sticking out of the cat flap, surrounded by a congealing lake of vomit.

Not my finest hour, I admit, but a rite of passage.

Hangovers

There not only needs to be a degree of proof of just how good the evening had been but it's entirely fitting – an appropriate badge of honour, if you like – that it can't all be fond memories and waking up next to someone well above your pay grade.

When you start out on your drinking career, after an especially heavy evening you will probably be waking up with a headache so severe you actually feel a bit like crying… except you can't because you have so little water left in your body you literally have no tears to call on. In fact, it's very hard to open your eyes at all, which have somehow glued themselves shut and, once you do, they seem to have lost the ability to swivel in their sockets. Instead, with a heroic effort, you eventually manage to turn your head and register that there is someone in bed next to you.

Oh dear sweet Jesus, you think as you realise who it is.

The tears finally come, ridding your body of its last few precious milligrams of moisture. You have become a locked-in mummy of your former self – a dried husk – as the person you have slept with stirs. And now they will want cuddles.

Even so, you think, as you close your eyes and pray for death, that last flaming Sambuca was still worth it.

On God

After my pilgrimage to Selfridges, I've got off the tube at Sloane Square and walked down the Embankment (which is always further than one remembers), past the boat in Cheyne Walk, and onto the New Kings Road with its antique shops full of gilded furniture and paintings that look like they have been stolen on order from museums. I am walking to meet friends in Fulham and thinking about how – or, more importantly, why – I started going to church again regularly back then. Obviously, as a society, we've gone beyond equating piety with goodness. What is beyond doubt, though, is that having religion drummed into me early on in life is a source of comfort.

On the face of it, mainly when I'm talking to people who didn't go to school with me, I'm rational about the whole subject of religion in that the only reasonable way to view it is through the hazing lens of agnosticism: that is to say, it is impossible to be sure either way, so it comes down to a personal choice – and one that no-one has the right to feel superior about. On the other hand – privately (well, until now!) – I cannot shake this belief in a benign God. One with a beard and a kindly manner who has our best interests at heart. And who sits on a cloud.

Proper, physical proof is one thing, but imagination is as important as what is rational. Our minds are made for both, and I've never thought either should hold sway on how we view our place in the Great Consciousness.

Perhaps unfairly, for those lacking in imagination – or unwilling to use it for purposes of theory or philosophy – I happen to think that a conviction, that when we die there is nothing, lacks verve. It feels like a cop out, to me. It's so much easier to say there's nothing out there and the end is simply The End. It's one less thing to worry about for most people.

But my belief is partly empirical, as well.

I'll explain quickly and then get back to the narrative: when I look at trees, pleasant faces, mountain streams, stars, children's faces, the human form, you name it – what *I* see is Intelligent Design. If I was to throw a bag of nails in the air, how they fell would look a random mess, but the way pebbles gather on a beach with the tide, or wild flowers contrive to grow in a meadow… from the tumbling of fireflies to the constellations in the heavens, the rills of sand on dunes, ripples on calm water, the undulation of hills, the swell of a breast, the reassurance of a soft touch and the way hands are just right for holding – it might be nauseatingly sentimental for some, yet it feels like it has had some thought behind it. To me.

Almost everything one's senses lock into seems to be so perfectly in place as to have had someone with a great deal of good sense and taste to have said, *This should be so.*

I look at Cooper, our springer spaniel, and see that here is a life form that does not only enjoy licking his own testicles and eating cat poo, but there is also a fundamental goodness to him, an intellectual honesty, a loyalty and unalloyed *glee* in the world around him. And the almost limitless capacity for love that just can't be the result of how atoms interact.

Parts of the Bible also seem divinely inspired (I'm nearly done). I love the opening lines of the Book of Genesis because they so perfectly and poetically describe what we call the Big Bang a very long time before any scientist got around to explaining it. *Let there be light* is the most succinct, laden line in any book I've ever read. Nothing else a deity might have said when they got up and decided to create the Universe would carry such weight. As an introduction to one of our most important books, whether you are religious or not, the words beautifully describe the relationship between what we see as meaningless – a Void: one huge, black vacuum – and the sudden appearance of a Radiance, which stands for life, optimism and the one thing, as humans, we crave – the deliverance from darkness, both physical and intellectual.

And I love the fact that this miracle, this achievement above all others, this creation of something that came from nothing, did not trigger through some chemical reaction (although that certainly ushered it in) but with the thing I love most in the world: words. An utterance that made distinction between light, darkness and names for everything. John's Gospel even comes right out and says it, in his opening line:

In the beginning was the Word, and the Word was with God, and the Word was God.

That's the second-best line in the Bible, I think.

Atheists counter this with what they *see*, which is often as terrible as it is compelling as an argument for a cruel God or one who just never was: the senselessness of loss, hurt and death. The vulnerability of children in the face of the terrible things adults will do to them. We are so helpless that I do not blame anyone for raging that any loving God would take more care of us, because we obviously need it.

As I've said already, we have been given the tools to look after ourselves, which is so much more important. We have infinite love but finite cruelty. I honestly believe that.